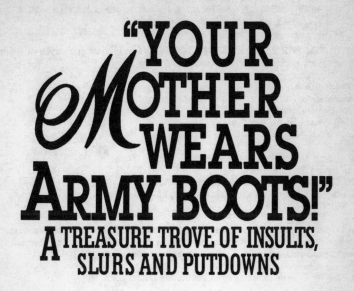

"YOUR MOTHER WEARS ARMY BOOTS!"

A TREASURE TROVE OF INSULTS, SLURS AND PUTDOWNS

JORDAN L. LINFIELD & JOE KAY

An Innovation Press Book

AVON BOOKS ◆ NEW YORK

"YOUR MOTHER WEARS ARMY BOOTS!" is an original publication of Avon
Books. This work has never before appeared in book form.

AVON BOOKS
A division of
The Hearst Corporation
1350 Avenue of the Americas
New York, New York 10019

Copyright © 1992 by Innovation Press
An Innovation Press Book
Published by arrangement with Innovation Press
Library of Congress Catalog Card Number: 92-4355
ISBN: 0-380-76591-8

Library of Congress Cataloging in Publication Data:

Linfield, Jordan.
    Your mother wears Army boots! : a treasure trove of insults,
slurs, and putdowns / Jordan Linfield and Joe Kay.
        p.   cm.
    1. English language—Slang—Dictionaries.   2. Invective—
Dictionaries.   I. Kay, Joe.   II. Title.
PE3721.L47   1992   92-4355
427'.09'03—dc20   CIP

First Avon Books Trade Printing: August 1992

AVON TRADEMARK REG. U.S. PAT. OFF. AND IN OTHER COUNTRIES, MARCA
REGISTRADA, HECHO EN U.S.A.

Printed in the U.S.A.

OPM   10   9   8   7   6   5   4   3   2   1

INTRODUCTION

The first insult may have been uttered three billion years ago when Lucy grunted to her companion something like "You clumsy ape, you're all fingers" as she tried to work her prehensile thumb. That quote has not yet been fully authenticated, but records of all peoples attest to the universality of the slur.

The Old Testament, the New Testament, and the Koran record such words. The works of the Greeks, the Romans, the ancient Hindus, and the Chinese attest to this aspect of human behavior. Perhaps no one has such an extravagant display of insults as Rabelais in his *Gargantua and Pantagruel*:

> ". . . . prattling gabblers, licorous gluttons, freckled bittors, mangy rascals, shite-a-bed scoundrels, drunken roysters, drowsy loiterers, slapsauce fellows, slabberdegullion druggles, lubbardly louts . . . drawlatch hoydens, flouting milksops. . . . ninny lobcocks, scurvy sneaksbies, fondling fops, base loons, saucy coxcombs, . . . noddy meacocks, blockish grutuols, . . . jobbernol goosecaps, . . . flutch calf-lolles, grouthead gnat-snappers, lobdotterels. . . . codshead loobies, woodcock slangams, ninnie-hammer fly catchers, noddiepeak simpletons, turdy-gut, shitten shepherds."

But the collections of the sixteenth century are of little value to those of us moving into the twenty-first century. *Your Mother Wears Army Boots!* is the only compendium of such words used in English today. Often the words are not pretty. They are rude, discourteous, uncivil, offensive, abusive, derogatory, invidious, defamatory, vicious, impolite, outrageous, contemptuous, hurtful, malicious, and just plain bitchy. But they are American words. They come out of American life and American experience. They mirror our culture, our history, and our language. They reflect the stresses and the strains that tear at our society and at our most personal relations.

Your Mothers Wears Army Boots! is as current and complete as years of serious research could make it. It is a collection of nouns, verbs, adjectives, and metaphors that have gained enough popular usage to be entered in the standard scholarly works of recorded English. American cultural life—contemporary novels, periodicals, ballads, proverbs, sayings, theatre, radio, TV, comics, underground newspapers, and rock and rap songs—have been examined for new insults, slurs, and put-downs. A quick perusal of the bibliography illustrates the breadth and scope of this book.

It deals with the principal categories of insults based on anatomy, physical appearance, mental ability, class, morality, character, age, sexual preference, political bias, ethnic, racial, and religious affiliations. Negative personality traits or behaviors such as bluffing and boasting, baseness and servility, self-righteousness and hypocrisy, theft and dishonesty, deception and lying, lewdness and depravity, stupidity and naivete, and the seven capital sins are dealt within their multiple variations.

Insults are double-edged. On one hand, verbal aggression can be an outlet that relieves pent-up anger and frustration; on the other hand, such words can escalate to a result that neither opponent intends. Ethnic, racist, sexist, and homophobic terms are particularly inflammable.

But most any noun can be used to insult or abuse. [Place the adjective 'dirty' or 'rotten' or 'damn' before it, and see what you have!] Conversely, even the most insulting terms are often used in jest, out of a sense of camaraderie.

Examining this fascinating vocabulary is vital for a better understanding of each other—the frailties that we share as well as those that push us apart. It is important to such diverse disciplines as psychology, social psychology, sociology, law, history, linguistics, and political science. As our allotted space shrinks and we are forced closer and closer together, civility becomes more necessary than ever. Understanding insults and slurs, their provenance, nuance, and development in time and place, is not just for academics, it is for each of us.

It is the conclusion of the authors that the demystifying of these words, many of which are taboo, is necessary to the development of a saner society. Demythologizing ethnic epithets is as essential to human accord as understanding male terms of abuse and control is to the change of traditional gender roles, or understanding homophobic terms is to acceptance of sexual diversity and pluralism.

The fault, dear reader, lies not in our words, but in ourselves.

The authors would be pleased to receive additional terms to be included in the next edition of *Your Mother Wears Army Boots!* We would appreciate mention of the source. Please include documentation wherever possible. All such submissions can be sent to *Your Mother Wears Army Boots!* Innovation Press, 373 Broadway, New York, New York 10013.

ABBREVIATIONS

adj	adjective
adv	adverb
e.g.	for example
imper	imperative
interj	interjection
n	noun
pron	pronoun
syn	synonym
v	verb

A **abandoned,** *adj.* Free from all moral restraint. ["An abandoned woman who has been so notoriously treacherous to us ..."—Samuel Coleridge.] *Syn.:* corrupt, debased, debauched, degraded, depraved, dissipated, dissolute, immoral, lewd, licentious, loose, profligate, reprobate, shameless, sinful, wanton, wicked, wild.

abashless, *adj.* Shameless, lacking in any sense of humility or guilt. ["This ... abashless mouth"—Robert Browning.]

abbreviated piece of nothing, *n.* A worthless person, an insignificant or petty person. ["The president's assistant acted like he was a big shot, but he was only an abbreviated piece of nothing."] *Syn.:* abbreviated piece of shit, banty, chicken feed, crumb, pimple, pissant, punk.

Abe, *n.* A Jewish man. [From *Abraham*, a personal name considered to be Jewish. "You got to soft-soap some of these Abie Kabibbles"—James T. Farrell, *Young Lonigan* (1932).] *Syn.:* Abie, Abie Kabibble, Hymie, Ike, Ikey, Ikey Mo, Izzy.

abhor, *v.* To regard with extreme disgust. ["Age, I abhor thee; youth, I adore thee"—William Shakespeare, *Venus and Adonis.*] *Syn.:* abominate, despise, detest, disdain, execrate, hate, loathe, nauseate. *Idioms:* make one's skin crawl, can't stand, can't stomach, view with horror.

ableist, *n.* One who discriminates or is prejudiced against handicapped people.

abominable, *adj.* Exciting disgust. ["Oh, my tongue, my abominable tongue! Why can't I learn to keep it quiet?" —Louisa May Alcott, *Little Women.*] *Syn.:* accursed, abhorrent, appalling, atrocious, base, damnable, despicable, detestable, disgusting, evil, foul, hateful, hellish, horrid, loathsome, odious, offensive, repellent, repugnant, repulsive, revolting, vile, villainous, wretched.

abortion, *n.* A messy failure, an also-ran, a disaster or fiasco in anything one tries. ["As a playwright you're an abortion. Give it up and get some honest work."] *Syn.:* catastrophe, disaster, miscarriage.

abracadabra, *n.* Gibberish, hocus-pocus. ["Psychology is either true knowledge concerning the spiritual nature of man or it is moonshine and abracadabra"—John Middleton Murry.]

abscess, *n.* A detestable person. [From *abscess*, collection of pus in a body cavity, hence an infection on the public weal. "That official is an abscess on the body politic."] *Syn.:* boil, carbuncle, furuncle, pimple, pustule.

absentminded, *adj.* Scatterbrained. ["The absentminded husband kissed the clock, wound up the cat, and put his wife out"—American folklore.] *Syn.:* blank, heedless, out to lunch, popcorn-headed, preoccupied, the lights are on but nobody's home, unconscious.

absolutely sanitary, *idiom.* Excessively fastidious, cold. ["The only . . . talent Miss Day possesses is that of being absolutely sanitary: her personality untouched by human emotions, her brow unclouded by human thought, her form unsmudged"—John Simon.]

absurdity, *n.* An extremely illogical or preposterous statement or action. ["Now is this not ridiculous?/Is this not preposterous?/A thorough-paced absurdity/—explain it if you can"—Gilbert and Sullivan, *Patience.*] *Syn.:* anomaly, asininity, daftness, foolishness, idiocy, implausibility, inanity, incongruity, nonsense.

abuser, *n.* A perverter, a seducer, as in child abuser, drug abuser. ["Nor adultrers, nor effeminate, nor abusers of themselves with Mankinde"—I Corinthians VI, 9.]

accommodationist, *n.* A black person who accommodates to the attitudes and desires of white people. [". . . make Uncle Toms, compromisers, accommodationists thoroughly ashamed"—Ossie Davis.]

accursed, *adj.* Damnable, detestable, worthy of a curse. ["A wretch accurst and hated by the gods"—Alexander Pope, *Iliad.*]

AC - DC, *adj.* Bisexual. [From labels on directional appliances that can be used with either alternating or direct current.] *Syn.:* ambidextrous, bi, bicycle, combo, Gillette blade, gold and silver, switch-hitter, two-way baby. *Idioms:* play both sides of the fence, caught between the pointers and setters.

ace of spades, *n.* A black person, especially one who is very dark. [From the color of the playing card.] *Syn.:* blackbird, black dust, blackout.

acidhead, *n.* A habitual user of LSD, an acid freak. [From *acid* (LSD), which produces hallucinations. "Stoned on pot and acid all day long, he calls it indulgence if we drink whiskey"—K. Millet, *Flying.*]

acquisitive, *adj.* Having an intense desire to acquire and hoard wealth. ["The natural man has only two primal passions, to get and to beget"—Sir William Osler, *Science and Immorality.*] *Syn.:* covetous, selfish, grasping, greedy, possessive, avaricious, grabby, mercenary, rapacious, voracious, insatiable. *Idioms:* have greedy guts, have the gimmies, have the grabs.

acrid, *adj.* Harsh, caustic. ["Their acrid temper turns, as soon as stirred,/The milk of their good purpose all to curd"—William Cowper, *Charity.*] *Syn.:* biting, nasty, acrimonious, vitriolic, acid, sarcastic.

activist, *n.* A politically or socially involved person who is often considered to be an extremist. ["To some black activists it sounded that their old liberal allies were saying that blacks could not manage a city of their own"—Costello and Wallace, *Signifying Rappers* (1990).] *Syn.:* hothead, radical, militant.

act like one's shit doesn't stink, *idiom.* To be haughty or act superior. *Idioms:* acts like shit wouldn't melt in his mouth, thinks she shits lollipops, thinks her ass is ice cream and everyone wants a lick of it

act your age, *imper.* Don't be stupid! *Idioms:* be your age, cut it out, cut the comedy, cut the crap, get your ass in gear.

addle-brained, *adj.* Applied to one who is confused or muddled. *Syn.*: addle-headed, addlepated, mixed up, muddled, befuddled, unglued, slaphappy, punchy, shook up, rattled.

adulterous, *adj.* Unfaithful to one's spouse. ["The adulterous Anthony, most large in his abominations"—William Shakespeare, *Anthony and Cleopatra.*] *Syn.*: fast and loose, two-timing, moonlighting, cheating, double-crossing.

afgay, *n.* A gay man. [From Pig Latin for *gay.*] *Syn.*: agfay, ansy-pay, eer-quay.

Afro-Saxon black, *n.* An African-American who tries to emulate his WASP counterpart. *Syn.*: Black Anglo-Saxon, NASP, Negro Anglo-Saxon Protestant.

afterbirth, *n.* One with an ugly face. [From the appearance of the placenta and membranes expelled from the uterus after a birth.]

ageist, *n.* One who is biased, or discriminates against someone on grounds of age. [Coined by Robert Butler, doctor and gerontologist, 1969.]

agitator, *n.* One who aggressively arouses others to change, at times induced by ego and self-interest. ["He was a great agitator for human rights, but during confrontations, he suddenly disappeared."] *Syn.*: extremist, militant, rebel.

ain't holding no air, you, *idiom.* You're unimpressive; you lack credibility; you don't know how to take care of yourself.

ain't shit, *idiom.* To be worthless. ["Black is beautiful,/Brown is slick./Yellow's okay,/But white ain't shit"—*Smoke Some Kill* (rock group)] *Syn.*: ain't nowhere.

ain't worth shit, *idiom.* ["He ain't worth shit in a handbag"—George Carlin.] *Syn.*: ain't worth the powder to blow it to hell, ain't worth a plug nickel, ain't worth diddly (or diddly shit).

airhead, *n.* A stupid, empty-headed, silly person. ["The usual crowd of airheads, phoneys, deadlegs, posers, bimbos, wallies, wannabees, hangers-on and gate-crashers . . ."—Cristena Appleyard, *Daily Mirror* (1989).] *Syn.*: airbrain, balloonhead, bubblehead, emptyhead, heliumhead, muddlehead, numbhead, softhead. [For full list of -head words, see **blockhead**.] *Idioms*: a few sandwiches short of a picnic, a few steps short of the attic, an idea would bust his head wide open, dead from the neck up, has a bad case of the simples, nobody home, doesn't know shit from shinola, playing with half a deck, someone blew out his pilot light, twelve cookies short of a dozen.

airy, *adj*. Empty-headed, has no idea where the brains should be. ["Him whose airy negligence puts his friends' affairs . . . in continual hazard"—Samuel Johnson, *The Rambler*.] *Syn*.: superficial, silly, flighty, harebrained, unsubstantial, empty, unreal, imaginary, speculative.

airy-fairy, *adj*. Fanciful, insubstantial, trivial. ["I am concerned with facts, not motives, suspicious, and airy-fairy nothingness"—F. Hoyle, *Black Cloud*.] *Syn*.: chicken feed, dinky, piddling, pissy-ass, popcorn.

albatross, *n*. A person who impedes the accomplishment of a project. [From the albatross killed by the ancient mariner in Samuel Coleridge's *The Rime of the Ancient Mariner*.]

alias man, *n*. A cheat, a hypocrite, an unethical person. [West Indian usage.]

Alibi Ike, *n*. A person who is always making excuses. [From Ring Lardner's short story of the same name (1924). "He always has an alibi, and one or two to spare"—T. S. Eliot, *Macavity, the Mystery Cat*.]

all behind like a fat woman, *idiom*. You're late or tardy.

alley apple, *n*. A worthless person. [From a piece of horse manure.] *Syn*.: horse apple, road apple.

alley cat, *n*. A sexually promiscuous person. [Refering to an alley cat, Dorothy Parker said, "That woman speaks eighteen languages, and she can't say no in any of them."] *Idiom*: have more pricks than a secondhand dart board.

alley rat, *n*. A villainous, corrupt, thieving person.

all guts, *n*. An obese person. *Syn*.: all belly, all ass (and no body).

all piss and wind, *idiom.* You're all talk and no action. ["All wind and piss like a tan yard cat." James Joyce, *Ulysses* (1922).]

allsbay, *interj.* Denotes disbelief. [From the Pig Latin for *balls.*] *Syn.*: utsnay.

all that meat and no potatoes, *idiom.* A man's exclamation on seeing a well-built or a fat woman.

all thumbs, *idiom.* Clumsy, awkward, inept. ["He tried to undress her, but he was so anxious that he was all thumbs."]

all tits and teeth, *idiom.* An unattractive woman who uses her smile and big breasts to attract attention.

all vines and no taters, *idiom.* A facade, a false front. ["He deceived his investors by throwing fancy parties on his yacht. But his pretense fell apart. He was all vines and no taters."] *Syn.*: all hat and no cattle.

all wet, *idiom.* Very wrong or mistaken. ["His position on the recession was all wet, but he wouldn't admit his error."]

almond eye, *n.* A person of Asian descent. ["... the washee-washee almond eye"—Eugene Field, *The Fair Limousin.*]

aloof, *adj.* Standing apart from others, remote. ["Young people ... tend to become arrogant and hard, ignorant of the problems of adult life, and quite aloof from their parents"—Bertrand Russell.] *Syn.*: cold, indifferent, standoffish, chilly, stuck-up, snobbish, withdrawn, remote, pretentious.

also-ran, *n.* A perennial loser, a useless person, a failure. ["Stassen never seemed to mind being an also-ran as a presidential candidate."]

alter kacker, *n.* A dirty old man, a seasoned lecher, an old fart. [From the Yiddish word *kack* = defecate. Pronounced as "cocker."] *Syn.*: A.K., old codger, old fogy, antique, dodo, foozle, fossil, geezer, mossback, old shit.

amazon, *n.* An extremely strong, masculine woman. [From a race of female warriors who, the fable says, removed one breast so as to not interfere with shooting arrows. "To the men an Amazon never fails to be forbidding"—Fordyce (1767).] *Syn.*: boon-dagger, bull bitch, muscle moll.

ambisinistrous, *adj.* Clumsy, klutzy. [From having two left hands. "In wedlock, he (the Prince of Wales) was certainly more than ambisinistrous"—Lord W. P. Lennox, *Biographical Reminiscences.*]

amoeba-brain, *adj.* A stupid, slow-witted person.

Amy-John, *n.* A lesbian, especially one who plays the dominant role. *Syn.*: butch, diesel dyke.

analphabetic, *adj.* Illiterate, ignorant, benighted.

anal-retentive, *adj.* Uptight, rigid. ["... anal-retentive, cacademician cretins"—Reinhold Aman.]

anathema, *n.* An object of abhorrence. [From the ecclesiastical curse of excommunication. "All plays are anathema to him, and he even disapproves of dancing bears" —Quiller Couch.]

androcrat, *n.* A male supremacist. ["Androcracy: government by a group of males"—*A Feminist Dictionary* (1985).]

androgyne, *n.* Having the physical characteristics of both sexes; a hermaphrodite, an effeminate man, a eunuch.

angelcake, *n.* A woman. [One of many words equating women and food. The idea of eating is often associated with oral sex. "She's good enough to eat" = "She's a good candidate for cunnilingus"] *Syn.*: bit of jam, cake, cheesecake, cherry pie, creampuff, crumpet, cupcake, dinner, dish, eating pussy, eating stuff, flavor, furburger, fur pie, honey, hot dish, hot potato, meat, morsel, peach, peacherooni, peacherino, pie, piece of mutton, plum, pork, pound cake, pumpkin, rabbit pie, sweet patootie, table grade, tomato.

angelface, *n.* An attractive woman. [One of the many words equating women with physical characteristics. Often used by men as complimentary, but considered by many women to be sexist and offensive.] *Syn.*: bathing beauty, beaut, beauty queen, centerfold, cheesecake, cover girl, cute chick, cutie, cutie pants, cutie pie, dazzler, dollface, eyeful, glamor girl, glamor puss, good looker, knock-out, looker, lovely, pinup, pinup girl, raving beauty, stunner, ten.

Anglo, *n.* A white person. [Originally Hispanic usage in the Southwest United States, distinguishing white Americans from Mexican-Americans. "Earlier this year the Anglos were for the first time tipped into the minority by accumulated Blacks, Hispanics, and Asians"—*Observer* (1984).] *Syn.*: blanco, gabacho, gringo.

anile, *adj.* Old-womanish, imbecilic. ["Puerile hallucinations and anile delierations"—*OED* (1652).]

animal, *n.* (1) A lecher, a whoremonger. *Syn.*: alley cat, dog, gay dog, goat, horseman, mink, parish bull, peach orchard boar, rooster, stallion, stud, wolf, buckfitch, bull, tomcat, town bull. (2) An aggressive, brutal person lacking sexual restraint, a human being without human qualities. ["Man is worse than an animal when he is an animal"—Rabindranath Tagore, *Story Birds* (1916).]

ankle, *n.* A despicable, contemptible person. ["An ankle is three feet lower than an asshole."]

Ann, *n.* A white woman to a black person, or a black woman who acts too much like a white one.

anorchid, *n.* A man without testicles. ["There was a young sailor named Bates/Who did a fandango on skates/He fell on his cutlass/Which rendered him nutless/And practically useless on dates"—G. Legman, *The Limerick.*]

another country heard from, *idiom.* A contemptuous response to someone who gives unwanted advice. ["Ah, another country heard from! Why don't you keep your nose out of this?"]

anti-Semite, *n.* One who has a hatred for or aversion to Jews. ["... hoarded with hate! A bull shitter, a biggot, an Anti-Semit (*sic*)—a real, 100%, flag-waving, Fourth of July American"—Albert Goldman, *Ladies and Gentlemen, Lenny Bruce* (1974).]

antisocial, *adj.* Opposed to the good of society, disinclined to mix in society, without social instincts. ["Some kinds of antisocial actions are so unreasonable . . . that we brand them . . . as insane"—George Bernard Shaw, *Fabian Essays on Socialism* (1889).] *Syn.*: disruptive, misanthropic, asocial, antagonistic.

antsy, *adj.* Anxious, disturbed. *Syn.*: uptight, jittery, nervous, bugged, spooked, fidgety. *Idioms*: have ants in one's pants, have kittens, in a sweat, jumpy as a cat on a hot tin roof, sweating bullets.

apathetic, *adj.* Showing lack of interest in people or things. ["There is too much apathy in the world today. . . . But who cares?"—Steven J. Paul.] *Syn.*: uncommitted, impassive, emotionless, unfeeling, cold, passionless, phlegmatic. *Idioms*: don't give a shit, don't give a damn, don't give a hoot.

apeshit, go, *idiom.* To go wild, to behave wildly or irrationally. ["After I'd left my last school, I pinched a wallet full of credit cards and went apeshit in about five different counties"—Stephen Fry, *Sunday Times Magazine* (1989).] *Syn.*: go ape, go bananas, freak out.

apostate, *n.* One who has abandoned his or her religion, principles, or party. ["Some wealthy Republicans felt to their dying days that Roosevelt was an apostate who deserted his class."] *Syn.*: renegade, heretic, traitor, defector, deserter, backslider, tergiversator, turncoat, turnabout.

apparatchik, *n.* A bureaucratic staff member, a flunky, a member of an existing power structure. ["White House apparatchiks who would suddenly throw the handsome hero to the criminal winds"—Carl Bernstein, *New York Times* (1987).]

appeaser, *n.* Someone who is willing to give in to an enemy in the hope that this will quiet him. ["An appeaser is one who feeds a crocodile—hoping that it will eat him last"—Winston Churchill.]

apple, *n.* A traitor to Native American Indian causes. [From being red on the outside, white on the inside.] *Syn.*: Uncle Tomahawk.

apple, bad or **rotten,** *n.* A no-good person who contaminates a whole group.

apple-knocker, *n.* An unsophisticated rural person. ["... them other sailors were appleknockers. They were so dumb they couldn't find their nose with both hands" —*The New Yorker* (1939).] *Syn.*: brush ape, clodhopper, hayseed, nose picker, shitkicker, yokel.

apple-polisher, *n.* A toady, a flatterer, a sycophant. [From the practice of bringing an apple to the teacher.]

applesauce, *n.* Nonsense, pretentious speech, insincere flattery. ["I know applesauce when I hear it"—Ring Lardner.] *Syn.*: apple butter, baloney, banana oil, bunk, hokum, cheese, fudge, crock, crock of shit, garbage, pile of shit, spinach, tripe, waffle, duck soup.

apron, *n.* A woman or one's wife.

apron strings, tied to one's, *idiom.* Overly influenced by one's wife or mother. *Syn.*: wimp, sissy, mama's boy.

Aqua Velva geek, *n.* A very reprehensible male ["Ohmigod, Stacey, OK, like this totally skanky Aqua Velva geek tried to pick me up, like he goes, 'Hey babe, let's take a walk on the wild side,' and like I go, 'Gag me with a spoon, slimeball!' "—Corey and Westermark, *Fer Shurr! How to Be a Valley Girl—Totally (1982).*]

Archie Bunker, *n.* A bigoted, unsophisticated, nationalistic lower-middle-class American. [From a principal character in the TV series "All in the Family." His counterparts are Alf or Ocker in Australia, and Alf Garnett in Great Britain.]

arctic, *adj.* Biting, cold, chilling, icy, unfriendly. ["She was not only frigid, she was absolutely arctic."] *Idioms*: colder than a cocksucker's knees, colder than a witch's tit, colder than a frozen fish's asshole, sitting on frozen custard.

armpit, *n.* Any cruddy place; one's home or place of work. ["My God! How can you work in an armpit like this?"] *Syn.*: craphouse, creepsville, dump, muckhole, nowhere city, shitheap, toilet.

arriviste, *n.* A person "on the make," an opportunist. ["An impoverished family of high breeding . . . sneers consolingly at vulgar arrivistes"—John Hersey.] *Syn.*: parvenu, upstart, nouveau riche, roturier.

arrogant, *adj.* Feeling and acting superior to others. ["He was arrogant, overbearing, conceited . . . without any rank that could excuse pride"—Anthony Trollope.] *Syn.*: overbearing, haughty, presumptuous, condescending, imperious, overweening, high-and-mighty, conceited, egotistical, self-important, disdainful, swaggering, insolent, scornful, lordly, pompous, biggety, bossy, dicty, siddity, snooty, snotty, uppity, stuck-up, high-nosed. *Idioms*: too big for one's britches, on one's high horse.

arsebender, *n.* A promiscuous woman, a whore. [—as used by John Barth, *The Sot-Weed Factor* (1960).] *Syn.*: backbender, bedbug, breechdropper, arsievarsie.

artsy-fartsy, *adj.* Pretentious, pompously or blatantly affected, overly intellectual/artistic, exhibiting superficial form and little positive content. *Syn.*: artsy-smartsy, artsy-craftsy.

asiatic, *adj.* Crazy, abnormal.

asinine, *adj.* Ridiculous behavior or remarks. [". . . A polite smile at what he thought was an asinine joke"—Dashiell Hammett.]

ass, *n.* A fool; a dull, stupid person. ["If three people say you are an ass, put on a bridle"—Spanish proverb.] *Compare*: badass, candyass, dumb ass, flat ass, horse's ass, lardass, pain in the ass, pissass, raggedy ass, rat's ass, shitass, smartass, soft ass, sorryass, stupidass, suckass, tightass, tiredass, wildass. *ass/assed.* Suffix used to give emphasis to adjectival phrases: e.g., bad-assed, funk-ass, half-assed, high-assed, jive-ass, pucker-assed, red-assed, trick-ass, tight-assed, strong-ass.

ass, my, *interj.* An expression of complete disbelief.

ass, piece of, *idiom.* A woman regarded as a sexual object. [One of the many sexist words based on anatomy for a woman, or women in general.] *Syn.*: ankle, butt, cooze, crack, crotch, cunt, cunt meat, hammer, hide, leg, pussy, rag and bone and a hank of hair, rib, slash, tail, belly-lass, cleave, cleaver, dangerous curves, dirtyleg, gash, hairy bit, hole, hot bot, nestlecock, openarse, piece of snatch, piece of tail, split-arse mechanic, willing tit, slotted-job, tit, snatch, tube, soft-jaw, soft-leg, split, wagtail, split tail, tickle tail, whisker, wool.

assassin, *n.* A person who mucks up things completely. [Allusion to the general meaning of the word as a killer. "Assassins!"—Arturo Toscanini to his orchestra when it played badly.]

ass-chewing, *adj.* Intensely angry. ["My boss was in an ass-chewing mood because I blew the sale."] *Syn.*: choleric, pissed, pissed off, shirty, waxy, wrathful, wrathy, wrothful, wrothy.

assface, *n.* One who is gross, ugly, and makes one nauseous. ["His pet name for his ex-wife was assface."] *Syn.*: snot-face, cuntface, fartface, fishface, shitface, toilet face, turd-face, zitface. *Idioms*: face like a douche bag, face like a toilet seat.

asshole, *n.* (1) A rude, obnoxious person; a mean, cruel person; a stupid, irritating person; a despicable person; a worthless, annoying person. ["Jesus loves you! Everyone else thinks you are an asshole!"—American graffito.] *Syn.*: A.H., a-hole, birdturd, bugger, bastard, butthole, dick, schmuck, dickhead, dipshit, prick, dirtbag, crumb, double-clutcher, horse's ass, piece of shit, rat's asshole. (2) The worst of all places. ["... if not the asshole of the world, is within a farting distance of it"—Stephen King, *Sunday Times Magazine*.]

assimilado or **assimilationist,** *n.* A minority person who turns his back on the causes of his people and tries to be like the majority. ["You are a nation, sick-ass assimilado" —Imamu Baraka, *The Nation Is Like Ourselves*.]

ass is grass, your, *idiom.* You're in deep trouble. ["Your ass is grass, and I'm the lawn mower"—U.S. Army saying.]

ass is so close to your mouth, *idiom.* You're an insulting toiletmouth. *Idiom:* when he has a mouthful of shit he always wants to spit it on you.

ass-kicker, *n.* An aggressive person, a bully. [From the expression "kick ass and take numbers" = to identify and punish severely—U.S. Army saying.]

ass-kisser, *n.* A sycophant, a groveler, someone who would do absolutely anything to get ahead. ["Its a short step from lip-service to ass-kissing"—Saul Bellow.] *Syn.:* arse-crawler, ass-licker, ass-sucker, asswipe, automatic tongue wiper, butt-wipe, boot-lick, kiss-ass, fart-licker, boot-licker, bum-licker, butt-lick, catch-fart, egg-sucker, fart-sucker, foot-licker, kissbutt, lickdish, lickspit, stroker, suck-ass, toad-eater, truckler, tuft-hunter.

ass-man, *n.* A homosexual man. ["He was the house ass-man"—M. Thomas, *Someone Else's Money* (1982).]

assy, *adj.* Bitchy, nasty, mean, malicious.

atheist, *n.* A person who denies the existence of God. ["I'm an atheist still, thank God"—Luis Buñuel.]

atrabilious, *adj.* Hypochondriac, splenetic, acrimonious. [From the Latin for *black* + *bile*.]

Attila the Hen, *n.* A woman deemed to be aggressive and powerful. [From the comparison to Attila, leader of the rapacious Huns.]

attitude, or **tude** *n.* Bad, hostile, snobbish, or generally unpleasant behavior.

audacious, *adj.* Overly bold to the point of being insolent. *Syn.:* impudent, fresh, cheeky, impertinent, brazen, shameless, rude, outrageous, presumptuous.

aunt, *n.* An elderly whore. ["Summer songs for me and my aunts,/While we lay tumbling in the hay"—William Shakespeare, *The Winter's Tale.*]

Aunt Thomasina, *n.* A woman considered as not supporting militantly the women's liberation movement. ["Accommodators and temporizers within the Woman's Lib movement were spoken of as Aunt Thomasinas"—*Atlantic Monthly* (1970).] *Syn.*: Aunt Jane, Aunt Tabby, Aunt Tom.

Aunt Jemima, *n.* The female counterpart of an Uncle Tom. ["Aunt Jemima is dead"—James Baldwin, *Notes of a Native Son* (1955).] *Syn.*: Aunt Jane, Aunt Tabby, Aunt Tom.

auntie, *n.* An aged male homosexual. ["Some mincy auntie in a cell with flowered curtains"—Peter Ustinov.] *Syn.*: aunt, aunteater.

authoritarian, *adj.* Misusing authority or power. ["But man, proud man/Drest in a little brief authority/Most ignorant of what he is most assur'd/His glassy essence, like an angry ape,/Play such fantastic tricks before high heaven,/As make the angels weep"—William Shakespeare, *Measure for Measure.*] *Syn.*: tyrannical, imperious, autocratic, repressive, oppressive, iron-handed.

autolotrous, *adj.* Worshiping oneself.

avaricious, *adj.* Extremely covetous. ["Avarice is generally the last passion of those lives of which the first part had been squandered in pleasure, and the second in ambition"—Samuel Johnson.] *Syn.*: greedy, money-grubbing, rapacious, miserly, penurious, niggardly, closefisted, penny-pinching.

ayatollah, *n.* Any despotic, repressive, rigid, fundamentalist person. ["... he was banished from godly Boston by the ayatollahs of his day"—Alfred Kazin, *New York Times Book Review* (1989).]

 babbitt, *n.* A conforming, bourgeois businessman who has little use for art or intellectual pursuits. [From Sinclair Lewis's novel *Babbitt* (1922).] *Syn.*: bourgie, citizen, clyde, cube, plastic, square.

babblemouth, *n.* An inveterate, indiscreet, and often erroneous gossip. ["Babble, babble; our old England may go down in babble"—Alfred Lord Tennyson, "Locksley Hall

Sixty Years After."] *Syn.*: babbler, bibble-babbler, big-mouth, big noise, blabber, blabberer, bucketmouth, chin-wagger, gabblemouth, gabbler, jawsmith, long tongue, loudmouth, motormouth, quidnunc, ratchetmouth, satch-elmouth, tongue-wagger. *Idioms*: all jaw, bat one's gums, beat one's gums, dish the dirt, flap one's chops, have diar-rhea of the mouth, run off at the mouth.

babe in the woods, *n.* A naive, gullible person; a dupe. ["She was such a babe in the woods. She thought a hump was a camel's back."] *Syn.*: cluck.

baboon, *n.* An awkward jerk, often called big baboon, a cluck. ["He (Mario Cuomo) didn't mind ridicule, he said. Lincoln was once called a baboon"—*New York* (1992).] *Syn.*: ape, (big) boob, lug, big dummy, chump, lunkhead, clown, dumbo, yahoo, geek, goop, jibone, lob, ox, pa-looka.

babu, *n.* A Hindu or Pakistani, particularly one with a bit of Western education.

baby, *n.* A sexually desirable girl or woman. [This is deemed offensive and condescending by many women, who object to the notion of babies as immature, childlike, and passive. "You've come a long way, baby. In the wrong direction" —Jane Gallion, "The Woman as Nigger."] *Syn.*: babe, ba-bydoll, doll, dolly, sweet baby, honey, honey bun, sweet-heart, sweet momma, sweet stuff, sweet thing.

baby blimp, *n.* A fat girl or woman. [Allusion to *blimp* = dirigible.] *Syn.*: beef, lotta momma, Big Bertha, cow, heavy cream, hefty hussy, hippy hussy, Miss Piggy, two-ton Tessie. *Idioms*: so fat that if she had to haul ass she'd have to make two trips, heavier than a ton of lard in a bucket of molas-ses, looks like ten pounds of shit in a five-pound bag, so fat that you can't tell which wrinkle she'll open to talk, her ass is built too close to the ground, her behind looks like two ferrets in a sack, it must be jelly because jam don't shake like that.

baby butch, *n.* A boyish-looking, teenaged lesbian. *Syn.*: dinky dyke, semi-diesel.

babyface, *n.* (1) An effeminate or boyish-looking man. *Syn.:* angel, angelface, buttercup, chicken, pussy. (2) An attractive, innocent woman. ["Man is willing to accept woman as an equal, as a man in skirts, as an angel, a devil, a babyface . . . a bosom, a womb, a pair of legs, an encyclopedia, an ideal or an obscenity. The only thing he won't accept her as is a human being"—D. H. Lawrence.]

baby-kisser, *n.* A campaigning politician who feigns interest in children and families.

baby pro, *n.* A young prostitute under the age of legal consent. ["He was nothing but a chicken hawk looking for a baby-pro."]

baby snatcher, *n.* A person who marries or has an affair with a much younger person. *Syn.:* body snatcher, cradle snatcher.

bac, *n.* A born-again Christian, a fundamentalist. ["The trouble with born-again Christians is that they are even bigger pains the second time around"—Herb Caen columnist.]

bacchanalian, *adj.* Drunken or orgiastic revelry. ["The bacchanalian orgies came to an abrupt end after the starlet was found floating in the pool."] *Syn.:* debauched, bacchaic, dionysian, dissolute, frenzied, licentious, maenadic, saturnalian.

bachelor bait, *n.* An unmarried woman. *Syn.:* bachelor girl, bachelor woman, old maid.

bachelor's baby, *n.* An illegitimate child, a bastard. ["Motherhood is a matter of fact, fatherhood is a matter of opinion"—American proverb.] *Syn.:* bachelor's son, come-by-chance baby, bantling, briar-patch child, buzzard baby, momzer, by-blow, ditch-edge child, Sunday baby, strawfield child, yard child. *Idioms:* born on the wrong side of the blanket, her baby is descended from the long line she listened to.

back, be on one's, *idiom.* To annoy, to anger, to keep bothering. *Idioms:* be in one's face, bust chops, break balls, gripe one's ass, nudzh one, yank one's chain.

backbiting, *adj.* Saying spiteful things about another. ["... jealousy and intrigue and backbiting, producing a poisonous atmosphere"—Bertrand Russell] *Syn.*: bad-mouthing, catty, belittling, calumnious, defamatory, villifying, traducing, derogating, denigrating, slanderous, spiteful.

back-breaker, *n.* A slave-driving boss. *Syn.*: ass-breaker, back-buster, ball-buster, bun-buster, butt-buster, conk-buster, gut-buster.

backdoor man, *n.* A married woman's clandestine lover. [From the picture of one who comes in the back door as the husband is leaving by the front door. "Tell your back-door man, I won't be your fool no more"—"I Ain't Gonna Be Your Fool" (blues song).] *Syn.*: creeper, creeping man, mean jumper, sneakin' deacon, sweetman, bit on the side.

back jumper, *n.* The leading partner in anal intercourse. *Syn.*: backdoor man, moon tripper, Greek, ring snatcher, topman.

back in your box, get, *imper.* Shut up! *Idioms:* back off; butt out; button your lip; hold your water; keep your nose out of this; listen, this is my duck, let me milk it; stay out.

back number, *n.* A has-been, an out-of-date person. ["It's sad to see those older actors, all back numbers, accepting bit parts and stupid roles in order to stay in the public's eye."]

back o' me hand to you, the, *idiom.* A traditional Anglo-Irish rebuff or threat.

back-patter, *n.* A servile, flattering self-seeker. *Syn.*: ass-kisser, apple-polisher, back-scratcher, boot-licker, brownnose, toady, ear-greaser, flannelmouth, lickspittle, mealymouth, soft-soap artist, clawback, sycophant.

backseat driver, *n.* One who gives unwanted advice.

backslider, *n.* A person who abandons his religion or principles. ["The way of the backslider is full of splinters"—American proverb.] *Syn.*: defector, defaulter, misbeliever, recreant, recusant, renegade.

backstabber, *n.* One who slanders or betrays others in an underhanded or sly manner.

back talk, *n.* Vociferous, balky contradiction; impertinent retorts; insolent dialogue. ["Don't give me none of your back talk."] *Syn.*: lip, back sass, jaw, sass.

backward, *adj.* Mentally deficient. *Syn.*: dull, retarded, dense, dim-witted, dull, half-witted, feebleminded, imbecilic, laggard, moronic, simpleminded, sluggish.

baconbelly, *n.* A very fat person. *Syn.*: blubberbelly, barrelbelly, tub of lard, double guts, beerbelly, fatass, big bunch of fat, blubberguts, gross, tubby, porcine, elephant, fatguts, fat lips, fatso, five-by-five, hippo, gutbucket, guts-tosell, guts-and-garbage, jellybelly, lardass, pusgut.

bad actor, *n.* A troublemaker, a difficult and contentious character. *Syn.*: smartass, wiseguy.

badass, *n.* A mean, belligerent, worthless person. ["He's one bad-ass motherfucker."]

badass(ed), *adj.* Inferior in character, ability, or performance. ["That rock group put on one badass performance, as if they were just going through the motions."] *Syn.*: second-rate, bush-league, cheesy, half-assed, mickey mouse, cotton-pickin', piss-poor, crappy, cruddy, crummy, dipshit, grungy, no-account, schlocky, raggedy-ass, rat-ass, rinky-dink, shitty, ticky-tacky, yucky, zero-minus.

bad baby, *n.* A rough, threatening man; a thug. *Syn.*: ape, badass, roughneck, big tuna, hood, bully, gorilla, goon, hoodlum, hooligan, mug, plug-ugly, ugly customer, yegg.

bad broad, *n.* An ugly woman. ["Beauty is skin-deep, but a bad broad's ugly goes clear to the bone"—American saying.] *Syn.*: airedale, bad head, vinegar puss, bat, cow, sourpussy, beast, clock-stopper, crock, crow, dog, dogess, douche, garbage can, hatchetface, horror, mud duck, pig, scag, scuzz, skank, witch. *Idioms*: homely enough to curdle milk, stomp-down ugly, so ugly the tide would not take her out, ugly as homemade sin, bag-over-the-head job, bag with a sag.

bad dude, *n.* A womanizer, a lecher. ["I think Wilt Chamberlain's claim to 20,000 seductions makes him the all-time bad dude"—Anon.] *Syn.*: bad mother, swinger, letch, gashhound, meathound, heavy hitter, tomcat, horny bastard, skirt-chaser, wolf, hot nuts, lady-killer, lecher, makeout artist, masher, rip, stick daddy, studhammer, tail-chaser, wencher, whorehound.

bad lay, *n.* A poor sexual performer. ["In spite of his vaunted claims of conquest and great performance, several actresses claimed that the stud was really a bad lay."] *Syn.*: cold cookie, dead battery, dryhole, dud, punk dunk, rock.

bad-mouth, *v.* To denigrate, to belittle, or to poor-mouth. *Syn.*: dump on, slam, gate-mouth, slag. *Idioms*: cut one into small pieces, lay a slur, scandalize one's name.

bad news, *n.* An unpleasant or dangerous person. *Syn.*: bad shit, bad medicine, tsuris, bad scene, poison, deep shit, hot grease, deep trouble, mind-fucker, pain in the ass, tough stuff.

bad pay, *n.* A person who does not repay debts on time or at all. *Syn.*: beat, deadbeat, welsher.

bad shit, *n.* A thoroughly despicable person. *Syn.*: deep shit, shitheel, sleazeball, slimebucket. *Idiom*: lower than a snake's belly in a wagon rut.

bad smell, *n.* A rotten egg. *Syn.*: son of a bitch, shit, bastard, stinker, turd.

bad-timing, *v.* Sexually unfaithful. ["She was too trusting to believe that he was bad-timing her."] *Syn.*: chippying, noshing, two-timing, yarding, cheating. *Idioms*: getting a little on the side, slippin' the traces, stepping out on someone.

bafflegabber, *n.* Politicians, bureaucrats, and academics who use pompous, complicated language in order to obfuscate. ["The bafflegabbers devised all kinds of analyses of poverty except one: the lack of money."]

bag, *n.* (1) An elderly woman. *Syn.:* hag, old bag, old bat, old broad, old hen, old witch. (2) A smelly, slovenly, over-the-hill hooker. *Syn.:* pig, garbage can, glueneck, gutter slut, hay bag, zook. (3) An unattractive woman. *Idioms:* fit to stop a clock, no oil painting, no prize, something the cat dragged in. (4) A promiscuous female. ["There goes the famous good time that was had by all"—Bette Davis,] referring to a promiscuous actress. *Syn.:* good-time girl, bat, baloney, hard baby, popover, swift baby, rough baby, wild baby. *Idioms:* have more pricks than a secondhand dart board, lead pipe cinch.

bag ass, *v.* To leave, to get lost. ["She had no intention of having lunch with him and that was that. . . . Why couldn't she simply tell him to bag his ass?"—Elmore Leonard, *The Switch*.]

bagel bender, *n.* A Jewish person. [From the doughnut-shaped hard roll popularized by Jews.] *Syn.:* bagel, Jew-bagel.

baggage, *n.* An easy lay.

baggy, *adj.* Fat and flabby. ["The chorus was made up of a lot of baggy hoofers."] *Syn.:* sagging, droopy, unshapely, flaccid, paunchy, bloated.

bagholder, *n.* A dupe who is left with all the blame or losses. ["His partners looted the company, took off for Brazil, and he was left as the bagholder."] *Syn.:* buck-taker, goat, patsy, dupe.

bag it, *interj.* ["Get out of my sight! Just forget it! Drop dead! Don't die, suffer!"]

bagman or **baglady** *n.* A trusted flunky who collects money from and/or for bribers, extortionists, or mobsters. ["Before I got promoted I used to be a bagman . . . just nickel and dime stuff"—*The Big Easy*, U.S. film (1986).]

bag of shit tied up with a string, *n.* A shapeless or scruffy person.

bag-over-the-head job, *n.* Sex with an ugly woman, or the woman herself. *Idiom:* don't look at the mantlepiece when you are stoking the fire.

bag-twister, *n.* An aggressive woman. [From *bag* = scrotum.]

bag your face, *imper.* (1) Stop talking! *Idioms:* shut up, shut your mouth and give your ass a chance, button your lip, can it, clam up, dry up, dummy up, knock it off, pack it up, pipe down, shut your ass, shut your head, shut your face, stow it. (2) You're repulsive! *idioms:* cover your face, go away.

bag your ass, *imper.* Go to hell!

Bahama mamma, *n.* An obese, unattractive black woman. *Syn.:* bear, pig(ger), pigmouth, shuttlebutt, teddy bear, Judy with the big booty.

bait, *n.* (1) A person police use to entrap homosexuals. (2) A sexually attractive young woman, often underaged. *Syn.:* jailbait, bedbait, johnny-bait. (3) An effeminate man or a masculine woman who attracts homosexuals. (4) An attractive man or woman who shills for a con artist or fronts for a mugger. ["He went for the bait and was hooked, but good."] (5) A bad-smelling woman.

balderdash, *n.* Idle, nonsensical talk. ["Psychology is the youngest of the sciences, and hence chiefly guesswork, empiricism, hocus-pocus, and balderdash."—H. L. Mencken.] *Syn.:* nonsense, poppycock, bullshit, tommyrot, crap, tomfoolery, trash, claptrap, bunk, buncombe (or bunkum), bosh, twaddle, drivel, bull, hot air, crock, gibberish.

bald-headed row, *n.* Old men who love to ogle women. [From the presence of many older men in the front rows at burlesque shows.]

baldie, *n.* A bald person. ["He's balder than Buddha's balls"—*Maledicta* VIII.] *Syn.:* bald coot, bald eagle, cueball, baldy, skinhead, egghead, suedehead.

bale of straw, *n.* A white girl or woman, especially a blonde. *Syn.:* Lady Snow, white meat, Little Eva, Miss Amy, snow, Miss Ann, Miss Lillian, pinktoes, silk.

ball-and-chain, *n.* One's wife or sweetheart. From the notion that a woman is a shackle. ["He was relieved when his divorce was final and he was free of his ball-and-chain."] *Syn.:* block and tackle, chief of staff, first sergeant, front office, war department.

ball-bearing hostess, *n.* A male airplane cabin attendant.

ball-breaker, *n.* A woman considered threatening or "castrating" by men, often because of her drive, brains, or success. ["... ball-breaker, that's one of the nicer things men have called me"—Caroline Hennessey, *I, B.I.T.C.H.* (1970).] *Syn.:* ball-tearer, ball-wracker, bitch kitty, bone-breaker, de-baller, gorgon, harpy, harridan, hellcat, nut-cruncher, pecker-wrecker.

ball-buster, *n.* A person who assigns extremely difficult tasks. *Syn.:* bun-buster, butt-buster, killer.

ball-crusher, *n.* A woman who exhausts a man sexually, as opposed to a ball-breaker, who hurts a man psychologically.

balls, *interj.* Exclamation of disgust and incredulity. *Idioms:* the hell you say, in a pig's eye, you're pissin' on my leg.

balls, have someone by the, *idiom.* To have one at a disadvantage and helpless to resist or fight back. *Idiom:* have one by the short hairs, have one by the curlies, your ass belongs to me.

balls, man with fuzzy, *idiom.* A white man.

balls, man with no, *idiom.* A coward or an impotent man. *Syn.:* candyass, limp-dick, doormat, wimp, wuss, pussy, jellyfish, mother's boy, namby-pamby, pantywaist, rabbit, sop, weak sister.

ballsey, *adj.* Very aggressive and impulsive. This has a negative connotation for a woman. ["She was labeled as too ballsey for the job."]

baloney, full of, *idiom.* Completely mistaken. ["You're full of baloney if you think people will vote for an ex-actor for president."] *Syn.:* all wet, full of crap, full of it, full of shit.

bam, *n.* A female marine. [Acronym for "*b*road-*a*ss *ma*-rine."]

'bama chucker, *n.* A white, Southern hick.

bamboozle, *v.* To cheat, often by confusing or misleading someone. ["What Oriental tomfoolery is bamboozling you?"—Albert Henry Newman.] *Syn.*: baffle, dupe, befuddle, deceive, con, trick, cheat, take, swindle, rook, victimize, defraud, cozen, gull, gyp, hoax, swindle, delude, hoodwink. *Idioms:* blow smoke, deal from the bottom of the deck, do a number on, jerk or rattle someone's chain, run a game, take someone to the cleaners, throw the hooks into someone, use smoke and mirrors.

bamboozler, *n.* A deceiver, a trickster, a swindler. *Syn.*: blindsider, fast-talker, con artist, dipsy-doodler, four-flusher, flimflammer, grifter, hornswoggler, shucker, yentzer.

banana, *n.* (1) A sexually attractive light-skinned African-American woman. *Syn.*: cafe au lait, high yella, high yeller, pinky, lemon, quadroon, octoroon, peola, pink toes, sealskin, bird's-eye maple, tush, yellow girl. (2) An Asian-American who identifies with white society. [From being yellow on the outside but white on the inside.] (3) A person from Central America. [From the advertisements for Chiquita bananas.] (4) A male homosexual, especially a fellator. [From *banana* = penis.]

bananas, *adj.* (1) Crazy, insane, demented. (2) Homosexual.

bandit, *n.* A homosexual who uses violence to gain sexual partners. [From prison use.] *Syn.*: ass bandit, biscuit bandit, bun bandit, kiester bandit.

band moll, *n.* A girl or young woman who trades sex for permission to be around pop or rock musicians. *Syn.*: groupie, prom queen, band rat, starfucker, celebrity fucker.

bandy-leg, *n.* A person with bowlegs. ["Never trust a man who is a bandy-leg—his brains are too near his bottom" —adapted from Noel Coward.]

bang, *n.* A woman regarded as a sexual object.

bangster, *n.* A drug addict who shoots up with a needle. *Syn.*: banger, hype shooter, mainliner, jabber, jaboff, junk hawk, junk hog, junkhound, junkman, needle fiend, needle jabber, needle knight, needle nipper, needle rusher, pinhead, pinjabber, vein shooter, zoner.

banty, *n.* A short person. ["Cagney portrayed a banty little rooster to the hilt."] *Syn.*: half-pint, little feller, runt, shrimp, shorty, a little drink of water.

baragouinist, *n.* One whose speech is outlandish and unintelligible.

barbarian, *n.* An insensitive, uncivilized person; a fierce and cruel person. ["... in Hitler's time, I saw what collective barbarians the Germans could become. ... The German people became possessed of an evil spirit, which brutalized them and degraded them"—William L. Shirer.]

barber's chair, *n.* A promiscuous girl or woman who is used by all.

Barbie doll, *n.* A mindless woman; typical all-American WASP; superconformist, fashion-conscious, consumerist, airhead, and self-conscious sexpot. [From the blue-eyed, blond-haired, big-busted, designer-labeled plastic doll. "Our Barbie doll president and his Barbie doll wife" —Hunter S. Thompson.]

barfbag, *n.* A despicable person. [From *barf* = vomit. "Word on the street is that you barfbags are giving the kids in the seventh grade a hard time"—*Vice Versa*, U.S. film (1988).]

barfly, *n.* A heavy drinker who spends lots of time at bars. ["Benchley was a barfly whose favorite quip was: Let's get out of these wet clothes and into a dry martini."]

barfola, *interj.* Dammit!

barf out or **barfola,** *interj.* This is terrible! How god-awful! Spare me!

barfy, *adj.* Vomity, nauseating, puky. ["He hated those Valley girls who called everyone and everything barfy at the slightest provocation."] *Syn.*: barf city, barf me out, barfulous, bletcherous,

bargeass or **barge,** *n.* One with exceptionally big buttocks.

barge pole, I wouldn't touch it with a, *idiom.* A put-down by a man of a woman he finds sexually repulsive.

bar hustler, *n.* A male prostitute who solicits customers in bars.

bark, *n.* A person of Irish descent.

barn-burner, *n.* A member of a political party who is willing to destroy his party in pursuit of a principle or personal gain. [From an early American reformer who said he was willing to burn down the barn in order to get rid of the rats.]

barnyard, *adj.* Pertaining to someone or something coarse or vulgar. *Syn.:* dirty, disgusting, fescennine, filthy, foul, indecent, salacious, scabrous, raunchy, smutty, vulgar.

barracuda, *n.* A predatory person who would stoop to any means, a killer who goes for the jugular, a piranha. ["He has a reputation of being a barracuda, but he was nevertheless gobbled up by the Wall Street sharks."]

barrelbelly, *n.* An exceptionally fat person.

basket case, *n.* A helpless, hopeless, mentally disturbed person.

basketeer, *n.* One who ogles male crotches, a basket-watcher.

bastard, *n.* A mean, despicable, self-serving person. ["Life is a God-damned, stinking, treacherous game and nine hundred and ninety-nine men out of a thousand are bastards"—Theodore Dreiser.] *Syn.:* motherfucker, prick, whoreson, heel, knave, lowlife, miscreant, son of a bitch, scoundrel.

bastarda, *n.* A female bastard.

bastardly-gullion, *n.* A bastard son of a bastard, bell-bastard.

bastrich, *n.* A despised person [A blend of *bastard* + *bitch.*]

bat, *n.* (1) An unattractive woman. ["It's a thankless job to butt in and tell a man that in your important opinion his wife is a vampire bat"—Sinclair Lewis.] *Syn.*: bag, beldam, biddy, crone, drab, old bat, trot, witch. (2) A crazy or eccentric person. ["The old bat would scream curses at everyone who passed her window."] (3) A woman of easy morals. (4) An older woman who seeks out younger men.

bat carrier, *n.* A stool pigeon, an informer, a snitch.

bathetic, *adj.* Overly or falsely sentimental. *Syn.*: anticlimactic, clichéd, hackneyed, stale, trite.

bato or **vato,** *n.* A Mexican or other Hispanic person.

battle-ax, *n.* An ill-tempered, mean woman. ["One of the American males' favorite put-down words for a strong, fist-shaking, foot-stamping rights-demanding woman" —Barbara Miles, in *A Feminist Dictionary* (1985).] *Syn.*: battleship, beldam, crone, spitfire, virago, termagant.

battyman, *n.* A homosexual. [West Indian usage.]

b.a.v., *n.* Someone who has not engaged in sex for a very long time. [From *b*orn-*a*gain *v*irgin.]

bawdy, *adj.* Relating to obscene language or behavior. ["It's a bawdy planet"—William Shakespeare, *Winter's Tale.*] *Syn.*: blue, coarse, dirty, gross, indecent, lascivious, lecherous, lewd, off-color, libidinous, licentious, lustful, pornographic, prurient, purple, raunchy, ribald, risqué, salacious, smutty, vulgar, lowdown and dirty.

B.B., *n.* A free-basing drug user who is seriously impaired. [Short for *base burnout.*]

B.B. head, *n.* An unattractive, sloppy woman, often with short, nappy hair.

B.D. woman, *n.* An aggressive, masculine lesbian. [Abbreviation of *bulldagger.* "B.D. women, they done laid their claim/They can lay their jive like a nach'l man"—"B.D. Woman's Blues (song)."]

beach bum, *n.* A man who loafs on beaches; a self-indulgent, strutting stud. ["He's just a beach bum whose only thought is the size of his pecs and lats."]

beach bitch, *n.* The homosexual equivalent of a beach bum. ["This beach bitch spent his summers on Fire Island, and his winters in Hawaii."]

beach bunny, *n.* A girl or woman who struts her sexuality on beaches.

bead-counter, *n.* A Roman Catholic. [From the reference to rosary beads.] *Syn.*: bead-puller, statue-lover.

beaded lady, *n.* A homosexual hippie.

beak, *n.* A mayor, a judge, or a lawyer.

beamy bimbo, *n.* A fat person.

bean-eater, *n.* A Mexican-American. ["Bean eater: A nickname for a Mexican"—Ramon Adams, *Western Words* (1948).] *Syn.*: bean, bean bandit, beaner, beano, burrito, chili-chomper, bean-choker, greaser, greasegut, pepperbelly, pinto bean, taco, taco-bender, beaner, tacohead.

bean juice, *n.* A despicable, disgusting person. [From a word for anal exudate. "You're nothing but bean juice, buster!"] *Syn.*: fart slime.

bear, *n.* An especially unattractive woman. *Syn.*: booga bear, beast, beastie, beastess, buzzard.

beard, *n.* A conventional man or woman who serves as a public cover for a gay or lesbian friend. ["The in-the-closet star was always accompanied by a beard on his promotional tours, but that didn't slow him down."]

beard-splitter, *n.* A lecherous man. [From *beard* = pubic hair.] *Syn.*: beard-jammer, hairmonger.

beast, *n.* A white person. ["... the beast's backing up. His ass/is grass"—A. B. Spellman, "The Beautiful Day #9."]

beasty, *adj.* Pertaining to a person repulsive due to either physical deformity or lack of social grace. *Syn.*: yukky, odious, unsightly, dorky.

beat the shit out of, *idiom.* To defeat soundly, to whip. *Idioms*: knock the shit out of, beat the can off, beat the bejesus out of, beat the living tar out of, beat the living daylights out of, break in half, brown-slice [West Indies usage], hang one out to dry, have one's guts for garters, jam one up, shove a fist down one's throat.

beat with an ugly stick, be, *idiom.* Very ugly. ["Boy, get the puss on that one. She was sure beat with an ugly stick."]

beaver, *n.* Any woman. [From *beaver* = pubic hair.] *Syn.*: beetle, fox, canary, doe, squirrel, heifer, bitch, chick, mouse, chicken.

beaver-shooter, *n.* A person addicted to peering at female genitals, a voyeur.

bebopper, *n.* A naive, inept, disliked person. ["He's thirty years old and still acts like a bebopper."] *Syn.*: bopper, bubblegummer, dud, feeb, frip, half-pint, lightweight, Melvin, one-eyed scribe, pint-size, pipsqueak, pissant, small change, teenybopper, twerp. *Idioms*: bit of fluff, no big deal, no great shakes, nobody to write home about.

bed bunny, or **bedbug,** *n.* A loose woman.

beddo, *n.* An Arab. [From *bedouin* = desert dweller.] *Syn.*: ay-rab, camel jockey, sand nigger, towelhead.

bed-swerver, *n.* One who is false to his or her marriage vows. *Syn.*: spouse-breacher.

beef, *n.* A sexually attractive young man or woman.

beekie, *n.* A person who spies on his fellow workers for the boss.

beerbelly or **beer gut,** *n.* A man with a huge paunch.

beer can player, *n.* An athlete who would rather sit on the bench than play; hence, a politician who is reluctant to enter the ring.

beginner brown, *n.* A light-skinned African-American. ["strong boned/beige beauty/was afro american in the twenties/turn 'negro' in the forties/proud-american in the sixties. . . . —Edward S. Spriggs, "My Beige Mom."] *Syn.*: beige, black-and-tan, bleached ebony, bird's-eye maple, lemon.

begonia, *n.* A black gay man, or a white gay man who prefers black men. *Syn.*: Beulah, hence, Beulah lover.

beige, *adj.* Boring, insipid, bland, strictly ho-hum; hence, someone who is boring, bland, insipid.

be in someone's crack, *idiom.* To be nosy. [From *crack* = buttocks' cleavage.] *Syn.*: be in someone's face.

belcher, *n.* A stool pigeon.

belch-guts, *n.* A drunk.

believer, *n.* A captured enemy soldier. [A "true believer" is a dead enemy soldier.]

bellyacher, *n.* A chronic complainer. *Syn.*: beefer, faultfinder, griper, grouser, grumbler, kicker, kvetch.

belly-god, *n.* A glutton. *Syn.*: belly-gut, belly-slave.

belly-lass or **belly-piece,** *n.* A mistress.

belt up, *imper.* Stop talking! Shut up!

bemused, *adj.* Tending to have one's mind wander. *Syn.*: absentminded, befuddled, fuddled, preoccupied, muddled, muted, stupefied.

bench jockey, *n.* A player who sits on the sidelines and gives advice or needles the opposition.

bench warmer, *n.* A second-rate player, a nonessential member of a staff or team.

beni, *n.* Human excrement; hence, a piece of beni or piece of crap.

benighted, *adj.* Primitive, uncultured, unsophisticated. *Syn.*: ignorant, backward, unenlightened, pig-ignorant, uncivilized, illiterate, know-nothing, empty-headed, unhip.

bent-wrist or *bent, n.* An effeminate homosexual.

benumbed, *adj.* So overwhelmed as to be paralyzed.

berkshire, *n.* A very black-skinned person. [From the color of Berkshire hogs. West Indian usage.]

besmearer, *n.* A person who sullies or smears another person's reputation.

besotted, *adj.* Overwhelmed by drink or emotion. [". . . seemed absolutely besotted about the damned woman"—Agatha Christie.] *Syn.*: drunk, befuddled, confused, inebriated, stupefied, witless, infatuated.

bespatterer, *n.* A slanderer.

bestial, *adj.* Pertaining to the character or conduct of beasts. [". . . inclined to describe any sexual indulgence of which he does not approve as bestial"—Joseph Wood Krutch.] *Syn.*: animal, barbaric, barbarous, brutal, brutish, carnal, degraded, depraved, feral, inhuman, savage, subhuman, swinish.

better-than-thou, *idiom.* A pious hypocrite.

B-girl, *n.* A promiscuous girl or woman, especially one who works as a hostess in a bar.

bi, *n.* A bisexual.

biased, *adj.* Favoring a group or viewpoint regardless of fact or logic. *Syn.*: bigoted, colored, blinkered, distorted, embittered, jaundiced, loaded, partisan, one-sided, partial, predisposed, prejudiced, slanted, tendentious, twisted, unfair, warped.

bibble-babbler, *n.* Someone who talks a lot and says nothing.

Bible-banger, *n.* A pious, straitlaced person; a strict follower of a religion, particularly a Protestant fundamentalist. ["All the candidates catered to the Bible-bangers when they went down South; no sex out of marriage, right-to-life, and a dose of homophobia."] *Syn.*: amen-snorter, Bibleback, Bible-basher, Bible-pounder, sky pilot, Bible-thumper, Bible-puncher, Christer, Holy Joe, knee-bender.

bibulous, *adj.* So drunk you don't know what is happening. *Syn.*: alcoholic, boozy, swacked, crapulous, inebriated, plastered, shikker, pickled, sottish, sucking in. *Idioms*: drunk as a skunk, drunk as a lord.

biffer, *n.* A homely woman who offsets her looks by being sexually loose.

bigass, *adj.* Consumed by one's importance.

big baby, *n.* (1) A weak, silly person. (2) A massive woman. *Syn.:* Big Bertha, biggie, big number, box, big belly, fatty.

big-belly, *n.* A very fat person.

big breeze, *n.* A person who talks excessively.

Big Brother, *n.* A dictatorial and sinister leader of a party or organization. ["Big Brother is watching you"—George Orwell, *Nineteen Eighty-Four* (1949).]

big Dick from Boston, *n.* A loud, vulgar tourist. ["When you go to Europe, don't act like big Dick from Boston"]

big diesel or **big diesel dyke,** *n.* A swaggering, cigar-smoking lesbian.

big ears, *n.* An overly inquisitive person.

big eyebrow, *n.* A white man.

big fart, *n.* A person who basks in self-importance. *Syn.:* tush hog, big head, swelled head, big noise, big shit, big stiff, big Swede, big cheese. *Idioms:* big dog in the meat house, big buck at the lick, tall hog at the trough.

biggety or **biggity,** *adj.* Pertaining to one who is cocky or conceited. *Syn.:* smartass, bold, cheeky, fresh, haughty, impudent, nervy, sassy, smart-alecky, swaggering, putting on airs.

big hunk of nothing, *n.* A small or unimportant person or object. *Syn.:* a mediocrity, a nobody, small potatoes, nebbish, small fry. *Idioms:* (long thin) streak of piss, nothing to write home about, not worth a plugged nickel, not worth a hill of beans.

big macher, *n.* A wheeler-dealer, an operator.

bigmouth, *n.* A talkative, boastful person; a smartass; a know-it-all. *Syn.:* armchair general, bag of wind, big noise, blow-hard, bullshit artist, crapper, gasbag, gatemouth, hot-air artist, loudmouth, braggart, Monday morning quarterback, popoff, satchelmouth, windbag.

bigot, *n.* A blind, obstinate zealot; devoted to a particular creed or party. ["The mind of the bigot is like the pupil of the eye; the more light you pour upon it, the more it will contract"—Oliver Wendell Holmes.] *Syn.:* chauvinist, dogmatist, fanatic, racist, xenophobe, sectarian, sexist, white supremacist, misogynist.

big shit, *n.* A big shot.

big sucker-and-egg man, *n.* An important, gullible person.

big-time operator, *n.* A wheeler-dealer, a lecher, or a hustler. ["M. was a big-time operator who overextended himself and whose empire ultimately collapsed."]

big woman, *n.* A very effeminate man.

big yawn, *n.* A boring, tedious person.

bike, *n.* A sexually promiscuous woman. [From the idea that anybody can ride her.]

bilge artist, *n.* A braggart, a bullshit artist.

bilious, *adj.* Terribly ill-tempered or grouchy. *Syn.:* irritable, sour, peevish, angry, nasty, cranky, crabby, petulant, testy, snappish, short-tempered, cantankerous.

bilker, *n.* One who cheats or reneges on debts.

billingsgate, *n.* Coarse or abusive language. [From the language used by the fishmongers at the Billingsgate market in London. "The more I humbled myself, the more he stormed . . . provoking me with scandalous names that I could not put up with; so that I . . . returned his billingsgate"—Tobias Smollett.]

bimbette, *n.* A frivolous young woman.

bimbo, *n.* (1) A mean, menacing man; a bozo; a goon. (2) A sexually loose woman. (3) An empty-headed woman. ["Not all women in pop are brainless bimbos lured into lurex by cynical rock business shitheads"—*Ms London Magazine* (1989).]

bircher, *n.* A member of any extremist group. [From the right-wing John Birch Society.]

bird, *n.* (1) A girl or woman. (2) An eccentric person, an odd bird. (3) A prostitute.

bird bandit, *n.* A womanizer, a lecher.

birdbrain, *n.* A person of meager intelligence; a stupid, foolish person. ["You're a birdbrain, and I mean that as an insult to birds"—George S. Kaufman.] *Syn.*: addlebrain, antbrain, B.B. brain, bottlebrain, brockbrain, bubblebrain, cockbrain, crackbrain, crapbrain, dickbrain, doodlebrain, dorkbrain, fatbrain, featherbrain, fiddlebrain, fleabrain, gnatbrain, giddybrain, goobrain, hairbrain, harebrain, lackbrain, rattlebrain, scatterbrain, shutterbrain, skitterbrain, squarebrain.

bird dog, *n.* A chaperone or one who tails a person.

birdie, *n.* A homosexual man.

bird-taker, *n.* (1) A sodomite. (2) A male whore.

birdturd, *n.* A despicable, obnoxious person.

birdwatcher, *n.* A fanatical environmentalist, an eco-nut. ["Developers complained that the birdwatchers were wrecking the economy."]

birl, *n.* An effeminate man. [From *boy* + *girl*.]

biscuit bandit, *n.* The aggressive partner in gay anal intercourse.

bit, *n.* A woman considered as a sexual object. *Idioms:* bit of fluff, bit of crumpet, bit of muslin, bit of stuff, bit of mutton, bit of skin, bit of skirt, bit of straight.

bitch, *n.* (1) A woman. ["... & she smiles/he wd either mumble curses/'bout crazy bitches/or sit dumbfounded"—Ntozake Shange, *For Colored Girls Who Have Considered Suicide When the Rainbow Is Enough*.] (2) A malicious, rude, or heartless woman; a woman who undermines masculinity; a ball-buster. ["That bitch. That fucking hillbilly whorehouse junkie dyke bitch"—Lenny Bruce, in Albert Goldman's *Ladies and Gentlemen, Lenny Bruce* (1974).] *Syn.*: broad, cunt, cat, dogess, fury, harridan, fishwife, shrew, battle-ax, termagant, virago, vixen, witch. (3) A mean, insolent, flaunting male homosexual. (4) A slut. ["He married the bitch/With the seven-year itch./And the band played on"—Ed Cary, *The Erotic Muse* (1972).]

bitch, *v.* To gripe, to kvetch.

bitch in heat, *n.* A sexually ravenous woman.

bitch kitty, *n.* A disagreeable or disliked woman. *Syn.*: bitch on wheels.

bitch's bastard, *n.* A nasty, revolting man.

bitch's blind, *n.* A girlfriend or wife who is a "cover" for a gay male.

bitchy, *adj.* Mean, malicious, and spiteful. *Syn.*: backbiting, catty, complaining, cruel, despiteful, evil, hateful, nasty, poisonous, rude, snide, snorky, spikey, venomous, vicious, vindictive, vixenish, waspish, wicked.

bite me, *interj.* Shut up! *Idioms*: you make me sick, get out of here, kiss my ass, fuck you.

biter, *n.* A con man, a cheat.

bit of black velvet, *n.* A woman of color, a bit of ebony.

bit of fluff, *n.* (1) An insignificant or ineffectual person. (2) An easy, empty-headed woman. ["Although he considered himself an intellectual, when it came to sex he preferred a bit of fluff."]

bit of jam, *n.* A woman considered as a sex object. *Syn.*: bit of crackling, pie, cake, hot tamale, hot tomato, mutton, peach, barbecue, cherry pie, dish, tomato, tart.

bit of spare, *n.* An unattached female attending a party or other event.

bit of stuff, *n.* An easy woman.

bit of tripe, *n.* One's wife.

bitter-ender, *n.* A person who stubbornly resists change. *Syn.*: conservative, diehard, fundamentalist, old-liner, reactionary, right-winger, stand-patter, stick in the mud, tory.

bitter half, *n.* One's wife. [A play on the expression "better half."]

blab, *v.* To inform. ["If he sees cards and actual money passing, he will be sure to blab, and it will be all over the town in no time"—Joseph Conrad.] *Syn.*: peach, snitch, squawk, squeal, be a stoolie.

blabbermouth, *n.* One who talks too much and reveals secrets, a gossip. ["We have drugs to make women speak, but none to keep them silent"—Anatole France.] *Syn.*: babblemouth, babbler, banderlog, big breeze, bigmouth, blabber, blabmouth, ear-bender, gabber, gabblemouth, gabbler, gatemouth, gibble-gabble, jabberer, liverlip, loud-mouth, magpie, motormouth, prater, prattler, quidnunc, tongue-wagger, yapper, yenta.

black, *n.* or adj. An African-American man or woman. ["White is right/Yellow mellow/Black, get back!/ Do you believe that Jack?/ Sure do!/ Then you're a dope for which there ain't much hope./ Black is fine!/And, God knows,/It's mine!"—Langston Hughes, "Argument."] [Although *black* has been the preferred term of address for some time for a person of some African ancestry, the following terms are usually considered offensive, especially if used by non-blacks.] *Syn.*: ashy black, coal black, dead black, deep black, honest black, jet black, near black, pale black, rusty black, thoroughbred black, won't-stop black, black tar baby, dark black, light black, navy black, off black, scrubby black, smooth black.

black-baiter, *n.* A person prejudiced against blacks, a racist.

blackball, *v.* To reject, to deny membership. ["They black-balled him from membership in the country club for the third time."] *Syn.*: blacklist, shit-list, stink-list, tincan. *Idioms*: put on the crap list, put on the ditch list, put on the shit list.

blackball, *n.* An especially dark-skinned black person. *Syn.*: blackbird, black dust, black cloud.

black boy or **blackfellow,** *n.* An adult black man.

black fay, *n.* A black who is deferential to whites, an Uncle Tom.

blackie, *n.* A black man or woman. *Syn.*: blackhead, blackout.

black Jew, *n.* A West Indian black who lives in the United States.

blackmailer, *n.* One who extorts money or favors by threatening to expose someone's real or imaginary misdeeds. ["Some say J. Edgar Hoover was a notorious blackmailer who threatened all sorts of politicos high or low."] *Syn.:* bleeder, blister, bloodsucker, extortionist, leech, shakedown artist, shark, vampire.

black meat, *n.* A black person viewed solely as a sex object. ["That sweet and sassy sister looks like the finest black meat."]

black plaguer, *n.* A person who plants unfounded rumors against political opponents, a rat-fucker.

black Protestant, *n.* (1) A Protestant deemed prejudiced against Roman Catholics. [Roman Catholic usage.] *Syn.:* black bastard. (2) A non-practicing Protestant. [Protestant usage.]

black sheep, *n.* A disreputable family or group member. ["That unemployed bum is the black sheep of my family."] *Syn.:* disgrace, outcast, pariah, reprobate, prodigal, wastrel.

blah, *adj.* Boring, dreary, humdrum, monotonous, plodding.

blala, *n.* Brother. [An insult when used by whites, an affectionate term when used by peers. Hawaiian usage.]

blank, *n.* A cold or unresponsive woman. *Syn.:* Frigidaire, an ice cube with a hole in it, block, cold cookie, burned bearing.

blanket ass, *n.* A Native American.

blankety-blank, *adj.* [Used as a euphemism for a taboo, profane, or vulgar word.] *Syn.:* bleeping, bliggey, so-and-so, you-know-what.

blarneyer, *n.* A flattering liar.

blasé, *adj.* Unimpressed or bored by one's surroundings, activities, or friends. ["Lying on the beach at St. Tropez, the Eurotrash star stared at her boy toy with a blasé smirk."] *Syn.:* apathetic, jaded, bored, dulled, sated, glutted, surfeited, weary, world-weary. *Idioms:* been around twice, done it all.

blasphemous, *adj.* Speaking of God in impious or irreverent terms, or flouting religious sensibilities. ["A pox o' your throat, you bawling, blasphemous, uncharitable dog" —William Shakespeare, *The Tempest.*] *Syn.:* execrative, hubristic, imprecatory, irreligious, irreverent, profane, sacrilegious, ungodly, godless.

blast, *v.* To condemn strongly. ["If he dares open his mouth just one more time, I am going to blast him."] *Syn.:* abuse, berate, denounce, excoriate, impugn, lambaste, roast, scorch, snipe, sock, vilify, whale. *Idioms:* lay into, let fly at, let loose on, pile into, pitch into, sail into, skin alive, sock it to.

blatherer, *n.* A long-winded, empty talker.

bleeding dirt, *n.* An extortionist who preys on homosexuals. ["Keep out of that club. It is a hangout for bleeding dirt."]

bleeding heart, *n.* A person seen as excessively softhearted toward the underprivileged. Often used by conservatives to condemn the politically liberal. ["... a man who would make Attila the Hun, by comparison, look like a bleeding heart"—Russell Baker, *New York Times* (1972).]

blemish, *n.* A person who is an embarrassment. ["I never take that blemish to a party. You never know what kind of stunt she'll pull."] *Syn.:* flaw, blotch, blot, taint, zit.

blimp, *n.* (1) A fat person, a fatty. ["When I was playing tennis, I was just a fat blimp waddling, round the court" —Annabel Croft, *Today* (1989).] (2) An elderly, incurable conservative. [From David Low's British cartoon character Colonel Blimp.]

(the) blind leading the blind, *idiom.* The ignorant trying to teach the unlearned.

blinking idiot or **blithering idiot,** *n.* A gross fool. ["The portrait of a blinking idiot"—William Shakespeare, *The Merchant of Venice.*]

bliss ninny, *n.* A person so ecstatic as to seem mad. ["Stop being a bliss ninny, just because he asked you for a date."]

blister, *n.* An annoying person. *Idioms*: blister on the bleeding bloody bollocks of biology, pimple on the petrified prong of progress.

blivit, *n.* An obsese or disgusting person. [Described as ten pounds of shit in a five-pound bag.]

blizzardhead, *n.* A very blond person. *Syn.*: bale of straw, bottle baby, peroxide baby, suicide blonde.

bloated aristocrat, *n.* A wealthy person bursting with self-importance. *Syn.*: bloated plute, Mr. Moneybags.

blob, *n.* A dull, heavy, useless lout; a nothing.

blockhead, *n.* A stupid, unthinking person. ["A learned blockhead is a greater blockhead than an ignorant blockhead"—Benjamin Franklin.]

blockhead, *n.* A stupid or silly person. *Syn.*: addlehead, airhead, applehead, asshead, bakehead, balloonhead, bananahead, beanhead, beefhead, beetlehead, blubberhead, blunderhead, bonehead, boofhead, bubblehead, buckethead, bumhead, bufflehead, bullhead, bunhead, cabbagehead, cementhead, cheesehead, chickenhead, chowderhead, chucklehead, clodhead, cluckhead, clunkhead, cokehead, conehead, corkhead, crumbhead, deadhead, dickhead, diphead, doughhead, dolthead, dullhead, dumbhead, dunderhead, dungeonhead, emptyhead, fathead, fiddlehead, flathead, foolhead, fuckhead, giddyhead, hammerhead, hardhead, jarhead, jolterhead, jughead, knobhead, knothead, knucklehead, lardhead, leatherhead, lughead, lunkhead, melonhead, mallethead, meathead, muddlehead, mullethead, musclehead, mushhead, mutthead, muttonhead, noodlehead, numbhead, peahead, pighead, pinhead, pointedhead, pointhead, pointyhead, poophead, potatohead, puppyhead, puddinghead, puttyhead, puzzlehead, rattlehead, roundhead, saphead, sheepshead, shithead, softhead, stupehead, stupidhead, tackhead, thickhead, timberhead, tottyhead, watermelonhead, wethead, woodhead, woodenhead, yaphead.

blondie, *n.* (1) A blond woman. (2) A white woman.

bloodclaat, *n.* A disgusting person. [From the West Indian word *bloodclaat* = menstrual cloth.]

blood of a bitch, *n.* (1) A descendent of a bitch, a son of a bitch. (2) A person who is not a genuine Protestant. [Canadian usage.]

bloodsucker, *n.* A murderer, a blackmailer, a leech. *Syn.*: extortioner, parasite, barnacle, freeloader, sponger, spiv, sponge, sucker.

bloomer, make a, *v.* To do something stupid. *Idioms*: do the crazy act, fuck up, make a prick of oneself.

blotcher, *n.* A disgusting person. [From the idea of one who emits a liquid fart that stains his underpants.]

bloviater, *n.* A verbose, windy person.

blow boy, *n.* A fellator.

blowen safen, *n.* A deflowered woman. *Syn.*: damaged goods.

blowhard, *n.* A boastful egomaniac. ["The new boss turned out to be a blowhard who couldn't deliver on anything."] *Syn.*: know-it-all, boaster, bigmouth, big talker, blower, bullshit artist, fanfaron, gasbag, grandstander, hotdogger, gascon, rodomontader, show-off, windbag.

blow-off, *n.* A goof-off.

blowin' off, *v.* To boast, to brag. *Idioms*: loudin' off, mouthin' off, runnin' off at the mouth, talking big.

blow smoke up someone's ass, *Idiom.* To try to fool someone.

blowtop, *n.* A hot-tempered, violent person; a hothead. ["That's the musical mania of the blowtops"—M. Mezzerow, *Really the Blues* (1946).]

blowzer, *n.* An unattractive, slovenly woman.

blowzy, *adj.* Frizzled and unkempt, looking like what the cat dragged in. ["Years of an unhappy marriage led to her constant blowzy appearance."] *Syn.*: bedraggled, disheveled, draggletailed, frowzy, messy, mussy, raunchy, slobbery, sloppy, sluttish, tousled.

blubberbelly, *n.* An obese person. *Syn.:* blubberguts, blubberpot.

blue-ball, *n.* A man who can't find a sexual outlet. [From the folklore that a male gets a case of "blue balls" from continued congestion with no outlet.]

bluebeard, *n.* A lecher, a womanizer.

blue-eyed devil, *n.* A white person.

blue-gum, *n.* A black person. *Syn.:* blue, blue boy, blue-gum moke, blue-lips, blue-skin.

bluenose, *n.* A puritan, a killjoy, a straitlaced person. ["The bluenoses are coming back in fashion."] *Syn.:* comstock, goody-goody, Mrs. Grundy, nice Nelly, prig, prude, wowser.

bluff, *n.* A lesbian who is either active or passive. [A blend of *butch* + *fluff.*]

boanthrop, *n.* A person who is dumb as an ox.

boborahead, *n.* A Japanese immigrant or a Hawaiian resident.

bobtail, *n.* (1) A woman who masturbates. (2) An impotent man.

boeotian, *n.* A fool.

bog-lander, *n.* A person of Irish descent. *Syn.:* bog-hopper, bog rat, bog-trotter, boiled dinner.

bogus, *adj.* Pertaining to a fake or dishonest person or action. ["She's genuinely bogus"—Christopher Hassal, about Dame Edith Sitwell.] *Syn.:* phony, bullshit, ersatz, fake, false, fraudulent, pinchbeck, pseudo, sham, spurious.

bohak or **bohawk,** *n.* A Lithuanian.

boho, *n.* An ineffectual person, a loser. [Presumably related to *bohunk* = an inept bungler, stupid.]

bohunk, *n.* (1) An immigrant from central Europe or Eastern Europe. (2) A stupid, clumsy, foolish person. *Syn.:* baboon, chucklehead, clod, gaum, gawk, hallion, klutz, looby, lubber, lump, palooka, yahoo.

boil, *n.* A disgusting or annoying person. ["Fred is such an obnoxious boil of a character. Instead of wanting to release him, you want to deposit him in a tree grinder" —*Newsday* (1991).]

boing-boing, *n.* A tourist.

boll weevil, *n.* A nonunion worker or a new lower-paid worker who threatens the job of a senior worker. ["All hell is going to break loose if the boll weevils continue to come into the plant."]

bombastic, *adj.* Pertaining to pompous and excessively flowery expression. *Syn.*: bloated, euphuistic, fustian, Gongoristic, grandiloquent, high-flown, histrionic, inflated, magniloquent, verbose.

bomb thrower, *n.* A politician who won't compromise.

bomfogger, *n.* A speaker heavy on saccharinely lofty or bombastic rhetoric and weak on substance. [From the acronym *bomfog* = Brotherhood Of Man, under the Fatherhood Of God, a catchphrase much used by Nelson Rockefeller.]

bone-breaker or **bone-bender,** *n.* A physician.

bone-cracker, *n.* A chiropractor.

bone-idle, *adj.* Especially lazy or sluggish. ["He was one bone-idle bastard. Dynamite or threat of firing could not get him moving."] *Syn.*: born tired, doggy, drag-assed, indolent, niggerish, otiose, rumdum, shiftless, work-shy.

boner, *n.* A blunder, an egregious mistake. ["He never lived down his boner in the playoffs."] *Syn.*: bitchup, bloop, blooper, bonehead play, botchup, clinker, flub, flummox, foozle, foulup, fuckup, gaffe, goofup, howler, louseup, muckup, muff, screwup, snafu.

bone-top, *n.* A stupid or foolish person.

bonkers, *adj.* Insane. ["You've gotta be bonkers if you think I am going to go out with you, you dweeb."] *Syn.*: bonzo, crackers, gonzo, gonzo city, meshuggah.

boob, *n.* An innocent and gullible person, a dupe, a patsy. ["Boobus Americanus"—H. L. Mencken.] *Syn.:* chump, fall guy, gobshite, lollipop, mark, mug, puppethead, pushover, sap, soft cop, soft touch, turkey on a string.

boodler, *n.* A corrupt, bribe-taking politician. ["No matter how often we turn the boodlers out, new ones come in to fleece us."]

boogerboo, *n.* A phony.

booger-bear, *n.* An ugly black woman.

boogers, *adj.* Unimpressive. [From *booger* = snot. "Kelly LeBrock thinks she's great/She's just cold boogers on a paper plate"—Julie Brown, in *The Village Voice* (1991).]

boogie, *n.* A black person.

boogie-joogie artist, *n.* One who deals in nonsense and trickery.

boojie or **buzhie,** *n.* A middle-class black, a member of the black bourgeoisie.

bookburner, *n.* A censor who takes it upon himself to decide what you may or may not read.

boondagger, *n.* A masculine woman or aggressive lesbian.

boor, *n.* A coarse, rude, or awkward person. ["Love makes gentlemen even of boors, whether noble or villian" —Henry Adams.] *Syn.:* chuff, churl, clodhopper, goop, Goth, Grobian, keelie, kern, lout, oaf, peasant, philistine, rustic, vulgarian, yahoo.

bootlips, *n.* A black man or woman.

boozehead, *n.* One who loves alcohol. ["This particular generation gap might almost be called chemical warfare—the potheads versus the boozeheads—or more accurately, religious warfare"—Leslie Fiedler.] *Syn.:* alkie, blotter, boozer, booze freak, boozer-heister, boozehound, boozer, bottle baby, guzzler.

borborologist, *n.* A person who uses foul or gross language, a filthy talker. *Syn.:* boborygmite.

bore, *n.* A tiresome, dull person. ["A bore: A person who talks when you wish him to listen"—Ambrose Bierce, *The Devil's Dictionary*. 1906.]

born loser, *n.* A person who habitually fails.

borrowed pecker, I wouldn't screw her with a, *idiom.* Said of a woman who is undesirable for any reason.

boss, *n.* An overbearing, racist white person; a term of mockery used by blacks.

Boss Charley or **Big Charlie,** *n.* A white person, especially one in authority.

boss lady, *n.* A woman in authority.

boss's automatic tongue-wiper, *idiom.* A toady, an asshole polisher.

bossy, *adj.* Imperious and demanding. ["I said to that bossy bitch, 'Who died and left you boss?' "] *Syn.:* authoritarian, domineering, autocratic, hectoring, demanding, despotic, dictatorial, exacting, high-handed, oppressive, overbearing, peremptory, tyrannical.

bottle, lose one's, *idiom.* To become scared. ["Some of the warders lost their bottle and just fled"—*News of the World* (1990).]

bottle blonde, *n.* A bleached blonde. [From the time when hair bleaching was considered a sign of a promiscuous woman.] *Syn.:* boxie.

bottom of the heap, *idiom.* A person who is obscure and insignificant. *Syn.:* lightweight, nobody, nebbish, a nothing. *Idiom:* low-rent, not amounting to a piss in the ocean, small-time, small change, small potatoes.

bourgeois, *adj.* Conformist, conservative, pedestrian, dull, hidebound, humdrum, materialistic, middle-class, square. ["Destroy him as you will, the bourgeois always bounces up. Execute him, expropriate him, starve him out en masse, and he reappears in your children"—Cyril Connolly.]

bowels in an uproar, don't get one's, *idiom.* Don't get overly excited.

bow-and-arrow, *n.* A Native American.

bowwow, *n.* An ugly or obnoxious woman, a real dog.

boy, *n.* (1) A black man. ["Captain, the boy who is playing the piano ... somewhere I have seen him"—Spoken by Ingrid Bergman, referring to Dooley Wilson, a man of almost sixty years, in the movie *Casablanca* (1943).] (2) A male hustler.

boy scout, *n.* An effeminate man or boy.

the boys in the back room, *idiom.* A group of men who control the inner workings of an organization. ["Even after years of political reform, the boys in the back room pick the mayor of this town."]

the boys uptown, *n.* (1) The political bosses of a city. (2) A group of anonymous criminals.

bozo, *n.* (1) A stupid person, a clown, a jerk. (2) A intimidating man, a goon, a thug.

bra-burner, *n.* A militant proponent of woman's rights. ["Bras were never burned. Bra-burning was a whole-cloth invention of the media"—Robin Morgan, *Sisterhood Is Powerful.*]

brace and bit, *n.* Women considered as sexual objects. [British rhyming slang for *tit.*]

bracketface, *n.* One who is extremely ugly.

brain, *n.* An intellectual, an egghead.

brain is wrapped loose, his, *idiom.* His roof ain't nailed on tight, his traces ain't hooked up right.

brainless, *adj.* Asinine, witless, buffleheaded, daft, fatuous, simple, foolish, half-witted, hen-witted, idiotic, mindless, nitwitted, senseless, stupid, weak-minded. ["If I ever needed a brain transplant, I'd choose a sportswriter because I'd want a brain that had never been used"—Norm Van Brocklin.]

brain-picker, *n.* A person who takes the creative work of others and palms it off as his own.

brass ankle or **black ankle,** *n.* A person of mixed white-black-Indian ancestry.

brassbound, *adj.* Unable to understand another's point. ["Those brassbound flag-wavers could not stomach her opposition to the war."] *Syn.*: bigoted, close-minded, dogmatic, hidebound, illiberal, intolerant, narrow-minded, rigid, small-minded.

brassy, *adj.* Brash, brazen, saucy, cheap, flamboyant, sassy, flashy, gaudy, insolent, meretricious, poncy, pushy, shameless, tawdry, vulgar. *Idioms*: all dressed up like a pox doctor's clerk, flashy as a Chinky's horse, flashy as a rat with a gold tooth.

bravo, *n.* (1) A Mexican or Spanish-American. (2) A hired killer or thug. ["... the hired bravos who defend the tyrant's throne"—Percy Bysshe Shelley.]

breed, *n.* A Native American with Indian and white forebears. *Syn.*: crossbreed, half-breed, quarter-breed.

breeder, *n.* A heterosexual or a married homosexual with children. [Gay slang.]

brenda, *n.* A foolish or unintellectual person.

brewery, couldn't run a pissup in a, *idiom.* A total screwup.

brigaty or **biggity,** *adj.* Arrogant, haughty.

bright, *n.* (1) A dandy. (2) A light-skinned African-American. *Syn.*: bright-bright, bright mulatto.

bright-skin, *n.* (1) A person with light-brown, golden, or tan coloring. (2) A white person.

broad, *n.* (1) A woman. ["We've got Dustin Hoffman fighting Meryl Streep for a four-year-old in *Kramer vs Kramer*. ... Thirty years ago, the Duke would have slapped the broad around and shipped the kid off to military school"—Bruce Feierstein, *Real Men Don't Eat Quiche*.] *Syn.*: bird, bozette, butt, canary, chick, chicken, cooz, cow, crack, cunt, cunt meat, cutie, dame, dearie, dish, doll, dolly, fem, femme, filly, fluff, frail, frau, gal, ginch, girlie, hammer, heifer, hen, hide, honey bun, honey-bunny, jane, jenny, job, klooch, leg, mama, mare, mat, moll, momma, mouse, pet, piece, pussy, quail, rib, skirt, slash, snatch, squab, squaw, sweet momma, sweet thing, tail, tart, tomato, twist, wench, witch, wool, wren. (2) A promiscuous woman. *Syn.*: bimbo, bum, chippie, cooze, dead cert, dirty leg, easy lay, easy ride, floozie, free for all, gash, little Miss Roundheels, lust dog, motorcycle, mount, nympho, paraffin lamp, pig, punchboard, pushover, quickie, quiff, screamer and a creamer, scrubber, shack job, shagbag, slag, sleepy-time girl, steamer, stinker, town bicycle, town pump, town punch.

broadnose, *n.* An African-American.

broken-rib, *n.* A woman who has been divorced.

bronco, *n.* (1) A awkward novice in homosexual relations. *Syn.*: belle, butterbox, chicken, cornflakes, daughter, debutante, ga-ga, lamb, pogue, poggler, tender box, tail, twinkie, tinkerbelle. (2) A catamite. *Syn.*: angelina, aunt, ball-and-chain, bender, bimbo, bindle boy, bitch, bo, boong-moll, bottoms, boxer, brat, brown, brunser, bumboy catch, cherry-picker, chuff, fag, fairy, fruit, gal-boy, gash, gay-cat, gazook, gazooney, ginch, gonsel, hide, hump, ingle, kid lamb, kife, little lady, miss nancy, mustard pot, nan-boy, nance, painted willie, pansy, pathic, peddle-snatch, peg boy, pink pants, poger, possesh, prushun, punce, punk, punk kid, receiver, ringtail, ringtail wife, road kid, roundeye, snatch-peddler, trug, twidget, willie. *Idioms*: comfort for the troops, one of the brown family, piece of snatch.

bronco-buster, *n.* An elderly man who loves young boys, a chicken hawk. ["The police could never stop the bronco-busters who came downtown."]

Bronx Indian, *n.* A Jewish person.

bronze, *n.* A person with some African ancestry.

brothel or **whorehouse, couldn't organize a fuck in a,** *idiom.* Completely incompetent.

brothel creeper, *n.* A whoremonger. *Syn.*: whore-hopper, chippy-chaser, cunthound.

brother-girl, *n.* A lesbian.

brother in black, *n.* An African-American.

brow, *n.* A lowbrow.

brown, *n.* or *adj.* (1) A person with some African ancestry, an African-American with brown skin tone. ["An' she laughs and chaffs with every brownskin man she meet" — "Black Snake Blues."] *Syn.*: brown-and-tan, brownie, brown polish, brownskin, chocolate brown, cocoa brown, cream brown, creole brown, dark brown, deep brown, deep yellow brown, fair brown, high brown, light brown, low brown, medium brown, muddy brown, reddish brown, sealskin brown, shit brown, solid brown, teasing brown, velvet brown. (2) A Mexican-American, a Puerto Rican.

brown bagger, *n.* A very ugly woman. [From the idea of one who should cover her face with a bag.]

brown bisquit, *n.* A brown-skinned person who follows white establishment standards against blacks' interests, a coco.

brown brother, *n.* A Pacific Islander or Malayan.

brown girl, *n.* A woman with a brown skin tone, especially if sexually attractive. *Syn.*: brown-skin baby, brown sugar.

brownie, *n.* A gay man who prefers anal sex. *Syn.*: brown hatter, brownie king, brownie queen, one of the Browning family, browning queen, browning sister.

brownnose, *n.* A fawner, a toady, a sycophant. *Syn.*: candy-tongue, apple-polisher, back-patter, back-slapper, boot-licker, browner, browntongue, bucker, cringer, egg-sucker, fawner, kiss-ass, stooge, suck-off, TL, TLer, tochus-licker, yes-man.

brown-shoes, *n.* A straight person who rejects drugs, a square.

brown-skin white folks, *n.* People who are called white by white Americans, but whom black people deem nonwhite.

bubble-and-squeak or **bubble,** *n.* A Greek person.

bubble gum, *adj.* Silly or shallow. [Relates to young adolescents, the bubble gum set.]

buck, *n.* (1) A young male Native American, or a young black man. (2) A womanizer.

bucket-broad, *n.* A promiscuous woman or hooker who engages in anal intercourse. ["Even the bucket-broads are starting to practice safe sex."]

buckethead, *n.* A German.

bucketmouth, *n.* One who uses obscene language, a toilet-mouth.

bucket worker, *n.* A bucket shop racketeer, a swindler. ["During the eighties, the bucket workers were working around the clock fleecing the suckers with get-rich schemes."]

buckle-my-shoe or **buckle,** *n.* A Jewish man or woman.

buck nigger, *n.* A black man

buck-passer, *n.* One who cannot accept responsibility for mistakes.

buckra, *n.* A white man, a cracker.

buck-taker, *n.* A scapegoat.

buckwheat, *n.* A light-skinned black person. ["I forgot no one was working. Everyone had Buckwheat's birthday off"—Norman Christopher, Maryland town commissioner on why he had trouble contacting county employees on Martin Luther King Jr. day, *Newsweek* (1992).]

buddahead or **buddhahead,** *n.* An Asian or a person of Asian extraction.

buffer, *n.* A pleasant old fool.

buffalo or **buff,** *n.* An obese woman.

buffalo butt, *n.* A person with large buttocks. ["He was inordinately attracted to the new buffalo butt in the office."]

buffarilla, *n.* An unattractive young woman. [A blend of *buffalo* + *gorilla*.]

bufflehead or **buffle,** *n.* A jerk.

bufu, *n.* A homosexual. [Valley girls' abbreviation for *buttfucker*.]

bug, *v.* To annoy or aggravate. ["He bugs the hell out of me."] *Syn.*: burn, chivy, discombobulate, dog, drug, get, gravel, gripe, hassle, hock, hound, miff, needle, nudge, nudzh, peeve, pick on, push, rib, ride, rile, roust, shag, sound. *Idioms*: be in one's face, be on one's back, break chops, flake off, get someone down, get down on, get on someone's back, get on someone's case, get under one's skin, get up someone's nose, give someone the needle, push someone's button, rattle someone's cage.

bug or **bugs,** *n.* An eccentric or crazy person, a nut.

bug bunny, *n.* A scientist working on bacteriological warfare. ["The easing of global tensions still hasn't put the bug bunnies out of work."]

bug doctor, *n.* A psychologist or psychiatrist.

bugger, *n.* (1) A sodomite, a pederast. ["Thus spoke the king of Siam/For women I don't give a damn./But a fat-bottomed boy/Is my pride and joy./They call me a bugger! I am'"—Norman Douglas, *Some Limericks* (1927).] (2) A heretic. (3) A nasty person. *Syn.*: bastard, louse, prick, puke, scum, shit, shithead, sod, stinker, toad.

buggy, *adj.* Crazy or neurotic. *Syn.:* bugs, nuts, batty, buggy, bughouse.

bug off, *interj.* Get out!

bugout, *n.* A quitter, a slacker.

bugs in the brain, have, *idiom.* To be eccentric.

built like a brick shithouse, *adj.* Describes a sexually attractive woman. *Syn.*: built like a shit brickhouse.

bujak, *n.* A person of Slav descent.

bulbous, *adj.* Fat-bellied, bloated, bulging, convex, potbellied, swollen.

bull bitch, *n.* A mannish woman, a virago.

bulldagger, *n.* A tough, aggressive lesbian. ["Now the hostess of the evenin' was Free-Turn Flo'/She bought fifteen bulldaggers to put on a show"—"Freaks Ball" in Bruce Jackson, "Get your Ass in the Water and Swim Like Me."] *Syn.:* boondagger, bull, bulldicker, bull dyke, bull dike, king, mason.

bulldog, *n.* A stubborn person, a mule.

bulldog Indian, *n.* A Native American who has only Indian ancestry.

bulldoze, *v.* To fool, to con. ["... through the sheer strength of his reputation and the force of his will bulldozing them into making loans"—F. L. Allen.]

bullshit, *n.* Nonsense, pretentious or deceitful speech. ["When his cock wouldn't stand up he blew his head off. He sold himself a line of bullshit and he bought it" —Germaine Greer about Ernest Hemingway.] *Syn.:* bull, apple butter, apple strudel, balloon juice, banana oil, batshit, beans, bibble-babble, bilge, blarney, blather, blatherskite, booshwah, borax, bosh, BS, bull's wool, bull, bullcrap, buncombe, bunk, claptrap, crap, crapola, crock, crud, dogshit, eyewash, flannel, flapsauce, fudge garbage, gas, gash, goulash, guff, hen piss, hockey, hog slosh, hogwash, hooey, horseshit, hot air, hot cock, humbug, jack shit, jive, moonshine, mumbo-jumbo, oil of tongue, oil, pigshit, pile of shit, piss and wind, poop, shit for the birds, shit, tommyrot. *Idioms:* crock of shit, bunch of ant paste, bunch of tripe, bunch of bug pukky, concentrated applesauce.

bullshit artist, *n.* A liar, a pretentious talker, a know-it-all. *Syn.:* bullshitter, bullshooter.

bully, *n.* A mean, cowardly fellow. *Syn.:* bouncer, browbeater, bucko, bully-boy, Drawcansir, intimidator, killcrow, persecutor, ruffian, termagant, tormentor, tough.

bum, *n.* (1) A hobo. (2) A promiscuous woman. (3) An incompetent fighter, a stumblebum. (4) A habitual beggar, a moocher.

bumblepuppy, *n.* An indifferent bridge player.

bummer, *n.* (1) A sodomite. (2) An unpleasant or negative experience.

bummerkeh, *n.* A loose woman.

bumper, *n.* A mannish lesbian. [From *bumping pussies* = tribadism.]

bumpkin, *n.* A rustic. ["... bashful country bumpkins" —Washington Irving.] *Syn.*: boor, chawbacon, clodhopper, clown, cornball, country jake, yokel, hillbilly, jake, looby, lubbard, lubber, lummox, oaf, peasant, provincial.

bump on a log, *idiom.* A social failure.

bumptious, *adj.* Disagreeably conceited. ["... every bumptious adventurer and fluent charlatan"—George Bernard Shaw.] *Syn.*: arrogant, cocky, egotistic, impudent, pompous, presumptuous, pushy, bodacious, swaggering, full of oneself.

bun, *n.* A wife or girlfriend.

bun bandit, *n.* The active partner in anal intercourse. *Syn.*: bunger, bunker.

bunco artist or **bunko artist,** *n.* A con man. ["The bunco artists swarmed over the festival like flies."]

bunco-steerer, *n.* A con man's accomplice.

bundler, *n.* A male sadist.

bun-duster, *n.* An effeminate male.

bungler, *n.* A sexually incompetent or impotent married male. *Syn.*: blunderer, butterfingers, duffer, footler, foozler, fumbler, botcher, lubber, muddler.

bungo, *n.* A boorish, ignorant black person. [West Indian usage.]

bunk lizard, *n.* A goof-off.

bunny, *n.* (1) A groupie. (2) A prostitute who serves either sex. (3) A sexually uninhibited woman.

bunny cake queen, *n.* The active partner in gay anal sex.

bunny-fuck, *v.* To procrastinate.

bunny-fucker, *n.* (1) One who finishes sex quickly. (2) One who wastes time.

bunter, *n.* (1) A thieving hooker. (2) An effeminate homosexual.

bunty, *n.* A small, middle-aged woman.

buppie, *n.* A middle-class upwardly mobile black, a black yuppie. ["Bryant Gumbel and Vanessa Williams are both Buppies. Of course, it wouldn't be Yuppie to be Miss America unless you are the first black one"—*People* (1984).]

burbed out, *adj.* Dressed like a middle-class surburbanite.

burn artist, *n.* A professional swindler or a seller of phony narcotics.

burner, *n.* A swindler or a tease.

buron, *n.* A combination of *bureaucrat* and *moron.*

burrhead, *n.* A black person.

bush, *adj.* Mediocre, second-rate. ["He thought he was a big shot the way he strutted his stuff. But everyone knew he was strictly bush."] *Syn.*: bush-league, cut-rate, garden-variety, low-rent, narrow-gauge, piddling, pissy-ass, scrub, small-beer, small-bore, small-potato, a sort a, so-so, tacky, tinhorn, two-bit.

bush bitch or **bush pig,** *n.* An ugly girl.

bushel bubby, *n.* A woman with large, pendulous breasts.

bush leaguer, *n.* A second-rate player on a sports team; hence, an inconsequential person. ["Although he had only been a bush leaguer, he became an outstanding manager."]

bushwa or **bushwah,** *n.* Bullshit. ["When are you going to stop shoveling the bushwa?"]

business boy, *n.* A male prostitute.

business girl, *n.* An independent hooker.

bust, *n.* A loser or an unresponsive woman or a bore.

bustle-puncher, *n.* A man who rubs against a woman while hiding in a crowd.

bust-out man, *n.* A person who switches to crooked dice.

butch, *n.* An aggressive lesbian, a bull dyke.

butcher, *n.* (1) A brutal and sanguinary ruler. ["He was known as the butcher of Baghdad."] *Syn.:* destroyer, killer, murderer, slaughterer, slayer. (2) A careless and incompetent surgeon.

butcher boy, *n.* A gay man who engages in sex with a lesbian.

butch queen, *n.* A gay man whose virile activities cloak his orientation.

butchski or **butchsky,** *n.* A Czechoslovak.

butter or **butter baby,** *n.* A sexy woman.

butterbag or **butterbox,** *n.* A Dutchman.

butterball, *n.* A fat person. ["The tackle looked like a butterball, but he was all muscle."]

butt boy, *n.* (1) A gay man. (2) A jerk.

butter-boy, *n.* A novice. *Syn.:* beginner, greener, greenhorn, new fish, rookie, wetfoot.

buttercup, *n.* An effeminate man. ["I'm called Little Buttercup—dear Little Buttercup"—W. S. Gilbert, *H.M.S. Pinafore.*]

buttered bun, *n.* A woman who engages in serial sex.

butterfly, *n.* A flashy person.

butterfly or **butterfly boy,** *n.* An effeminate homosexual. ["The butterflies were obvious targets for homophobic gangs."]

butterfly case, *n.* A nut.

butterhead, *n.* (1) A black person who is deemed to be a discredit to the black community. (2) A fool whose brains are as soft as butter.

buttermilk, *n.* An ugly girl or woman.

buttermouth, *n.* A Dutchman.

buttfucker, *n.* One who engages in anal intercourse.

buttinsky, *n.* A rude, intrusive meddler. ["His mother-in-law was an insufferable buttinsky."] *Syn.:* butterinsky, buttinski, butt-in, kibitzer.

buttlicker, *n.* An ass-kisser.

buttly, *adj.* Extremely ugly.

buttoner, *n.* The shill in the three-card monte con.

button man, *n.* A low-ranking mafia soldier. ["He advanced from button man to second in command due to his loan-sharking success."] *Syn.:* button player, button soldier, soldier.

button up, *interj.* Stop talking! Shut up! Shut your trap!

button your lip, *imper.* Stop talking! Shut up! Shut your face!

butt-peddler, *n.* A pimp or a hooker.

butt pirate, *n.* A homosexual man.

buy off, *v.* To shirk one's responsibility.

buy the dick, *v.* Get into trouble, get hurt.

buzzcatcher, *n.* A woman who masturbates with a vibrator.

buzzed, *adj.* High, loaded, fucked up, blitzed.

C

cabbagehead, *n.* (1) A brainless, thickheaded person. (2) A German or a Dutchman.

cabron *n.* A bastard. [Spanish usage, pronounced kah-bron.]

caca, *n.* Dung, feces, shit. [From Spanish *cagar* = to discharge excrement. "They're spreading that caca all over the barrio." Puerto Rican and Mexican usage.] *Syn.*: cack, kaka.

cacademic or **cacademoid,** *n.* A university professor who is detested for having shit in his blood or head. [A blend of *caca* + *academic* + *oid,* coined by Reinhold Aman, editor, *Maledicta.*]

cacafogo or **cacafuego,** *n.* A difficult or troublesome person. ["Keep away from her. She's a real cacafugo." Literally, "shitfire."]

cack-handed, *adj.* Clumsy, awkward. ["What a cack-handed lummox he turned out to be."]

cacophonous, *adj.* Harsh-sounding. ["The scold loosed with her cacophonous-sounding screech"—as quoted in *Oxford English Dictionary.*] *Syn.*: jarring, dissonant, discordant, harsh, raucous, strident, screechy, grating.

cacozeliac, *n.* A person who uses pedantic and ludicrous words in speech and writing. ["His lectures are totally useless. He is nothing but a cacozeliac."]

cad, *n.* A vulgar and ill-mannered man. ["You cannot make a vulgar offensive cad conduct himself as a gentleman" —*OED* (1868).] *Syn.*: bounder, louse, rotter, lout, churl, dastard, heel, scoundrel, rascal, knave, rouge.

cadet, *n.* A new drug user.

cagey, *adj.* Not frank, secretive. ["His business dealings were so cagey that even his sons didn't know what he was doing."] *Syn.*: sneaky, wily, cunning, crafty, shifty, slippery, sly, foxy, shrewd.

caitiff, *n.* A base, despicable person; a wretch.

cake, *n.* A sexually attractive woman. [From *cake* = female genitals.]

cake-eater, *n.* A lecher, a womanizer, or an effeminate man.

callous, *adj.* Emotionally hardened. ["Piety . . . is made callous and inactive by kneeling too much"—Landor.] *Syn.:* hard-bitten, hard-boiled, soulless, thick-skinned, unfeeling, cold, insensitive, uncaring, hard, hard-hearted, heartless.

callow, *adj.* Inexperienced. ["I don't date callow youths."] *Syn.:* immature, raw, shallow, awkward, unsophisticated, naive, artless, childish, jejune, juvenile, infantile, puerile, sophomoric, green behind the ears.

calumny, *n.* A deliberate or malicious false statement harmful to another's reputation. [". . . calumnies/like women that will wear their tongues out"—*OED (1611).*] *Syn.:* libel, slander, lie, traducement.

camel-jammer, *n.* An Arab or other Middle Eastern person.

camois-nosed, *adj.* Pug-nosed.

camp, *n.* Effeminate stylized or theatrical and artificial behavior, such as a mincing gait, fluttering gestures, or a pronounced lisp. ["... a camp queen's lisp and waggle"—Costello and Wallace, *Signifying Raps* (1990).]

camp it up, *idiom.* To overdo effeminate or ultratheatrical behavior and dress.

canary, *n.* (1) A stool pigeon. [From the idea of singing. "The capos were worried that he was singing like a canary to the Feds."] (2) A Chinese person.

candle-basher, *n.* A spinster or a female masturbator. [From the folklore allusion that candles are used for that purpose.]

candyass or **candybutt,** *n.* A coward, a timid person, a weakling ["Oh, the dirty little coward/That shot Mr. Howard,/Laid Jesse James in his grave"—Anon., 1880s.]

candyfloss or **cotton candy,** *n.* Shallow ideas or proposals. ["I can't buy that suggestion. It's about as substantial as candyfloss."]

candy man, *n.* A man who sells drugs, women, or any other "pleasurable" commodity. ["The candy men hang around the major highway to service commuters."]

can it, *idiom.* Shut up!

canned goods, *n.* A male or female virgin. [From the idea of being unopened. "I knew her before she was a virgin"—Oscar Wilde.]

cannibal, *n.* A man or woman who performs oral sex with a male. *Syn.*: maneater, nosher.

cantankerous, *adj.* Bitter, ill-humored, or irritable. ["Lionel Barrymore perfected the role of a cantankerous old man."] *Syn.*: cankered, contrary, cranky, cross-grained, grouchy, huffy, rantankerous, vinegarish, perverse, grumpy, waspish, waspy.

Canuck, *n.* A French-Canadian. ["That's a Canuck for you, ain't been a son to your ma"—*OED* (1965).] *Syn.*: Frite, Jean Baptiste, Pepsi.

canvasback, *n.* A promiscuous woman, a mattressback. [From the allusion to lying on one's back.]

capo, *n.* The chief or captain of a local Mafia unit.

cap on, *v.* To insult or degrade someone.

capon, *n.* An effeminate man, or a eunuch. [From *capon* = castrated rooster. "If there is a capon in Christendom, I'll make thee one"—*OED* (1691).]

capoop, *n.* A despicable person. [From a word for dung.]

capricious, *adj.* Led by whim. ["He judged her to be capricious, and easily wearied of the pleasure of the moment"—Wharton.] *Syn.*: fitful, fickle, erratic, flighty, skittish, mercurial, indecisive, vacillating, shilly-shallying.

caprine, *adj.* Goatlike. ["That which in their physiognomy is canine, vulpine, caprine"—quoted in *OED.*]

captious, *adj.* Ready to take offense or find fault. *Syn.*: carping, nitpicking, quibbling, hair-splitting, picky, caviling, petulant, picayune, niggling, cutting, belittling, peevish, testy, snappish.

cardophagus, *n.* A donkey, an ass. ["Kick him and abuse him, you who have never brayed, but bear with him all honest fellow cardophagi"—William M. Thackeray (1857).]

carminative, *adj.* Expelling flatulence.

carnalist, *n.* A lascivious person obsessed with sexual desires. ["Shallow, narrowhearted carnalist"—*OED*.]

carnivorous, *adj.* Flesh-eating. ["The carniverous brokers on Wall Street eat suckers like you for breakfast."] *Syn.*: predatory, predacious, victimizing, plundering.

carpetbagger, *n.* A plunderer. [From *carpetbag* = a traveling bag made of carpet. The name given to people who went south after the Civil War to enrich themselves.]

carving knife, *n.* One's wife.

Caspar Milquetoast, *n.* A cowardly, weak person. [From the central character in the comic strip "The Timid Soul," created by H. T. Webster.]

castaway, *n.* A reprobate, one who is rejected. ["Why do you call us Orphans, Wretches, Castaways"—William Shakespeare, *Richard III*.] *Syn.*: bum, outcast, pariah, unperson, leper, untouchable, nonperson.

castrate, *n.* To cut off the testicles. ["Nazi doctors castrated prisoners as part of their medical 'experiments.'"] *Syn.*: de-ball, alter, change, dehorn, desexualize, devirilize, emasculate, knacker, nut-cut.

cat, *n.* A spiteful and malicious woman who, often subtly, criticizes and denigrates other women.

catch it (or get it) in the neck, *idiom.* To be severely rebuked or punished, to catch hell.

catch-fart, *n.* A toady, a sycophant. [From one who follows closely behind his boss.]

catch shit, *idiom.* To be verbally abused, to catch hell, to be scolded. ["If I get in after 1 A.M., I sure am going to catch shit."]

catty, *adj.* Discrediting others, nastily gossipy. ["Her catty talk resulted in her being dropped from her consciousness-raising group."] *Syn.*: malicious, mean, malignant, malevolent, spiteful.

celebrity fucker, *n.* A person who screws his or her way to success. *Syn.*: groupie, screamer and creamer, plaster caster, star fucker, third assistant cocksucker in a Mongolian cluster-fuck.

centerfold, *n.* A sexually desirable person, usually a vacuous, siliconed woman. [From the two-page photograph featured in *Playboy*.]

chair-warmer, *n.* An idle and dispensable worker. [From the idea of one who does nothing but keep a chair warm.]

chalk, *n.* A white person.

chalker, *n.* A black who acts white or who spends so much time with whites that it's rubbing off on him like chalk.

chamberpot, *n.* A promiscuous woman. [As used in John Barth's *The Sot-Weed Factor* (1960).] *Syn*: swilltrough, bedpan, slop jar.

character assassin, *n.* One who conducts a slanderous campaign to disgrace another's reputation. ["A period of the big lie, of the furtive informer, of the character assassin"—*American Speech (1951).*] *Syn.*: McCarthyite.

charcoal, *n.* An African-American. [From the color of charcoal.]

charity girl, *n.* A sexually promiscuous young woman. [From the idea of one who gives it away for free.] *Syn.*: charity dame, charity moll.

charlatan, *n.* One who fakes knowledge or skill, a pretentious impostor. ["... replaced by the charlatans and the rogues—by those without learning, without scruples, or both"—Asher Moore.] *Syn.*: quack, cheap Jack, mountebank, quacksalver, quackster, saltimbanque.

Charles, *n.* A white man. ["He assumed . . . his ancestors were happy, shiftless, watermelon-eating darkies who loved Mr. Charlie and Miss Ann"—James Baldwin, in J. H. Clarke's book *Harlem.*] *Syn.*: Charlie, Chuck, Mr. Charlie, Chahlie, Big Charlie.

Charlie Hunt, *n.* A fool, a despicable person. [From British rhyming slang for *cunt.*]

chattermucker, *n.* A blabberer, a gossip, a magpie, a prattler.

chatty, *adj.* Infested with lice. *Syn.*: lousy, slovenly, crab-infested.

chauvinist, *n.* (1) A superpatriot. [After Nicholas Chauvin of Rochefort, a soldier under Napoleon whose demonstrative patriotism was celebrated and then ridiculed as excessive by his fellow officers.] *Syn.*: blind patriot, flag-waver, jingoist, militarist, nationalist. (2) A person who believes in the superiority of his group or cause and is prejudiced against others. [". . . her treatment of Edmund—female chauvinist"—*Rolling Stone* (1977).] *Syn.*: ethnocentrist, racist, male chauvinist.

chaw or **chawmouth,** *n.* A person of Irish descent.

chawbacon, *n.* A bumpkin or a rustic boor. ["Half a dozen grinning chaw-bacons watching him"—*OED* (1880).] *Syn.*: apple-knocker, boonie, bumpkin, bushwacker, carrot-cruncher, rube, clod, clodhopper, hayseed, hick, honyock, neck, redneck, shitkicker, swede, woolyback, yob, yokel.

cheap, *adj.* (1) Of inferior or bad quality. *Syn.*: cheapjack, cheesy, cheapshit, crummy, crappy, piss-poor, lousy, schlocky, shoddy, cheap and nasty. (2) Pertaining to a woman who lacks sexual control. ["You're nothing but a cheap woman."]

cheap date or **cheap drunk,** *n.* A woman who needs very few drinks to become "agreeable." ["His lack of self-esteem led him to go for cheap dates."]

cheap shanty Mick, *n.* A person of Irish descent, especially a poor one.

cheapskate, *n.* A stingy, ungenerous person. *Syn.*: cheapie, cheapo, el cheapo, skinflint.

cheeky, *adj.* Insolent, impudent, presuming. ["If he is cheeky/he doesn't respect you/for not punishing him/ for not respecting you./He won't respect you/if you don't punish him/for not respecting you"—R. D. Laing, "Knots."] *Syn.*: smart-ass, snotty, impertinent, cocky, gutty, lippy, nervy, sassy, smart-alecky, snotty, wise-ass.

cheese-cutter, *n.* A person who releases bad-smelling intestinal gas. [From *burnt cheese* = foul-smelling fart.] *Syn.*: cheezer, fart-cutter.

cheese dong, *n.* A stupid and foolish person. *Syn.*: cheese-head, cheesemeister.

cheese-eater, *n.* (1) A Dutchman. (2) A person who is not Catholic. [A reciprocal word for the use of *fish-eater* as a derogatory name for a Catholic.] (3) An informer, a stool pigeon, a rat.

cheesy, *adj.* (1) Lacking in taste, vulgarly shabby. ["Hare and rabbit fur are utterly revolting and cheesy"—R. Macaully, *Staying With Relations* (1930).] *Syn.*: cheap, tacky, phony. (2) Disloyal, false, hypocritical.

cherry, *n.* A virgin or a novice at a given task.

cherry-picker, *n.* A libertine who likes young women, or one who prefers sex with young girls. *Syn.*: cherry-copper.

cherry pie, *n.* A sexually loose woman. [Allusion to *cherry* + *as easy as pie*.]

Cheskey or **Czezski,** *n.* A person of Czechoslovakian descent.

chew someone's ass out, *idiom.* To bawl out, to scold severely. *Syn.*: chew someone's balls off, chew out.

chichi, *adj.* Prissy, ostentatiously showy, overelaborate. ["The sort of real Italian country cooking that is a revelation after so much chichi Italian food dished up in London" —*Daily Telegraph* (1969).] *Syn.*: garish, flashy, vulgar, gimcrack, flamboyant, pretentious.

chick, *n.* A woman, especially a young woman. ["Chicks are the preoccupation of the unemployed"—Albert Goldman, *Ladies and Gentlemen, Lenny Bruce* (1970).] *Syn.:* chickie, chicken, chicken dinner, chicklet.

chicken, *n.* (1) A coward, a timid person. *Syn.:* candyass, fraidy-cat, puckerass, scaredy-cat, sissy, weak sister, yellowbelly, chickenheart, chickenshit. *See also:* wimp. (2) An underaged boy used for sexual purposes.

chicken feed, *n.* A worthless person, small potatoes.

chicken-grabber or **chicken-choker,** *n.* A despised wretch, a masturbator. [From the reference to the penis as a chicken neck.]

chicken hawk, *n.* A man who seeks young boys for sex. ["I don't do chickenhawk and/I don't do rough trade and/I don't do men's rooms"—M. Thomas, *Green Monday* (1980).] *Syn.:* chicken queen, hebophile.

chicken in the basket, *n.* A young boy available for gay sex.

chicken out, *v.* To back off from a course of action because of fear. *Syn.:* funk out, turn chicken, turn yellow.

chicken shit, *n.* The rules and meanness of a minor and pretentious bureaucrat or person in authority. ["He spent all his time on chicken shit, and never dealt with policy or real problems."]

chickenshit, *adj.* Pertaining to anything that is despicable or worthless. ["She's a slut, just a chickenshit whore"—Chester Himes, *Blind Man With a Pistol* (1969).]

Chico, *n.* A Chicano, a Hispanic, or a person from the Caribbean. ["... Chico/up from Cuba Haiti Jamaica"—Langston Hughes, "Good Morning."]

chili bowl, *n.* A dirty, unkempt person. *Syn.:* dirtball.

chilly mo, *n.* An aloof and uninvolved person.

Chinaman, *n.* A Chinese man.

chingado, *n.* Motherfucker. [From Spanish *chingar* = to fuck.]

China doll, *n.* A young Chinese woman.

Chink, *n.* A person of Chinese descent. ["The Barman was a broadfaced Chink"—John Dos Passos, *1919* (1932).] *Syn.:* Chinee, Chinky, Chino, pong, ricebelly.

chinless wonder, *n.* A person with a weak character.

chintzy or **chinchy,** *adj.* (1) Ill-made but showy. ["The effect is chintzy and would be unbecoming"—George Eliot, *Letter* (1851).] *Syn.:* cheap, shoddy, unfashionable. (2) Stingy, parsimonious. ["I'll have to revise my attitude to the chintzy old bastard"—Len Deighton, *Funeral in Berlin* (1964).] *Syn.:* tight, tight as Kelsey's nuts.

chippie or **chippy,** *n.* A young promiscuous woman. ["She's no better than a regular little chippie"—Thomas Wolfe, *Look Homeward Angel* (1929).]

chippy-chaser or **chippymonger,** *n.* A lecher, a man who chases women hoping to have sex if he catches one. ["I awake one morning to find myself chained to a toilet in Hell with all the other chippy-mongers in the world." —Philip Roth, *Portnoy's Complaint* (1969).]

chocolate or **chocolate drop,** *n.* An American black.

choke up, *v.* To become tense and perform poorly under pressure. *Syn.:* blow it, choke, tense up, clutch up, screw up.

Cholo, *n.* A Chicano, a Pachuco, or any Hispanic. ["Don' be callin' to ese Cholo or Chico if you don' be knowin' d' dude, 'cause he'll righteously fire on you"—in Edith Folb, *Runnin' Down Some Lines* (1980).]

chop, *v.* To insult someone with a dig or criticism. *Syn.:* chop down, cut, tear down, dig.

chop cock, *n.* A Jewish male. ["So coons (blacks) chop cocks (Jews) and dagos (Italians) came in for special bashing" —Sanford H Margalith, *Maledicta, X.*]

chop-logic, *n.* A person who uses absurdly convoluted and illogical arguments.

chopped liver, *n.* An insignificant person, one who doesn't matter. ["What am I, chopped liver?"]

chopstick, *n.* A person of Asian descent.

chowhound, *n.* A glutton.

Christer, *n.* A straitlaced, overzealous, overpious, sanctimonious Christian. ["It doesn't matter to me if he's a chauvinist, a little Christer, or a nearsighted pedant"—Henry Miller, *Tropic of Cancer* (1934).] *Syn.*: holier-than-thou, Holy Joe, Jesus freak, plaster saint.

Christ-killer, *n.* A Jewish man or woman. [From the libel that the Jews were responsible for Jesus's death. "Because I'm Jewish, a lot of people ask why I killed Christ. What can I say? It was an accident. It was one of those parties that got out of hand. I killed him because he wouldn't become a doctor"—Lenny Bruce.]

chubbette, *n.* A plump, well-rounded girl or woman.

chuck, *n.* A white man. [From the diminutive for *Charles* = white man. "Let me run down/Just a little/of my/Case against you/Chuck!"—Bobb Hamilton, "Brother Harlem Bedford Watts Tells Mr. Charlie Where It's At."]

chuck you, Farley, *interj.* Fuck you, Charlie!

chuff, *n.* (1) A boy kept by a gay man. (2) A fat, coarse person.

chuff-nut, *n.* A disgusting person. [From fecal or seminal matter clinging to the anal or pubic hairs.]

chump, *n.* A dupe, a sucker, or a stupid person. ["So you chumps, you punks, you faggots/who ain't movin' yet/PLEASE, get your mind together...."—Bob Bennett, "It is Time for Action."]

chungo bunny, *n.* A black person.

churlish, *adj.* Intentionally rude and boorish. ["We found the people more churlish than usual"—David Livingstone, *Zambesi*, (1865).] *Syn.*: surly, grouchy, crabbed, rancorous, quarrelsome, splenetic, irascible, petulant, testy, irritable, bilious, choleric, waspish, sour, tart, boorish, insulting, sullen.

chutzpah, *n.* Arrogant and offensive presumption, brazen impudence. ["Kennedy can get into Watts in his shirt sleeves, into working-class quarters with his gut Catholicism, and into a whole range of theoretically hostile environments with nothing more than *chutzpah*"—*New Statesman* (1968).] *Syn.*: ultrabrazenness, cheek, cheekiness, crust, gall, guts, effrontery, moxie, snottiness.

citizen, *n.* A conservative, well-established member of society; a square. ["Fools! Assholes! Devout Citizens!/Stop it! Go home to your radios"—Leroi Jones.]

civil serpent, *n.* A bureaucrat. [Play on the words *civil servant.*]

clam, *n.* A silent, rather dumb person. ["It will be lost on such an intellectual clam as you"—Mark Twain, *Sketches* (1872).]

clannish, *adj.* Cliquish, snobbish, and provincial. ["It was not always safe to have even a game of football between villages. The old clannish spirit was apt to break out"—Washington Irving (1849).]

claptrap, *n.* (1) Something showy or meretricious used to win applause. ["The piece at one point turns into deplorable dramatic claptrap."—*Illustrated London News* (1966).] *Syn.*: sham, humbug, fustian, gaudiness, quackery, hokum, blather, blarney, twaddle, baloney, flapdoodle, tripe, bilge, bosh. (2) A loose woman probably infected with gonorrhea. [From the word *clap* = gonorrhea.]

clarty-paps, *n.* A filthy woman. [From *clart* = dung.]

classist, *n.* One who is biased toward, discriminates against, or stereotypes people on the basis of socioeconomic status or background.

classy chassy, *n.* A young woman with an attractive figure.

clawback, *n.* A backscratcher, a sycophant. ["The puffers and earwigs and clawbacks and parasites surrounding her"—F. Rolfe, *Desire and Pursuit (1913).*]

clay eater, *n.* A native of the Piedmont lowlands of Georgia or South Carolina.

clay pigeon, *n.* A person who is easily fooled.

clean one's clock, *idiom.* To defeat someone thoroughly. *Idioms:* clean up on someone, clean up the floor with someone.

clean up your act, *idiom.* Correct your behavior, start acting properly. *Idioms:* act your age, clean up your shit, get your shit together, shape up or ship out, sprout wings, straighten up and fly right, suck it up.

cleaver, *n.* A sexually promiscuous woman.

Clem, *n.* A person who is easily duped.

clerks and jerks, *n.* Rear-echelon soldiers.

clever dick, *n.* A smart aleck, a know-it-all.

clinker, *n.* A loser, a washout. [From fecal or seminal matter adhering to the anal or pubic hairs, or from *clinkerballs* = balls of dried dung in sheep's wool.]

clip artist, *n.* A swindler. ["She was a clip artist working out of a Northside clip joint."]

clipped dick, *n.* A Jewish man. [Allusion to circumcision. "When they circumcised Herbert Samuel they threw away the wrong bit"—attributed to David Lloyd George.] *Syn.:* cut cock.

clit-hopper, *n.* A promiscuous lesbian. [From *clit* = clitoris.]

clit-licker, *n.* A person who performs cunnilingus.

cloak-and-suiter, *n.* A Jewish man.

clockwork orange, queer as a, *idiom.* A male homosexual. [From Anthony Burgess, *A Clockwork Orange* (1962).]

clodhopper, *n.* A rural person; a hillbilly; a farmer; a clumsy, awkward boor. ["Though honest and active they're most unattractive and awkward as can be. They're clumsy clodhoppers"—William S. Gilbert.] *Syn.:* hick, bumpkin, clumperton, hayseed, plowboy, redneck, yokel.

clone, *n.* A mindless copy of another person. ["The White House aides all looked like clones of their bosses."]

close-lipped, *adj.* Silent. *Syn.:* closemouthed, button-lipped, close-tongued, reserved, reticent, taciturn, tight-lipped, tightmouthed, uncommunicative.

closet case, *n.* One who takes part in homosexual activity but does not perceive oneself or admit to being gay or lesbian. *Syn.:* closet queen, closet queer.

clot or clod, *n.* A stupid or foolish person. ["She has marital thrombosis—she married a clot"—*Maledicta* (1977).]

cloth-ears, *n.* One who seems not to have heard an insult. ["Hey, cloth-ears, I'm talking to you!"]

clotheshorse, *n.* A person preoccupied with clothes.

cloud up and rain all over you, I'll, *idiom.* I'm going to beat the hell out of you!

cluck or dumb cluck, *n.* A dull, stupid person with the brains of a chicken.

clueless, *adj.* Ignorant or confused.

clunker, *n.* A clumsy person, particularly an unskilled athlete.

clutched, *adj.* Tense, uptight, nervous.

clyde, *n.* A foolish or stupid person, or a square.

coal mine, *n.* A dark-skinned African-American. ["In Chicago, they be callin' me 'coal mine' and 'blackbird' 'cause I was dark"—in Edith Folb, *Runnin' Down Some Lines* (1980).] *Syn.:* coal bin, coal chute.

cock, *n.* (1) An arrogant, swaggering male. ["He bruised his way to the perilous glory of being cock·of the school" —F. E. Trollope, *Charming Fellow* (1876).] *Syn.:* cock of the walk. (2) A woman viewed mainly as a sexual object. [From *cock* = vagina in the South.] (3) Nonsense, crap, rubbish. ["What he usually improvised was just a load of cock"—L. Deighton, *Expensive Place* (1967).] *Syn.:* cock-and-bull story, poppycock.

cockabaloo, *n.* A nasty boss or supervisor.

cockalorum, *n.* A small conceited man. [From *cocalorum* = little or small cock. "Lord James Butler was the high cockalorum of the Protestants"—quoted in *OED* (1881).]

cockaludicrous, *adj.* Pompously in error.

cockamamie, *adj.* Absurd, confused, mixed-up; or cheap, fake, worthless, fraudulent. ["You march into the precinct with a tight dress and a cockamamie bunch of alibis"— E. McBain, *Empty Hours* (1962).]

cock-bite, *n.* A castrating or bitchy woman.

cock cheese, *n.* A disgusting person. [From foul-smelling, rancid secretions of the penis or vagina.]

cock-chafer, *n.* A woman who is a sexual tease. ["... cockchafer: a girl in the habit of permitting all familiarities except the last"—J. S. Farmer, *Slang and its Analogues* (1891).]

cock-happy, *adj.* Describing a woman who is always ready and willing to engage in sexual activity.

cockhound, *n.* A man who aggressively seeks sex or places sex above all other interests. [From use in the South of *cock* = vagina.] *Syn.:* cock artist, cockfighter, cock of the game, cocksman, cocksmith, cum freak, fleshhound.

cock-queen, *n.* A woman whose husband or boyfriend has sex with other women.

cocksmitten, *adj.* Obsessed by men.

cocksucker, *n.* (1) A male (and sometimes a female) who performs oral sex with a male. ["If it weren't for the spooks wouldn't a damn one of you white cocksuckers ever get laid"—James Baldwin, *Another Country* (1962).] (2) A despicable and detestable person. ["My father said 'No' to one after another of the thousand little accessories the cocksucker wanted to sell us"—Philip Roth, *Portnoy's Complaint* (1969).] (3) A toady, a sycophant. [One of the strongest terms of abuse in the English language.]

cocksucking, *adj.* Despicable, contemptible, disgusting. ["Mother-raping, cocksucking, turdeating bastard, are you blind"—Chester Himes, *Blind Man With a Pistol* (1969).]

cocksure, *adj.* Arrogantly or smugly sure. ["Cocksure: to be positive; to be mistaken at the top of one's voice"—Ambrose Bierce, *The Devil's Dictionary* (1906).] *Syn.*: audacious, brash, bumptious, cheeky, cocky, conceited, chesty.

cock-teaser, *n.* A person who arouses a man sexually and then denies him completion. ["I hate a girl who says she will/And then says she won't"—Max Miller, *The Max Miller Blue Book* (1975).] *Syn.*: CT, prick-teaser, PT.

cocky, *adj.* Vain, arrogantly pert. ["He looked the cockiest little man of all little men"—quoted in *OED* (1863).] *Syn.*: arrogant, bold, conceited, overly assertive, pushy, smug.

coffee cooler, *n.* A person who avoids work. *Syn.*: goldbrick, shirker, goof-off, loafer.

cojones, no, *idiom.* No courage. [Spanish for "no balls," made popular in English by Ernest Hemingway.] *Syn.*: no huevos.

coke freak, *n.* A frequent or heavy cocaine user. ["All of a sudden the coke freaks were going back to smack."] *Syn.*: coke fiend, cokehead, cokey.

cold biscuit, *n.* A cold, unresponsive woman.

cold-blooded, *adj.* Unimpassioned, unfeeling. ["The instruments of his cold-blooded malice"—Thomas B. McCauley, *History of England* (1848).]

cold-cock, *v.* To hit someone hard verbally, leaving him with no comeback.

cold-decker, *n.* A cheat or a swindler.

cold fish, *n.* A passionless, unsociable person. ["The president's wife was regarded as an especially cold fish."] *Syn.*: chilly mo, iceberg, ice maiden.

cold shot, *n.* A verbal insult, a put-down.

color-struck, *adj.* Prejudiced against darker-skinned black persons, or preferring white aesthetic and racial values to those of people of color.

comatose, *adj.* Very stupid or unaware of what is going on around one. ["... wailing, stupid, comatose creatures" —Ralph Waldo Emerson.] *Syn.:* cataleptic, catatonic, drugged, narcotized, stuporous, unconscious, dead behind the ears.

come down hard, *idiom.* To punish severly, to clamp down on.

come unglued, *idiom.* To get angry or lose control. ["At the slightest criticism, he would come unglued."] *Syn.:* blow one's stack, come unstrung, come unscrewed, fall apart.

comma-counter, *n.* A person who overemphasizes minor details, a pedantic perfectionist. ["The editor was a great comma-counter who failed to see how boring the magazine had become."] *Syn.:* nitpicker, quibbler, pedant, pettifogger.

Commie or **Commy,** *n.* (1) A member of a Communist party or a supporter of Marxist-Leninist theories. [From abbreviation of *Communist.* "Every communist has a fascist frown, and every fascist has a communist smile"—Muriel Spark.] *Syn:* Bolshie, Bolshevik, com, commie symp, comrade, red. (2) A traitor, an enemy, a despised person. ["Fuck 'em all, fuck 'em all/The Commies, the U.N. and all"—U.S. Marine Corps song (1953).] (3) A hippie living in a commune.

common, *adj.* (1) Lower-class, ordinary. ["God must hate the common people because he made them so common"—Philip Wylie.] (2) Trashy, mediocre, low, rough. ["She's nothing but a common tramp, common as cat shit and twice as nasty."] *Idioms:* common as dishwater, common as dog shit.

company man, *n.* A person who sides with the boss, usually against the people he works with. ["The good company men were shocked when they were fired along with the others."]

computer geek, *n.* A hacker. ["One who fulfills all the dreariest negative stereotypes about hackers: an asocial, malodorous, pasty-faced monomaniac with all the personality of a cheese grater." Eric Raymond, *The New Hacker's Dictionary* (1991).] *Syn.:* turbo nerd, turbo geek. *Syn.:* biter, burn artist, burner, clip artist, cold decker, fleecer, flimflammer, four-flusher, gouger, grifter, gyp, hoser, jackleg, scammer, shark, skinner.

con, *v.* To trick or to cheat someone out of money. *Syn.:* do a number on, fool, hit on someone, shuck, snow.

conceited, *adj.* Having an exaggerated opinion of oneself. ["He was conceited like a cock who thought that the sun had risen to hear him crow"—adapted from George Eliot.]

conehead, *n.* A phony intellectual.

conk-buster, *n.* A phony intellectual.

con man, *n.* A confidence man, a swindler. ["Here lies Jed T. Whittaker, the greatest con man of all time/And I never saw the time, day or night, when he couldn't make hisself a dime"—"Herman From the Shark-Tooth Shore," a classic toast.]

conservative, *adj.* Opposing change, favoring traditional values. ["Being conservative is like trying to steal second base while keeping a foot on first"—adapted from Lawrence J. Peter.] *Syn.:* die-hard, fogyish, hard-shell, illiberal, old-line, old-school, orthodox, reactionary, right-wing, square, stick-in-the-mud, tory, traditional, unprogressive.

contemptible, *adj.* Deserving contempt. ["The one disgraceful, unpardonable, and to all time contemptible action of my life was to allow myself to appeal to society for help and protection"—Oscar Wilde.]

contentious, *adj.* Quarrelsome. *Syn.:* argumentative, belligerent, cantankerous, combative, pugnacious, ructious, truculent. *Idioms:* having a chip on one's shoulder, having a bone to pick, having a hard-on for.

contumacious, *adj.* Obstinately contrary, head strong, mulish. *Syn.*: disobedient, fractious, disrespectful, insolent, insubordinate, intractable, headstrong, perverse, pigheaded, recalcitrant.

cooch, *n.* A woman viewed only as a sex object.

cookie-cutter, *n.* A weak person, a wimp.

cookie-pusher, *n.* (1) A person who flatters superiors, a brownnoser. (2) A government bureaucrat or career officer. ["The cookie-pusher feared that defense cutbacks would wipe out their privileged positions."] (3) A lazy do-nothing, a wastrel.

cooler, *n.* An unattractive young woman.

coolie, *n.* One who works long hours at arduous tasks for very little money. [From *coolie* = a lower-class Asian.]

coon, *n.* An American black. [From shortening of *racoon.* "Desegregation became a fad/coons wore business suits/ sucked butts/but did not pick their noses/spoke, with egalitarian accents"—Stanley Crouch, "BLACKIE speaks on campus: a valentine for vachel lindsay."]

coosie, *n.* A Chinese person.

coot, *n.* An old, silly fool.

coo-yon, *n.* A crazy person.

cooz or **cuzzy,** *n.* A person, especially a woman, seen solely as a sex object.

cop out, *v.* To find a false excuse to get out of work or another commitment. ["It was easy for her to cop out of tough jobs; she was the boss's pet."]

copperhead, *n.* A traitor. [From a poisonous snake. A name given to Northerners who sympathized with the South during the Civil War.]

copper-hearted, *adj.* Likely to squeal on one, untrustworthy.

coprocrat, *n.* A believer in coprocracy, or rule by shits.

coprolaliac, *n.* One who uses dirty language excessively, a toiletmouth.

coprolite, *n.* A disgusting person. [From *coprolite* = fossilized dung.]

coprophagous, *adj.* Shit-eating, dung-ingesting. ["A gap-toothed and hoary ape . . . coryphaeus or choragus of his Bulgarian tribe of auto-coprophagous baboons"—Swinburne, in a letter to Emerson, 1874.]

copycat, *n.* An imitator, one who mimics. ["A lotta cats copy the Mona Lisa, but people still line up to see the original"—Louis Armstrong.]

coquette, *n.* A flirtatious, flighty woman. ["A coquette is a woman who arouses passion she has no intention of gratifying"—George Bernard Shaw.]

corksacking, *adj.* Disgusting, depraved. [Euphemistic form of *cocksucking,* coined by Anthony Burgess in the *New York Times.*]

corn, *n.* Maudlin sentimentality in literature, music, or art. ["His Broadway hits were nothing but pure corn—not a genuine emotion in any of them."] *Syn.:* corniness, drool, flapdoodle, glop, goo, mush, pure corn, schmaltz, slobber, slop, slush.

cornball, *n.* A naive, unsophisticated person who likes or produces mawkishly sentimental material.

cornholer, *n.* One who gooses someone, or engages in anal sex.

cornpone, *n.* A Southerner. [From the food of the same name.]

cotton-picking, *adj.* Damned, rotten, lousy, no-good, worthless. ["Get your cotton-pickin' hands offa me."]

couch case, *n.* An emotionally disturbed and agitated person.

couch potato, *n.* One who spends much time watching television or just sits around doing nothing. ["That new breed of American, the stay-at-home, VCR-watching couch potato . . ."—*Guardian*, (1988).]

couldn't organize a fuck in a whorehouse, *idiom.* Totally and utterly incompetent. *Idioms:* couldn't run a piss-up in a brewery, couldn't sell cunt in a jailhouse.

court holy water or **bread,** *idiom.* Insincere language, empty verbiage or flattery.

cousin, *n.* A dupe. ["There were always plenty of cousins around who fell for his get-rich-quick schemes."] *Syn.:* sucker, pigeon, mug, mark.

cow, *n.* A heavy, graceless, obese, placid woman. *Syn.:* heifer, silly cow, silly moo.

cow-and-kisses, *n.* A wife, or one's own wife. *Syn.:* cheese-and-kisses, plate-and-dishes [rhyming slang for *missus.*]

coward, *n.* A person lacking courage. ["I loathe people who keep dogs. They are cowards who haven't the guts to bite people themselves"—August Strindberg, *A Madman's Diary.*] *Syn.:* baby, caitiff, creamer, dastard, faint-heart, poltroon, scaredy-cat, yellow-belly, yellow-dog.

cowboy, *n.* (1) A person who is undisciplined or reckless, or a wild criminal. ["The L.A. cops were widely regarded as a bunch of cowboys."]

cow clap, *n.* A disgusting person. [From *cow dung.*] *Syn.:* cow cake, cow clod, cow dab, cow flop, cow pat, cow pie, cow plop, cow pucky, cow shard, cow shit, cow slip.

coxcomb, *n.* A fop, a dandy, a conceited fool.

coyote, *n.* A contemptible person, specifically one who brings illegal Mexicans into the United States and then robs them and betrays them to the authorities.

crab, *n.* A person who is irritable or disagreeable. ["He used his age as an excuse for being a crab, but he had always been the same grouch."] *Syn.:* crabapple, grouch, grump, griper.

cracked, *adj.* Crazy, eccentric, foolish, spaced-out, nuts, dim-witted.

cracker, *n.* A rural Southerner. ["It's all a thing of mind over matter/You don't mind—crackers don't matter" —Kuwasi Balogon, "If You Love Them, Wouldn't You Like to See Them Better Off?"] *Syn.*: Arkie, clay-eater, Georgia cracker, good old boy, ku kluxer, Okie, peck, woodchuck, woolhat.

crackfart, *n.* A person who boasts, a braggart.

cradle-snatcher, *n.* A person who seeks younger sex partners. *Syn.*: cradle-robber, baby-snatcher.

crank, *n.* An eccentric or grouchy person with weird ideas.

crank freak, *n.* A drug user who alternates between depressants and stimulants. *Syn.*: crank commando, cranker.

crank it on, *idiom.* To lie or tell a wild, tall tale.

crap, *n.* (1) Any poorly made item. ["Ninety percent of everything is crap"—Theodore Sturgeon, science fiction author.] (2) Dung, feces, shit. (3) Nonsense, lies, exaggeration, crapola. ["Stop bullshittin' me. That's a lotta crap."]

crapoid, *n.* A disgusting person.

crapper, *n.* A liar, a braggart, a person who exaggerates.

craterface, *n.* A person with many acne scars. *Syn.*: pizzaface.

crashing bore, *n.* An utter and complete bore.

crawfish, *n.* A person who is mean and stingy.

crawler, *n.* A sycophant, an ass-kisser.

crazie, *n.* A destructive political fanatic. ["The crazies alienated their potential supporters with their violent tactics."]

crazy, *adj.* Not sensible, mentally deranged, unusual, or bizarre. *Syn.*: apeshit, berserk, bugs, bugsy, cockeyed, crackpot, crazy-assed, daffy, dick-brained, fruitcakey, gonzo, goofy, insane, spaced out, squirrely, unhinged. *Idioms*: a few cards short of a full deck, crazy as cat shit, food for the squirrels, not tightly wrapped, half there, rowing with one oar in the water, elevator doesn't reach the top floor.

creaker, *n.* An elderly person.

creamie, *n.* A sexually attractive woman.

cream puff, *n.* (1) A weakling, someone easily pushed around. (2) An effeminate man.

creative accountant, *n.* An accountant who falsifies financial records.

credulous, *adj.* Tending to believe anything. *Syn.*: gullible, naive, unsophisticated.

creep, *n.* A loathsome person. ["But, step aside, creep, and watch a master"—"Mexican Rose," a classic toast.] *Syn.*: jerk, fool, crumb, nerd, crumb bum, creeping crud.

creeping Jesus, *n.* A whining, simpering, sanctimonious person.

creeps, give one the, *idiom.* To give one a feeling of revulsion. ["He gave me the creeps with all his talk of busting heads."]

cretin, *n.* A stupid, foolish idiot. *Syn.*: cretinoid, spas.

crill, *adj.* Very inferior, totally grody. ["I could totally freak out, like my mom, the Jell-O head, buys me this crill barf-pink terry cloth like strapless dress to wear to Cori's bat mitzvah"—Corey and Westermark, *Fer Shurr! How to Be a Valley Girl—Totally!*]

crisco, *n.* An obese person. [From the trademarked fat substance.]

crispy or **crispo,** *n.* A burnout, a jel, a space cadet. *Idiom*: one with fried brains.

critic, *n.* One who judges harshly, a fault-finder. ["Critics are like eunuchs in a harem: they know how it is done, they've seen it done every day, but they are unable to do it themselves"—Brendan Behan.] *Syn.*: carper, crabber, knocker, nitpicker, smellfungus, whiner.

criticaster, *n.* An incompetent critic.

croaker or **hungry croaker,** *n.* An unethical doctor who will illegally prescribe a drug. ["Everyone knows the croakers who run the Medical mill."]

crock of shit or **crock,** *n.* (1) A mass of lies and bullshit. ["We all saw his apparent concern for the middle class as a crock to win votes."] (2) A liar, a braggart, a worthless person.

crocodile, *n.* A rapacious hypocrite who feigns sorrow to deceive potential victims. [From the legend that crocodiles shed tears over the necessity of killing for food.]

cromagnon, *n.* An ugly man.

crone, *n.* An ugly old woman. *Syn.:* hag, witch.

cronky, *adj.* Corrupt, lying.

crony, *n.* An unqualified person appointed to public office because of his political connections. ["I am against government by crony"—Harold L. Ickes.]

crook, *n.* A professional thief or swindler. ["I am not a crook"—Richard M. Nixon.]

crookback, *n.* A hunchback.

crooked rib, *n.* A wife who nags and scolds.

crosspatch, *n.* A cranky, bad-tempered person. *Syn.:* crotcheteer, killjoy, sorehead, scold, shrew, sourpuss.

crotchhound, *n.* A womanizer, a lecher. ["I'd never seen such a crotchhound. I warned him that he's beginning to get a reputation about all the squak he's stabbing"—Trevanian, *The Main* (1977).]

crotch cheese, *n.* A disgusting and filthy person. [From a smelly substance found in unclean pubic areas.]

crotchety, *adj.* Short-tempered. *Syn.:* cross, cranky, crusty, contrary, crabbed, dotty, prickly, eccentric, fussy, grouchy, odd, peculiar, perverse, potty.

crotch rot, *n.* A disgusting, despicable person. [From an itching of the groin and scrotum, possibly due to disease.]

crotel, *n.* A disgusting person. [From *crotels* = small balls of hare shit.]

crow, *n.* An ugly or unpopular woman. ["It's amazing how many old crows marry good-looking men. Money doesn't hurt either."]

C.R.S., *adj.* Can't remember shit, forgetful, stupid. ["He's strictly C.R.S."]

crud, *n.* A contemptible and repulsive person. [From *crud,* curdle.]

crud, you, *interj.* Go to hell! Fuck you!

cruising for a bruising, *idiom.* Asking for trouble, risking violence. ["Keep that up and you're cruisin' for a bruising."]

crumb or **crumb bum,** *n.* A worthless person, or a dirty louse. ["God! The country that produced George Washington has got this collection of crumb bums!"—Barbara Tuchman on the 1980 presidential candidates.] *Syn.*: crumb bun, crum bun, crum.

crumblie, *n.* An older person. [From *crumble* = to decay. "The growing fashion among teenagers is to describe their parents as 'wrinklies' and their grandparents as 'crumblies.' A reader, however, tells me how she countered this when ... she described her own children, in their earshot, as 'pimplies.' "—*Daily Telegraph* (1987).] *Syn.*: wrinkly, dusty.

crumpet, *n.* An attractive woman viewed as available as a sexual partner. [From *crumpet* = a sweetened griddle cake.]

crypto, *n.* A person who conceals his or her true beliefs, a secret member of a party or sect. [Often used as a prefix. "Philby was a crypto-Communist since his Cambridge days."]

cube, *n.* A very conventional person, a square.

cubehead, *n.* A user of LSD or a user who takes a drug on a sugar cube.

cuckold, *n.* A man whose wife commits adultry. [From the cuckoo bird, who deposits its eggs in other birds' nests. "I had rather be a toad,/And live upon the vapour of a dungeon,/Than keep a corner in the thing I love/For others' uses"—William Shakespeare, *Othello.*] *Syn.*: buck's face, cuck, cuckoo, cornuto, green goose, half-moon, hoddy-peek, horn-grower, horn merchant, horn-wearer, ramhead.

cuckquean, *n.* A woman whose husband commits adultery.

cuddle-bunny, *n.* A young sexually loose woman.

cueball, *n.* An eccentric, odd person.

cuffee, *n.* An African-American.

culch, *n.* Rubbish, bullshit. [From *culch* = the floor of an oyster bed.]

cullud gal, *n.* A black woman. [From *cullud* = *colored.* ["I believe my old lady's/Pregnant again/Fate must have/Some kind of Trickeration/To populate the/Cullud Nation!"—Langston Hughes, "What So Soon."]

cullud gemman, *n.* A black man.

culture vulture, *n.* A pretentious devotee, and often exploiter, of the arts and intellectual pursuits; a culture snob.

cum freak, *n.* A woman who is interested solely in copulating. [From *cum* = semen.]

cunning as a shithouse rat, *idiom.* Deceptive, sly, underhanded, crafty.

cunny-hunter, *n.* A lecher, a womanizer. *Syn.*: cunthound.

cunt, *n.* (1) A rotten, contemptible woman; a bitch. [From *cunt* defined as "a nasty name for a nasty thing"—Francis Grose, *A Dictionary of the Vulgar Tongue* (1785).] (2) A woman regarded solely as a sexual object. (3) A unpleasant, despicable person. ["Tell him he's a cunt from me"—George Orwell, *Collected Essays* (1968).] *Syn.*: grumble-and-grunt, sharp-and-blunt, Sir Berkeley Hunt, untcay.

cuntfarter or **pussyfarter,** *n.* An unpleasant woman [From one who emits air from the vagina during copulation.]

cunt itch, *n.* Female sexual desire. ["She's suffering from you know what—a serious case of cunt itch."]

cunt-lapper or **cunt-sucker,** *n.* (1) A person who orally stimulates the genitalia of a woman. (2) A lesbian. (3) Any disliked person.

cunt meat, *n.* A generic term for women.

cunt-struck, *adj.* Obsessed with women.

cunt-teaser, *n.* (1) A man who arouses a woman sexually but refuses to copulate. (2) A woman who stimulates a lesbian but refuses sexual relations.

cupcake, *n.* (1) An attractive, cute woman. (2) An effeminate man.

cupidity, *n.* A strong desire for wealth. *Syn.*: acquisitiveness, avarice, avariciousness, avidity, covetousness, greed, rapaciousness, rapacity, voracity.

cur, *n.* A mean and despicable person. [From *cur* = a worthless dog, one of low breed. "Hang cur! Hang you whoreson . . ."—William Shakespeare, *The Tempest.*]

curly wolf, *n.* A tough, tricky character.

curmudgeon, *n.* An avaricious, salty-tongued, ill-natured person. ["Having a curmudgeon as his chief aide deflected most criticism from his office."]

curpel, *n.* A horse's ass.

curse you, *interj.* Damn you!

curtain lecture, *n.* A wife's angry or critical lecture to her husband in bed.

cushion-thumper, *n.* A clergyman.

cut, *v.* To insult someone, often sarcastically.

cut-cock, *n.* A Jewish man. [Allusion to circumcision.]

cut down to size, *v.* To attack a person with too high an opinion of himself. ["They loved to cut that officious spokesperson down to size."]

cutesie-pie, *n.* An attractive man. *Syn.*: cutie, cutie-pie.

cut someone a new asshole, *idiom.* To rebuke someone harshly. ["Come into my office and bring that report. I think I'm going to cut you a new asshole."] *Idioms:* cut one off at the knees, cut (or turn) off one's water, cut one's ass, cut the blood out of someone, cut your water and take the meter out.

cut out paper dolls, *idiom.* To behave in an insane manner.

cutthroat, *adj.* Very harsh, barbarous, murderous, sanguinary, ruthless.

cynic, *n.* One who thinks all acts spring from purely selfish motives. [From the Greek *kynikos* = doglike. "A cynic is a man who, when he smells flowers, looks around for a coffin"—H. L. Mencken.] *Syn.:* scoffer, Calamity Jane, misanthrope, doubter, faultfinder, knocker, misogynist, pessimist, spoilsport.

D

daffodil, *n.* An effeminate man. *Syn.:* buttercup, daisy, flower, lily, pansy, ansypay.

dabbler, *n.* A person who does anything in a trifling way and is not serious. ["The certainty of touch which marks the difference between an artist and the dabbler ... can come only after patient study"—Barrett Wendell.]

daffy, *adj.* Eccentric, foolish, stupid. ["How can you stand around with those daffy jocks."] *Syn.:* brain-sick, besotted, daft, dippy, dizzy, ditsy, unhinged, wacky, witless. *Idioms:* been in the sun too long, off one's nut.

dagger, *n.* A masculine lesbian. [Shortened form of *bull-dagger.*]

dagling, *n.* A despicable and detestable person. [From the word for sheep dung.]

dago, *n.* A person of Italian descent, used less often for a person of Portuguese or Spanish descent. [From Diego, a personal name.]

damaged goods, *n.* A woman who has lost her virginity.

dame, *n.* Any girl or woman, often with the implication of promiscuity. ["Dames will lie about anything—just for practice"—Paul Gauguin.]

dammit all, *interj.* A curse to express anger or pain.

damn, *n.* (1) A mild oath still considered profane. ["Bad language or abuse/I never, never use,/Whatever the emergency;/Though "Bother it" I may/Occasionally say,/I never use a big, big D"—W. S. Gilbert, *H.M.S Pinafore.*] *Syn.:* double-damn, D.D., bother, dern, consarn, dang, dast, durn, blame. (2) a little bit, the least bit. [Used negatively.]

damnation, *interj.* A curse of anger, pain, or disappointment. *Syn.:* blamnation, botheration, dangnation, hangnation, murderation, tarnation, thunderation.

damned, *adj.* Cursed, or condemned to hell. [Often used as an intensfier. "Get your damned cotton-picking hands off me."] *Syn.:* accursed, blamed, blanked, bleeding, bloody, browned, cotton-picking, dashed, detestable, doggoned, doomed, frigging, fucking, goddamned, motherfucking.

damn you, *interj.* Go to hell! *Idioms:* balls to you, cram it, God rot your soul, hope your rabbit dies, ram it, up yours.

damper, *n.* A person who depresses another's enthusiasm, a killjoy.

dandy, *n.* An effeminate man. ["... that he had the taste of a dandy, we learn from a letter of the time describing his 'smart white hat, kid gloves, brown frock coat, yellow cassimere waistcoat, gray duck trousers, and blue silk handkerchief carelessly secured in front by a silver pin'"—Thomas Walsh.]

dange broad, *n.* A sexually attractive black woman.

dangerous curves, *n.* An attractive woman.

dangler, *n.* (1) An exhibitionist, a flasher. (2) A gay man who wears tight trousers to show off.

dangus, *n.* A slovenly woman.

dap, *n.* A white person. [Reverse slang for *pad* = paddy, slang for an Irish person, hence a white person.]

darkie or **dark cloud,** *n.* A black person. ["There was a young woman named Starkie/Who had an affair with a darkie./The result of her sins/Was quadruplets not twins—/One black, one white, and two khaki"—English limerick.]

dark meat, *n.* A black woman viewed solely as a sex object.

dastard, *n.* (1) A coward. (2) A dimwit or a boor.

Day-Glo, *adj.* Gaudy and cheap.

dead, *adj.* Dull, blank, boring, doltish, flat, vapid, dreary, tedious, sluggish, drab, uninteresting. ["You can't keep a dead mind down"—Samuel Beckett.]

deadass, *n.* An impotent man. ["... us women know who got the spring and which is the unfortunate deadass" —Norman Mailer, *Why Are We in Vietnam?* (1967).]

deadbeat, *n.* A person who begs for money from his friends and does not pay them back. ["A deadbeat is a person who can't pay, gets another person who can't pay to guarantee that he can pay"—adapted from Charles Dickens.] *Syn.:* moocher, schnorrer, sponger, parasite, leech, freeloader, welsher.

dead duck, *n.* A person who is ruined or destined to fail. *Idiom:* a goner.

deadeye, *n.* A leering man who eyeballs and objectifies women.

deadfanny, *adj.* Dull, foolish, stupid.

dead from the neck up, *idiom.* (1) A particularly stupid person. (2) A conservative person who is resistant to new ideas. (3) A big bore.

dead in the water, *idiom.* Doomed to failure, kaput, stalled or defunct, down the drain. ["Your plan is dead in the water. Can't you ever come up with something that can fly?"]

dead meat, *n.* A stupid, dull dimwit.

deadneck, *n.* (1) A stupid person, an ignoramus. (2) A hippie who is into nature.

dead pigeon, *n.* A person who is sure to fail.

deadsville, *adj.* Dull, dreary, boring. ["Let's get out of here. This is deadsville."]

dealer, *n.* A person who peddles drugs. *Syn.*: bagman, bigman, broker, candy man, candy-pusher, connection, dope-peddler, dope pimp, ice-cream man, junker, junk-peddler, missionary, peddler, pusher, righteous dealer, tambourine man, viper, feed-and-grain man, good-time man.

deal in dirt, *idiom.* To gossip about or badmouth someone. *Syn.*: do dirt, dish the dirt.

debased, *adj.* Corrupted, tainted, perverted, degenerate, polluted, vitiated. ["Success permits him to see how those he has converted distort and debase his teaching"—Aldous Huxley.] *Idioms*: gone to the dogs, gone to hell.

debauched, *adj.* Depraved, corrupted. ["Debauchee: one who has so earnestly pursued pleasure that he has the misfortune to overtake it"—Ambrose Bierce, *The Devil's Dictionary*.] *Syn.*: degenerate, perverted, profligate, licentious, rakehell, lascivious, lewd, licentious, lecherous, dissolute, wanton, dissipated, immoral, degraded, tainted, rotten to the core.

decadent, *adj.* Lacking in moral vigor, decaying. ["Although he thought of his parents as decadent bourgeois, he continued to live off their largesse."] *Syn.*: corrupt, immoral, effete, degraded, degenerate, debased, depraved, fin-de-siècle, perverse, perverted, dissolute.

deceitful, *adj.* Duplicitous, treacherous. ["The fox barks not when he would steal the lamb. No, no, my sovereign! Gloucester is a man unsounded yet and full of deep deceit"—William Shakespeare.]

deceiver, *n.* One who misleads or is unfaithful. ["Sigh no more, ladies, sigh no more/Men were deceivers ever"—William Shakespeare, *Much Ado About Nothing*.]

deep pockets, *n.* A rich person, a plutocrat. ["When you are suing, always go after the deep pockets."]

deep shit, in, *idiom.* In serious trouble. ["You keep that up and you're going to be in deep shit, buster."]

deep throat, *n.* One who divulges secret information. [From Deep Throat, an unrevealed source of much of the information in the Watergate scandal.]

defective, *adj.* Deranged, mentally lacking, retarded, backward, simpleminded. ["In our culture a person who falls sick, hears voices, communicates with shadows, and acquires special abilities from them is inevitably classed as deranged"—Alfred Lewis Kroeber.] *Idioms:* not all there, soft in the head.

degenerate, *n.* (1) A person deemed by some to engage in "abnormal" sexual activities. *Syn.:* reprobate, pervert, bugger, sinner. (2) Heterosexual slang for a homosexual. *Syn.:* DG, deegy.

deknackered, *adj.* Castrated, de-balled, emasculated, denutted. ["You have as much courage as a denackered goldfish."]

demon from hell, *idiom.* Conniving, deceitful person.

derrick, *n.* A mannish-looking butch lesbian.

desipience, *n.* Foolishness, silliness.

despicable, *adj.* Detestable. ["The immorality of James' Court was hardly more despicable than the imbecility of his government"—J. R. Green.]

devil, the, *idiom.* A white person. ["Farrakhan-ite rappers tend to be more circumspect, saying 'devils' instead of 'white devils' and usually condemning the system rather than people who run it"—Jon Pareles, the *New York Times* (1992).]

deviant, *adj.* Abnormal. *Syn.:* bizarre, freakish, freaky, kinky, perverse, perverted, queer, twisted.

deviate, *n.* A homosexual man or woman.

devious, *adj.* Deceitful, disingenuous. ["The marks of the thoroughbred are simply not there. The man was blatant, crude, overly confidential, devious"—H. L. Mencken.]

diabolic or **diabolical,** *adj.* Damnable, devilish, satanic. ["People suffering from the paranoia of persecution often imagine that they are the victims of a diabolical secret society"—Aldous Huxley.] *Syn.*: fiendish, hellish, wicked, infernal, malevolent, demonic, iniquitous, impious, villainous, nefarious, monstrous, heinous, vicious.

diarrhea of the mouth, *idiom.* A condition of talking excessively and constantly. ["Can't you shut him up? He's got a bad case of diarrhea of the mouth"] *Idioms:* diarrhea of the jawbone, foot-in-mouth disease.

diatribe, *n.* An abusive, prolonged denunciation or harangue. ["Do I have to listen to your diatribes every time I come home?"] *Syn.*: tirade, tongue-lashing, jeremiad, invective.

dick, *n.* (1) An unattractive, egotistical man. (2) A stupid person, a jerk. *Syn.*: dickhead, peckerhead, dickwad, dickweed. (3) A mean, offensive person; a prick.

dick or **dick over,** *v.* To cheat, trick, or deceive someone.

dick around, *v.* To waste time. ["Stop dicking around and get on the ball."]

dick-drinker, *n.* Someone who performs fellatio. [From *dick* = penis.] *Syn.*: dick-licker, dickey-licker, dickey-taster, dick-sucker, spigot-sucker.

dick-for, *n.* A person dumb enough to ask "What's a dick for?"

dicktease, *n.* A woman who pretends to like a man, then turns cold on him.

dicky broad, *n.* A mannish lesbian.

dictatorial, *adj.* Authoritarian, despotic, doctrinaire, domineering, dogmatic, magisterial, overbearing. ["... a captain who has been entrusted with dictatorial power—Thomas B. Macaulay.]

dicty, *adj.* High-class, snobbish, high-hat, potty, snobby, snooty, haughty, imperious. ["Get a load of that dicty, hincty bitch."]

diddler, *n.* (1) A masturbator. (2) A cheater or deceiver.

diddly-shit, *adj.* Worthless, useless, trivial, or insignificant. *Syn.*: diddly, diddly-squat, doodly-squat, doodly-shit.

diddybopper, *n.* (1) A pretentious or pompous black person who identifies with white mainstream culture. (2) A socially inexperienced person.

didn't catch shit, *idiom.* Didn't impress anybody. ["She didn't get the role. Her singing and dancing didn't catch shit."]

diehard, *n.* An irreconcilable enemy of change. ["The Tory Die-hards in their clubs/they sing this plaintive tune." A.T. Hagg, *Labour Community Song Book* (1927).] *Syn.*: bitter-ender, conservative, fundamentalist, mossback, old-liner, old fogy, rightist, right-winger, standpatter, tory.

diesel dyke, *n.* An aggressive, masculine lesbian. ["What's the point of being a lesbian if a woman is going to look like a diesel dyke and act like an imitation man?"]

dig dirt, *v.* To gossip.

digithead, *n.* One who studies constantly, a grind.

dilberry or **dillberry,** *n.* A disgusting person. [From the word for fecal matter caught on the pubic or anal hair.]

dildo or **dill,** *n.* A foolish and despicable person. [From *dildo* = artificial phallus.]

dimbo, *n.* A dumb bimbo. ["That dimbo really thought the star invited her up to talk about politics."]

dim bulb, *n.* A stupid person. *Syn.*: bulb, dimwit.

dime-dropper, *n.* An informer. [From the time past, when a telephone call cost a dime.]

ding-a-ling, *n.* An old silly person. [From one who hears bells.] *Syn.*: ding-ding, ding-dong.

dingbat, *n.* (1) A stupid, vague, or inane simpleton. ["Stifle yourself, You dingbat"—"All in the Family," TV show.] (2) A person of Italian descent.

dinge, *n.* A black person. ["That big dinge took him by surprise . . . the big black bastard"—Ernest Hemingway, *Winner Take Nothing* (1933).]

dinge queen, *n.* A white homosexual who seeks sex with black men.

dingleberry, *n.* A stupid and disgusting person. [From *dingleberry* = a blob of fecal matter on the hairs around the anus. "Pick the dingleberries out of your teeth"—Norman Mailer, *Why Are We in Vietnam?* (1967).] *Syn.:* dangleberry, fartleberry.

dink, *n.* (1) A Vietnamese person. ["These are not people. . . . They are dinks and gooks and slant-eyed bastards"—*Guardian* (1970).] *Syn.:* Charles, Charlie, Chuck, dip, dipshit, Link the Chink. (2) A person of East Asian nationality or descent. (3) An American black.

dink, *n.* A member of a childless couple. [From the acronym for *d*ouble *i*ncome *n*o *k*ids.]

dinky, *adj.* Minor, undersized, insignificant, bush-league, small-time.

dinner, *n.* An attractive woman viewed as a sex object. [One of the many eating metaphors for women.]

dip or **diphead**, *n.* An eccentric person.

dipped, *adj.* Having some black heritage.

dipper, *n.* A Baptist.

dippermouth, *n.* A person with an overly large mouth.

dippy, *adj.* Balmy, crazy, harebrained, loony, nuts, preposterous, wacky.

dipshit or **dipstick**, *n.* A stupid, jerky, person; a loser. ["Try as he could to succeed, he never amounted to more than a dipshit."]

dipshit, *adj.* Second-rate or inferior.

dipsy-doddle, *n.* A deceiver, a con man, a swindler.

dirt, *n.* A despicable, scummy, worthless person. ["Her family warned her that she was marrying dirt."] *Syn.:* dirtbag, dirtball, crud, scumbag.

dirt-eater, *n.* A poor Southern white.

dirty, *adj.* Obscene, smutty. ["Is sex dirty? Only if it is done right"—Woody Allen.]

dirty dog, *n.* A contemptible, vile person; a man who mistreats a woman.

dirty dowager, *n.* A rich, aging homosexual.

dirty joke, *n.* A very ugly, stupid person.

dirtyleg, *n.* A promiscuous woman.

dirtymouth, *n.* A person who talks obscenely.

dirtyneck, *n.* A laborer, a farmer, a member of the working class.

dirty old man, *n.* (1) A lecherous elderly man, an old goat. ["You know inside every senior citizen is a dirty old man trying to get out"—Emlyn Williams.] (2) A male homosexual with a much younger partner.

dirty-pool player, *n.* A person who cheats by breaking the rules.

dirty puzzle, *n.* A sluttish, slovenly woman.

dirty tricks, *n.* Underhanded or dishonest practices, especially in politics. *Syn.:* dirty work, trickery, skullduggery, deception.

dis, *v.* To be disrespectful to someone. ["While taking a dispute to someone's home is the ultimate in 'dissing' . . . there are other insults that can be just as deadly . . . 'You dis, you die,' some youths say"—*Boston Globe* (1990).]

dish, *n.* A sexually attractive woman. ["I got pictures of this dame, she's a swell dish." H. Hobson, *Mission House Murder* (1959).] *Syn.:* charmer, cuddle-bunny, date bait, dreamboat, dream girl, fine hammer, fox, frail end, frail job, good looker, hammer, hot dish, lulu, mink, nifty number, oomph girl, poundcake, sex bunny, sex goddess, sex job, sex kitten, sexpot, sex queen, slick chick, stone fox.

dish-clout, *n.* A slattern.

dish it out, *v.* To punish or abuse. ["You can dish it out but you sure can't take it."]

dish the dirt, *idiom.* To slander or gossip maliciously.

dishy, *adj.* Very attractive or sexually desirable.

disloyal, *adj.* Unfaithful, faithless. ["Good party people think such open-mindedness disloyal; but in politics there should be no loyalty except to the public good"—George Bernard Shaw.]

dissolute, *adj.* Dissipated, corrupt, loose, debauched, unrestrained, immoral, abandoned, lewd, licentious, self-indulgent, sybaritic. ["See them spending and squandering and being irresponsible and dissolute and not caring twopence for the way two-thirds of the world live"—Rose Macaulay.]

distaff, *adj.* Pertaining to women. [From the term for the staff used in spinning flax. "Let's hear from the distaff side."]

ditsy or **ditzy,** *adj.* (1) Airheaded, vapid. ["I can't see how you go out with that ditzy blonde."] *Syn.*: silly, scatterbrained, addled, airbrained, frivolous, daffy, dippy, dizzy, fluffheaded, gaga, giddy, goofy, goo-goo, kooky, loopy, potty, rattlebrained, zerking. (2) Pretentious, haughty.

dittybop, *n.* A young person who adopts hip mannerisms unsuited to his personality.

ditz, *n.* A silly and inane person. ["Beauty is only skin deep, but it's a valuable asset if you're a ditz."] *Syn.*: dizzy Lizzie, dumb Dora, fluffhead, giddybrain, giddyhead, ninny.

dizzy, *adj.* Scatterbrained, crazy.

do a dump on someone, *idiom.* To criticize someone severely. ["Stop dumping on me. I'm a person too." Anon.]

do a number on someone, *idiom.* To harm or deceive someone. *Syn.:* do a job on someone.

do a snow job on someone, *idiom.* To deceive someone, especially through flattery.

Dr. Thomas, *n.* A bourgeois black person who has adopted white middle-class values. ["Spitballs and shouts of 'Dr. Thomas' or, more familiarly 'Tom' hit my neck. . . . 'You must think you're white." Darryl Pinckney, *High Cotton* (1992).]

doctrinaire, *adj.* Dogmatic, inflexible in one's beliefs or ideas. ["The most profound contribution to political thought in America, namely the Federalist, was not the work of doctrinaire thinkers but of men of affairs"—Felix Frankfurter.] *Syn.:* rigid, set, arbitrary, absolute, opinionated, pontifical, unshakable, pigheaded, biased, mulish, narrow-minded.

dodo or **dumb dodo,** *n.* A boring or stupid person.

doesn't know enough to come in out of the rain, *idiom.* An exceptionally stupid person.

dog, *n.* (1) An unattractive person. ["I can't stand to look at her. She's a dog."] (2) An untrustworthy, seducing, promiscuous man. ["You're Nothing But a Hound Dog"—Elvis Presley song.] (3) An old hooker. (4) A lousy product, a lemon, a dud. ["So many movies are dogs." *New Yorker* (1970).] (5) A white person.

dog, (dirty), *n.* (1) Any man who mistreats or demeans others, notably women. (2) A bad or evil-tempered man.

(that) dog won't hunt, that cock won't fight, *idiom.* That won't wash! *Idioms:* the hell you say, my hind foot, you're pissin' on my leg.

dog-ass, *adj.* Wretched, inferior, unpleasant.

dogcatcher, *n.* The least important office in any political entity. *Idiom:* a person so incompetent I wouldn't elect him dogcatcher.

dog doo, *n.* Dog shit.

dogfart, *n.* A despicable person. ["Windbag Hamill, sulfurous dogfart"—Donald Charles (pseud.), in *Maledicta V.*]

dogfish, *n.* A sharklike person.

dog-hearted, *adj.* Cruel, pitiless.

dog it, *v.* To avoid hard work, to shirk, to goof off, to fuck off.

dogleg, *n.* An untrustworthy person.

dogmatic, *adj.* Tending to fixed and arbitrary opinions. ["He was dogmatic when he was radical; he's dogmatic as a conservative. Same obstinate hard head."] *Syn.:* arbitrary, biased, prejudiced, stubborn, obstinate, intolerant, blind.

do-gooder, *n.* (1) A naive supporter of social causes; a pretentious, ostentatious "humanitarian." ["Give me the radicals, give me the conservatives, but God deliver me from the do-gooders."]

dog on, *v.* To talk badly about someone. *Syn.:* bag on, rag on.

dogsbody, *n.* A menial.

dog's dinner, *n.* An unattractive person.

dog shit, *n.* A person who is pretentious, despicable, and trashy. ["The Euro-trash think they're hot shit when they're really dog shit."]

dog's lady, *n.* A bitch. *Syn.:* dogess, dog's wife, puppy's mamma.

dog's nose, *n.* A paid stool pigeon.

dog's vomit, *n.* A disgusting person.

doll, *n.* (1) An attractive young woman. ["A living doll, everywhere you look./It can sew, it can cook,/It can talk, talk, talk./It works, there is nothing wrong with it./You have a hole, it's a poultice./You have an eye, it's an image./My boy, it's your last resort./Will you marry it, marry it, marry it"—Sylvia Plath, "The Applicant," *Ariel* (1966).]

Syn.: doll city, dollface, dolly, baby doll, bimbo, dollybird. (2) a conceited young woman.

dolt, *n.* An idiot, a blockhead. *Syn.*: jerk, dunce, nitwit, ass, ninny, imbecile, fool, blockhead, bonehead, moron, numskull, jackass, halfwit.

DOM, *n.* A elderly man obsessed with sex. [From the abbreviation of *d*irty *o*ld *m*an.]

domino, *n.* A dark-skinned black person.

Don Juan, *n.* A lecher or ladies' man. ["Don't trifle with her affections, you Don Juan." William M. Thackeray, *Vanity Fair* (1848).]

donkey, *n.* A stubborn person, or an ass, a fool.

donkey flogger, *n.* A male masturbator. [From *flog the donkey* = to masturbate.]

don't give a tuppeny fuck, *idiom.* Couldn't care less, don't give a damn. [British usage.]

don't give me that, *idiom.* Don't try to fool me. *Idioms:* don't bullshit me, don't pull my leg.

don't hold no air, *idiom.* Doesn't carry any weight.

don't know one's ass from a hole in the ground, *idiom.* To be particularly stupid.

don't know shit from shinola, *idiom.* As wrong as one can be. [Shinola is a shoe polish.]

don't know whether you're coming or going, *idiom.* Utterly confused, lost. *Syn.*: don't know up from down.

don't let your mouth overload your ass, *idiom.* Don't talk so tough or we're going to tangle assholes. *Idiom:* don't let your mouth write a check your ass can't cash.

doodle-dasher, *n.* A male masturbator.

doodle-shit, *n.* Nothing, or less than nothing. (Variations: doddly-squat, doodily-shit, doodley-shit, doodleesqua', squat, doodly-squat, doodly.)

doo-doo head, *n.* An idiot. [From *doo-doo* = shit.]

doof or **doofus,** *n.* A person who is odd, eccentric, or lacking social skills.

dooky, *n.* Excrement.

doormat, *n.* (1) A constant victim. ["People call me feminist whenever I express sentiments that differentiate me from a doormat or a prostitute"—Rebecca West.] (2) A weakling.

dork, *n.* (1) An eccentric person, an oddball. ["I love your husband but he's a real dork."/"Yes, but he's my dork"—*Someone to Watch Over Me*, U.S. film (1987).] (2) A despicable person. [From *dork* = penis.] (3) A stupid and worthless man. *Syn.*: dorkmunder, dorkbrain.

dothead, *n.* A Hindu who lives in the United States. [From the red dot worn by some on their foreheads.]

do the finger, *idiom.* Raise the middle finger to say "fuck you." *Syn.*: shoot the bird.

dotty, *adj.* Crazy, feebleminded, eccentric. [From being in one's dotage.]

double-assed, *adj.* Having a very fat behind.

double-bagger, *n.* A very ugly or unappealing person. *Syn.*: two-bagger.

double-clutcher, *n.* A bastard, a prick.

double-clutching, *adj.* Motherfucking.

double-crosser, *n.* A betrayer, or one who cheats on other cheats. ["The mob never killed double-crossers' families; but the new wave drug dealers make a point of hitting them."]

double-cunted, *adj.* Relating to a woman with large genitals.

double-damn, *n.* A very strong damn or condemnation.

double-dome, *n.* An egghead. ["That double-dome founded the most successful computer firm of all."]

double-dugged, *adj.* Big-breasted.

double-faced, *adj.* Hypocritical, dishonest, sneaky, double-dealing.

double-gaited, *adj.* (1) Strange, eccentric. (2) Bisexual or ambisexual.

double-hearted, *adj.* Treacherous.

double-minded, *adj.* Undetermined, wavering.

doublespeak, *n.* Deliberately unclear or obscure language used to deceive, evade, or impress. *Syn.*: double-talk, gobbledygook, mumbo jumbo, bullshit, crap, gibberish, nonsense, flimflam, balderdash, hokum, hocus-pocus, twaddle, blather, jabber, drivel, prattle, rubbish, palaver, baloney, bunk, jazz.

double-tongued, *adj.* Deceitful, self-contradictory.

double trouble, *n.* A very troublesome person, a pain in the ass.

douche bag, *n.* (1) A loathsome person. ["OK, we're going in there and anyone who doesn't act elegant is a douche bag"—*Satisfaction,* U.S. film (1988).] (2) An ugly girl or woman.

down and dirty, *idiom.* Vicious and deceptive.

downputter, *n.* A person who always knocks others.

doxy, *n.* A loose woman or a prostitute. *Syn.*: trull, strumpet, slattern, drab.

drag, *n.* (1) An unpleasant, boring person or experience. (2) Clothes associated with one sex but worn by someone of the opposite sex.

drag ass, *idiom.* To be morose, sluggish, whiny, or depressed.

dragon, *n.* (1) A wanton woman. (2) A fierce woman, a scold, a battle-ax, a war-horse. (3) A woman with masculine characteristics.

Dragon Lady, *n.* A powerful, intimidating woman. [From the comic strip by Milt Coniff.]

drag queen, *n.* A male homosexual who wears female clothing in public. ["A lot of queens, a lot of guys who do drag for special occasions, put on big false tits, and just act, they act like whores pretty much—that's their definition of what a liberated woman is"—Tede Matthews, in Judy Grahn's *Another Mother Tongue* (1984).]

dragsville, *adj.* Very dull, tedious. *Syn.:* draggy, dullsville, drat, damn.

drape queen, *n.* A gay man who pads his crotch with various items to give the illusion of bigger attributes.

dreck, *n.* Worthless crap. *Syn.:* garbage, junk, shit.

dreykop, *n.* A trickster, a fraud. [From the Yiddish for "twisted head."]

drip, *n.* A boring, conventional person. ["Drooling, drively, doleful, depressing, drosical drips"—Sir Thomas Beecham.] *Syn.:* square, droop, drizzle, drizzle puss, wet blanket.

drip-dry lover, *n.* A man with a small penis.

drivel, *n.* Stupid, childish language; nonsense. ["The ropy drivel of rheumatic brains"—William Gifford.]

droid, *n.* An inferior, mechanical type of person. *Syn.:* android, robot, semihuman drone.

drone, *n.* A boring person or a parasite, a leech.

drool, *v.* To talk foolishly. [From *drool* = secrete saliva.] *Syn.:* dribble, drivel, salivate, blabber, slabber, prattle, slaver, slobber.

droopy-drawers, *n.* (1) A dull and stupid person. (2) A sloppy woman, a slattern.

drop a brick, *idiom.* To blunder, to commit a gaffe, to screw up.

drop one's buckets, *idiom.* To make an embarrassing mistake, to goof.

drop dead or **D.D.,** *idiom.* An emphatic, scornful rejection. *Idiom:* go to hell.

drop-dead list, *idiom.* A list of persons one does not wish to associate with or favor, a shit list. ["Liz was very high on Donald's drop-dead list."]

drown in sweat, he'll never, *idiom.* He's too lazy to hit a lick at a snake, he's as slow as cream a-rising.

drugstore cowboy, *n.* An effeminate man or a ladies' man.

drumble, *n.* A fool, an inept drone.

dry goods, *n.* A woman considered as a sexual object. *Syn.:* bit of muslin, petticoat, calico, piece, dish, dolly, hunk of skirt, lift-skirts, light-skirts, loose-bodied gown, miniskirt, muslin, piece of stuff, skirt, smock.

dry hole, *n.* A cold, unresponsive woman.

dry up, *interj.* Shut up!

dub, *n.* A failure, a novice, a fool.

duck, *n.* (1) A young woman, considered sexually. ["They all thought of her as a pretty duck, when she was actually quite cold."] (2) An unappealing person. *Syn.:* misfit, nerd, geek.

duckbutt, *n.* A short person with a big ass.

duckey, *n.* An effeminate man.

duck-fucker, *n.* A person who has sexual relations with an animal. *Syn.:* pig-sticker.

duckhead, *n.* An unattractive, unkempt woman. *Syn.:* B.B. head, duck's butt.

duck-plucker, *n.* A despicable person.

duckspeak, *n.* Formal speech that is senseless, tautological, and asinine. [From George Orwell.]

duck-squeezer, *idiom.* An extreme or rabid conservationist and environmentalist. *Syn.:* ecofreak, eagle freak, econut, greenie, tree-hugger.

dude, *n.* an affected male, a fop. ["They were all mountain-wise, range-broken men, picked . . . for diplomacy in handling dudes"—*Scribner's Magazine.*]

dudley, *n.* A failure, a loser.

duffer, *n.* (1) An old man. *Syn.*: geezer, jasper. (2) A mediocre or poor performer, especially at golf. *Syn.*: hacker, scrub, second-rater, dub, muffer.

dull pickle, *n.* A heavy, stupid fool.

dullsville, *adj.* Boring, dull, tedious, blah, boh-ring, dead, deadsville, sleep city, dragass, draggy, hicksville, ho-hum, oofless, yawny. ["Let's leave; this party is dullsville."]

dull tool, *idiom.* An ineffective person. *Syn.*: dead one, loser.

dumbbell, *n.* A stupid or unthinking person. ["She's so dumb she couldn't add up to two without taking off her blouse"—"The Benny Hill Show."] *Syn.*: dunce, ignoramus, fool, schmuck, blockhead, oaf, stupe, clod, clown, dumbass, dumb dodo, dumb bunny, dumb cluck, dumdum, dumb fuck, dumb shit, dumski, dummy, jerk, numskull, simpleton, booby, nitwit, jackass, moron, imbecile, idiot, dimwit, dummkopf, dumbdumb.

dumb dora, *n.* A stupid, giddy, or vapid young woman.

dumb john, *n.* A person easily duped. *Syn.*: easy mark, patsy, sucker.

dumbo, *n.* (1) A big, stupid person. (2) A person with big ears. [From the cartoon elephant called Dumbo.]

dumb ox, *n.* A large, stupid person. ["While he was not dumber than an ox, he was not any smarter"—James Thurber.]

dumbsocks, *n.* A Scandinavian.

dump on, *v.* To yell or shout at, or abuse someone, often when it is undeserved. *Syn.*: to shit on, to crap on, to malign, to unload on.

dundering rake, *n.* A very lewd man.

dung, *n.* A detestable person. [From *dung* = fecal matter, usually that of animals.] *Syn.*: alley apple, B.M., body wax, booboo, bowel movement, bowels, ca-ca, cack, cacky, carrion, clart, compost, cow, cow cake, cow pie, cow pucky, cow slip, cradle custard, crap, danna, dead soldier, dirt, doo-doo, doody, dreck, droppings, duty, gerry, guano, hockey, horse and trap, horse dumpling, jank, job, jobber, ka-ka, manure, meadow dressing, merd, muck, mute, night soil, ordure, orts, pilgrim's salve, pony and trap, poo, pooh, poop, poo-poo, quaker, rich dirt, scharn, siege, sign, soft and nasty, soft stuff, sozzle, spraints, stool, tad, turd, waste, yackum.

dung-fork, *n*. A country bumpkin.

dunnigan, *n*. A thief who operates in public toilets.

dunt, *n*. A person who could be mistaken for someone of the opposite sex.

duplicity, *n*. Double-dealing, deceitfulness. ["I should disdain myself as much as I do him, were I capable of such duplicity as to flatter a man whom I scorn and despise" —Frances Burney.]

dust someone off, *idiom*. To give someone a beating.

dusty, *adj*. Having a bad attitude.

dustybutt, *n*. (1) An ugly hooker. (2) A short person whose behind is so low that it drags in the dust.

dutch widow, *n*. A whore.

dweeb, *n*. (1) A loathsome person. [" 'These Val guys are totally gross. They think they're real, but you can tell they're Barneys.' She says 'dweeby types' often 'snog right up' to her when she's wearing her 'floss,' or thong-back bikini"—*Wall Street Journal* (1990).] (2) A serious student. (3) An eccentric person, a nerd.

dyke or **dike,** *n*. A lesbian. *Syn.*: Amy-John, boon-dagger, bull, bulldagger, bull dyke, bull dyker, butch, diesel dyke, fem, femme, lez, lezzie, man.

dyspeptic, *adj*. Bad-tempered, ill-natured, ill-humored, crotchety, hot-tempered, irritable, irascible, crabby, bitchy, short-tempered, choleric, sour-tempered, waspish, grouchy, cantankerous, crabby, grumpy, ornery, fractious, contentious.

eagle-beak, *n.* A Jewish person.

ear-banger *n.* A person who tries to advance himself by sucking up to his boss.

early spurter *n.* A premature ejaculator.

earwig, *v.* To annoy one, or to try to insinuate oneself through flattery. ["Earwigging, feeding an officer's ear with scandal against an absent individual"—Smyth, *Sailor's Word Book* (1867).]

easy lay, *n.* A person who can be easily persuaded to engage in sex. *Syn.:* easy make, easy mark, easy meat, easy ride, easy stuff, easy virtue.

easy mark, *n.* A person who is easily victimized or cheated.

easy rider, *n.* A man who lives off a hooker's earnings. ["I wonder where ma easy rider's gone?/He done left me, put my new gold watch in pawn"—Blues Song, Langston Hughes.]

eat, *v.* To be forced to accept something unpleasant.

eat chain, *interj.* Drop dead! [Short for "Eat a chain saw."]

eat crow, *v.* To accept humiliation and insults meekly, to swallow one's pride. ["Maxwell's subordinates were often forced to eat crow, even when they had not erred."] *Syn.:* eat dirt, eat shit, eat it, lump it, take shit.

eatin' stuff, *n.* An appealing woman viewed as an object of oral sex. *Syn.:* bar-b-q, barbecue, eatin' pussy, good eatin', table grade.

eat it, *imper.* A command to perform oral sex.

eat me, *imper.* Derogatory or dismissive command. *Idioms:* drop dead, eat my shorts, fuck you, kiss my ass.

eat (or have) someone's lunch, *v.* To defeat someone decisively.

eat one's ass off, *v.* To criticize or to punish severely. *Syn.:* eat someone out, chew someone out.

eat your heart out, *interj.* Envy me.

ecovillain, *n.* A polluter of the environment. ["Tom Cruise will wear a shock of bright green hair in his next movie, fighting such evil characters as Sly Sludge . . . in an effort to wipe out those 'eco-villains who pollute the earth.' " —*Sunday Mail Magazine* (1990).]

Edsel, *n.* A dud, a real loser. [From the car of the same name that was the biggest flop in the history of the American auto industry. "Spiro Agnew: the human Edsel" —Graffito.]

eer-quay, *adj.* Refering to a homosexual man. [From the Pig Latin for *queer.*]

eff, *n. & v.* Euphemism for *fuck.*

effie, *n.* An overly effeminate homosexual.

effeminate, *adj.* Foppy, unbecomingly overrefined, self-indulgent, like a woman. ["Amphibious thing! that acting either part,/The trifling head, or the corrupted heart;/Fop at the toilet, flatt'rer at the board,/Now trips a lady, and now struts a Lord"—Alexander Pope, "Epistle to Dr. Arbuthnot."] *Syn.:* delicate, epicene, Miss-Nancyish, pansified, namby-pamby, pansy, soft, poofy [British usage], prissy, sissyish, sissified, womanish.

effete, *adj.* Lacking vigor. ["Those happy days of courtship before he became the lazy nincompoop, the effete fop, whose life seemed spent in card and supper rooms" —Baroness Orczy, *The Scarlet Pimpernel* (1906).] *Syn.:* weary, burned out, worn out, decadent, decrepit, enfeebled, dissipated.

egg got shook, his, *idiom.* He's clumsy.

egghead, *n.* An intellectual, a heavy thinker. ["An 'egghead' is a person who stands firmly on both feet in midair on both sides of an issue"—Senator Homer Ferguson.] *Syn.:* conehead, conk-buster, double-dome, high-brow, ivory-dome, mandarin, longhair, pointhead, pointyhead, brahmin.

eggo, *n.* A person who is behind the times and socially inept.

eggplant, *n.* An American black. [From the dark color of the eggplant.]

egg roll, *n.* A person of Asian descent.

egg-sucker, *n.* A person who seeks advancement through flattery.

egotistic, *adj.* Selfish, self-important. ["Egotist: A person of low taste more interested in himself than in me"—Ambrose Bierce, *The Devil's Dictionary.*] *Syn.*: big-headed, self-centered, egomaniacal, egoistic, self-absorbed, self-obsessed, self-serving, narcissistic, megalomaniacal, self-seeking, swollen-headed, vain, vainglorious. *Idioms*: be on an ego trip, think one's shit doesn't stink.

egregious, *adj.* Atrocious, flagrant, glaring, gross, notorious, monstrous, outrageous.

eightball, *n.* (1) A bumbler, one who is always in hot water. (2) An American black. (3) A conventional, unsophisticated person, a square.

eight-rock, *n.* A dark-skinned black.

80–90, *n.* A stupid fool. [From the numerical equivalents in the Hebrew alphabet for *p* and *tz*, a euphemism for *putz* = *prick.*]

el cheapo, *n.* A cheap person.

elitist, *n.* A person who favors a select part of society, one who is exclusory, snobbish, antidemocratic. ["Thompson doesn't know what to do with us? . . . Condemn us as quotation-mongers? Class us with elitists?"—*New Left Review* (1961).] *Syn.*: exclusionist, exclusivist.

elk, *n.* A square.

Elmer Gantry, *n.* A successful evangelist who is in reality a charlatan and a hypocrite [From Sinclair Lewis' *Elmer Gantry,* a novel that portrayed such a character. ". . . the godsons of Elmer Gantry got rich saving souls"—*Newsweek* (1988).]

emasculated, *adj.* Castrated, deprived of vitality, hence unmanly, effeminate. ["The emasculated bull reverts to the colour of the female"—Charles Darwin, *The Descent of Man* (1871).]

empty sack, he's an, *idiom.* Worthless. *Syn.*: ain't worth gully dirt, he's triflin', no 'count.

empty stack, *n.* A person with not much upstairs.

empty suit, *n.* A bureaucrat. *Syn.*: paper-shuffler, buck-passer, apparatchik, paper-pusher.

enigmatic, *adj.* Ambiguous. ["Being excessively reserved withal, he became not a little enigmatic"—Thomas Carlyle.] *Syn.*: secretive, baffling, perplexing, equivocal, cryptic, paradoxical.

enough to gag a maggot, *idiom.* Very disgusting, revolting, repulsive, repugnant.

epicene, *n.* A gay male. ["The hearty sportsman who is really epicene beneath his tweeds"—Wolcott Gibbs.] *Syn.*: bardache, invert, neuter gender, third-sexer, urning, uranist.

equivocal, *adj.* Meaning one thing and expressing another. ["Equivocation is halfway to lying"—William Penn *Some Fruits of Solitude.*] *Syn.*: imprecise, confusing, evasive, vague, undecided, hazy.

ergoist, *n.* One who slavishly adheres to protocol.

ersatz, *adj.* An inferior imitation of the real thing. [". . . ersatz tough/Heart full of green and running stuff"—Donald Charles (pseud.), in *Maledicta V.*]

ese, *n.* A Chicano or Hispanic person. *Syn.*: Felipe.

Esso-B, *n.* A son of a bitch.

Ethel, *n.* An effeminate man. *Syn.*: Betty, Dyna, Gussie, Jenny, Margery, Mary, Mary ann, Nancy, Nelly.

eunuch, *n.* (1) A castrated man. ["Eunuchs, Unite, You Have Nothing to Lose"—Graffito.] *Syn.*: abeilard, bobtail, capon, castrato, rascaglion, spado, wether. (2) A weakling. ["It seems that in Rhodesia one cannot remain neutral, that after all one is provoked to react, or become a political eunuch"—*Times* (1963).]

evil, *adj.* Morally wrong and reprehensible, or marked by spite. ["I'm evil, mean and funny, so don't come back with that line of jive"—Blues Song.]

ex-bitch, *n.* One's divorced wife. ["How much alimony did my ex-bitch say she wants a month—$12,000?"—*Maledicta IX.*]

execrable, *adj.* Accursed, damnable, heinous. ["The concurrent possession of great wealth and execrable taste . . ."—Philip Wylie.]

excess baggage, *n.* A useless person who slows down the action.

excrementivorous, *adj.* Shit-eating.

execrate, *v.* Abhor, abominate, curse, damn, excoriate, fulminate, revile, imprecate, vilify.

extremist, *n.* A person who is far out politically, a fanatic. ["What is objectionable, what is dangerous about extremists is not that they are extreme, but that they are intolerant. The evil is not what they say about their cause, but what they say about their opponents"—Robert Kennedy.]

eyeballer, *n.* One who ogles women. *Syn.:* deadeye dick, crude public peeper, eye-fucker.

eyewash, *n.* Bullshit, nonsense.

eyetie or itie, *n.* A person of Italian descent.

face, *n.* A white person [Short or *paleface.*]

face like a douche bag, *idiom.* Very ugly, gruesome. ["I never forget a face, but in your case I'll be glad to make an exception"—Groucho Marx.] *Idioms:* face like a toilet, ugly as a hairless monkey, ugly as a hatful of assholes, face that would sour buttermilk, so ugly they fed him with a slingshot.

face all plowed up, *idiom.* A creased and wrinkled face. ["No matter how many times she went to Helena Rubinstein, her face still looked all plowed up."]

face artist, *n.* A person who is adept at oral sex.

face card, *n.* An egotist, an ego-tripper, a swaggerer.

face man, *n.* A good-looking but fatuous young man. ["A face man never quite gets over the idea that he is a thing of beauty and a boy forever"—adapted from Helen Rowland.]

facist, *n.* One who puts excessive emphasis on what is traditionally defined as beauty, especially facial beauty.

factoid, *n.* One who keeps repeating fiction and untruth until it is finally accepted as truth.

fade, *n.* A white person, or a black person who is deferential to whites.

faded boogie, *n.* A black police informer.

faggot, *n.* (1) A gay man. ["Duffy was no queen, no platinum dyed queen, no screaming faggot"—H. Kane, *Killer's Kiss* (1962).] *Syn.:* faggart. (2) An odious and repellent male regardless of sexual preference.

faggoty, *adj.* Effeminate. ["And there are two things in Harlem I don't understand./It's a bull-dyking woman and a faggoty man"—Claude McKay, *Home to Harlem.*]

fag hag, *n.* A woman who hangs out with gay men. ["She is in fact, common; and her ... camping around merely makes her into that most degraded thing, an outré actress can decline into a fag-hag"—John Simon.] *Syn.:* fag-bag, fruit fly, faggot's moll.

fagin, *n.* An old crook who teaches one how to become a criminal.

failure, *n.* A person who can't perform. *Syn.:* bust, loser, lemon, a never-was and never-will-be.

fair sex, *idiom.* Women as a whole. ["Anyone who knows anything of history knows that great social changes are impossible without the feminine upheaval. Social progress can be measured exactly by the social position of the fair sex; the ugly ones included"—Karl Marx.] *Syn.:* weaker sex, distaff side.

fairy, *n.* A male homosexual. ["Ballet is the fairies' baseball"—Oscar Levant.]

fairy godmother, *n.* A gay man's male initiator and teacher.

fairy lady, *n.* A passive lesbian.

fairy nice, *adj.* Gay.

faithless, *adj.* Disloyal, perfidious, traitorous, treacherous, unloyal. ["He abandoned one wife and was faithless to another"—J. R. Green.]

fake, *n.* A fraud, a sham, a phony, a pseudo.

fake out someone, *v.* To trick or deceive someone.

faker, *n.* One who is adept at pulling the wool over another person's eyes. ["He is essentially a faker with a large contempt for the ignorance and gullibility of the American voter"—*Current History.*]

fall down and go boom, *idiom.* To take a tumble, to fall on one's face.

fall down on the job, *idiom.* To shirk an obligation, to fail to come through. ["She said that she decided to file for divorce because he fell down on the job."]

fall guy, *n.* One who is set up to take the blame for others, a patsy, a dupe. ["Assassination buffs felt that Oswald was just a fall guy."]

fall flat on one's ass, *idiom.* To fail miserably.

false, *adj.* Faithless, false-hearted, two-faced, double-dealing, devious, hypocritical, dishonest, treacherous, perfidious, deceitful, two-timing, tricky. ["Thou shalt not bear false witness against they neighbor"—*Exodus* 20:16.]

fanatic, *n.* An extremist, a zealot, a hothead, a crazie, a militant, a member of the lunatic fringe. ["A fanatic is a man that does what he thinks the Lord would do if He knew the facts of the case"—Finley Peter Dunne.]

fancy-Dan, *n.* A pretentious person.

fancy-pants, *n.* A sissy, an effeminate man.

fancy-schmancy, *adj.* Pretentiously ornate.

fanfaronade, *n.* Braggadocio, bragging behavior.

fan someone's tail, *idiom.* To spank someone, or to blast someone verbally.

fantastic, *adj.* Unbelievable, farfetched, ridiculous, unreal. ["These methods of interpretation . . . seem gratuitously farfetched, fantastic"—Edmund Wilson.]

far as a cat can spit, as, *idiom.* No way! *Syn.:* as far as you can throw a bull by the tail.

fart, *n.* A contemptible, worthless person. [From the word for anal emission of intestinal gas. "Cough and the world coughs with you. Fart and you stand alone"—Trevor Griffiths, *The Comedians.*] *Syn.:* fartkin, fartik, fart-blossom, fart-face, old fart, peo.

fart around, *idiom.* To waste time. ["I wish they would stop farting around and make up their minds."] *Syn.:* goof off, fart about, fart off, fartass.

fart-catcher, *n.* A toady, a sycophant, one who follows his boss or supervisor closely, a fart-licker, a fart-sucker.

fart-cracker, *n.* A disgusting person who passes gas in front of others. ["There was a young fellow from Sparta/A really magnificent farter./On the strength of one bean/He'd fart 'God Save the Queen'/And Beethoven's 'Moonlight Sonata' "—G. Legman, *The Limerick.*]

fart higher than one's ass, trying to, *idiom.* One's reach is higher than one's grasp. *Syn.:* trying to ride a horse when one can't ride a calf.

farthole, *n.* A person who is an asshole.

fart in a whirlwind, like a, *idiom.* To be ignored or unnoticed. ["The candidate made as much an impression on the crowd as a fart in a whirlwind."] *Syn.:* like a popcorn fart in hell.

fartleberry, *n.* A disreputable, disgusting person. [From the word for fecal matter in anal hair.]

fart-smelling, *adj.* Odious, repugnant.

fascist, *adj.* Rigid, authoritarian, doctrinaire, dictatorial, antidemocratic, totalitarian.

fast fanny, *n.* A sexually loose woman.

fast fuck, *n.* A premature ejaculator.

fast-talking Charlie, *n.* A Jewish person. *Syn.:* Goldberg, Jewie, Goldstein, Mr. Money, slick-em-plenty, three balls.

fat cat, *n.* A plutocrat, one of the rich, privileged elite who often control political campaigns. ["She was one of LBJ's fat cats."] *Syn.:* big cheese, biggie, high-muck-a-muck, mugwump, nabob.

fatherfucker, *n.* A male homosexual.

fatist, *n.* One who is biased or discriminates against fat people. ["*Fatist* is a refreshing new word to me, as opposed to *fattest,* which is much more familiar"—*Spare Rib* (1987).]

fat-mouth, *v.* To argue, to talk back, to sass.

fatso, *n.* An obese, gross person. *Syn.:* buffalo butt, fat, fatass, fatguts, fatty, fat stuff, biggie, blimp, blubberpot, chub, chubbette, crisco, elephant, hippo, jellybelly, jumbo, lardass, lardbucket, porky, pudge, pusgut, pustlegut, tub, tunny, tub of guts, tub of lard, walrus, whale.

fatuous, *adj.* Dull, dense, simple, inane, silly, witless, vapid, vacuous. *Idiom:* vacant in mind.

faultfinder, *n.* A persistent critic. *Syn.:* quibbler, carper, fussbudget, derogator, bellyacher, malcontent, pettifogger, faultin' person.

faust, *n.* An ugly female.

fawning, *adj.* Bootlicking, cowering, cringing, groveling, kowtowing, sycophantic, sycophantical, toadyish, truckling. ["Low-crooked curtsies, and base spaniel fawning"—William Shakespeare, *Julius Caesar.*]

fay or **fey,** *n.* A white person. [Short for *ofay.*]

fay, *adj.* Gay.

feak or **feague,** *n.* A filthy, disgusting person. [From *feak = anus.*]

feather-bed soldier, *n.* An expert womanizer.

featherlegs, *n.* A liar, a cheat.

feather-legged, *adj.* Craven, cowardly. [From cockfighting, where a cock with feathered legs is a poor performer.]

feather-plucker, *n.* A womanizer, or a euphemism for *motherfucker.*

fecal freak, *n.* A shit-eater.

feckless, *adj.* Fustian, good-for-nothing, ineffectual, meaningless, no go, pointless, purposeless, useless, worthless, careless, thoughtless, sloppy, lackadaisical.

feeb, *n.* A nutty person. [Shortened form of *feebleminded.*]

fegelah or **feygelah,** *n.* A gay male. [From the Yiddish word for bird.]

feh, *interj.* An exclamation of disgust.

feisty, *adj.* Crabby, crusty, cussed, fire-eating, grouchy, hard-nosed, mean, miffy, ornery, snarky, soreheaded, tetchy.

felch queen, *n.* A gay male who is stimulated by fecal matter.

fellator, *n.* A male who performs oral sex on another male.

fellatrice, *n.* A woman who performs oral sex on a male.

fellow traveler, *n.* (1) A person who sympathizes with a cause without public identification. (2) One who supports Communist causes without joining the party.

fembo, *n.* A gay male.

fembot, *n.* An unliberated woman who follows unthinkingly the role set for her by patriarchal society. *Syn.:* totaled woman.

femme or **fem,** *n.* (1) A lesbian who takes a passive, feminine role. (2) A male homosexual in the passive role.

femmoke, *n.* A black woman.

fence sitter, *n.* A person who hesitates to take a position on an important issue. ["I don't like those cold, precise, fence sitters, who in order not to speak wrong, never speak at all, and in order not to do wrong, never do anything"—adapted from Henry Ward Beecher.]

fenks, *n.* A rotten person. [From the word for rotten whale blubber.]

ferblet, *n.* An effeminate male.

ferry, *n.* A promiscuous woman or hooker. [From the idea that she gives "rides" to many men.]

fetid, *adj.* Stinking, malodorous, foul, ill-smelling, noisome, noxious, stenchy, mephitic, odious, rotten, putrid, nasty, vile.

fetus, *n.* A real loser.

fice, *n.* A repugnant person. [From the word for a strong-smelling silent fart.]

fiddle, *v.* To defraud.

fiddle-fart, *v.* To waste time, to mess around. *Syn.:* monkey-fart.

fiddlefucking, *adj.* Bad, rotten. [Used as an intensifier.]

fiendish, *adj.* Demonic, devilish, diabolical, satanic, serpentine. ["The fiendish joy that illumined his usually stolid countenance sent a sudden disgust and horror through me"—Geoffrey Francis Hudson.]

fifth columnist, *n.* A subversive, a hidden traitor, a copperhead. [From the boast of a Franco spokesman during the Spanish civil war that four columns were advancing on Madrid and that they would be joined by a fifth column inside the city.]

filly, *n.* A young woman; hence, filly-hunter, skirt-chaser.

filthbag, *n.* A despicable, disgusting person; a dirtbag; scumbag.

filthy, *adj.* (1) Wealthy, loaded, rich. (2) Obscene, dirty, salacious. ["... he was constantly drunk, filthy beyond all powers of decent expression"—James Kenneth Stephen.]

filthy rich, *n.* People who are very wealthy.

fine fryer, *n.* An attractive young woman, a chick.

F-ing, *adj.* A disguise for *fucking*.

finger artist, *n.* A lesbian.

finicky, *adj.* Fussy, hairsplitting, niggling, persnickety, squeamish.

fink, *n.* An odious, contemptible person; especially a stool pigeon, a scab or a traitor to one's race, class, sex, or ethnic group. ["Now the use of finks has become acceptable as union power has declined."]

fink out on, *v.* To renege on a promise, to cop out.

fish, *n.* (1) A woman. *Syn.*: fish tank, fish pond. (2) An easily deceived person. *Syn.*: easy mark, mark, mug, patsy, sucker.

fish-eater or **fish,** *n.* A Roman Catholic. *Syn.*: cheese-eater, mackerel-snapper, mackerel-snatcher, guppy-gobbler.

fish-eyed, *adj.* Staring in a cold, inhuman fashion.

fish or cut bait, *interj.* Make up your mind! *Idioms:* get the finger out of your ass, shit or get off the pot.

fishwife, *n.* (1) A shrewish, ill-tempered woman. (2) A woman who is the wife of a gay male.

five-and-dime, *idiom.* Small-time, cheap, penny-ante.

five-letter woman, *n.* A bitch.

fixer, *n.* A person who sets up shady and illegal deals.

flabby, *adj.* Limp, flaccid, soft, feeble, weak, floppy, drooping limply, doughy, baggy, spongy. ["Did you get a load of those flabby blimps on the beach in thongs?"]

fladge fiend, *n.* A masochist or a sadist.

flag-waver, *n.* A jingoist, a superpatriot.

flake, *n.* An eccentric person; or a boring, unpleasant person.

flaked-out, *adj.* Unconscious, out of it. ["After she became flaked-out on coke, three guys raped her."]

flake-out, *n.* A person who is a complete failure.

flaky, *adj.* Birdy, cracked, goofus, dizzy, goofy, half-cracked, half-nuts, haywire, kinky, loopy, eccentric, bizarre, nutty, squirrely, wacko, wacky, weird, dinghy, screwy.

flam, *n.* A scam. [Shortened from *flimflam.*]

flamer, *n.* A blatantly obvious gay man. *Syn.*: flaming faggot, flaming queen, flaming asshole, flaming fruitbar.

flaming, *adj.* Blatantly homosexual. [A word intensifier. "... a flaming faggot is just an outrageous obviously gay man. ... It doesn't mean the same as a drag queen" —Tede Mathews, in J. Grahn's *Another Mother Tongue.*]

flamtag, *n.* A dirty, unkempt woman.

flangehead, *n.* A Chinese man or woman.

flannel, *v.* To flatter a woman in order to seduce her.

flannelmouth, *n.* (1) An oily-tongued, mellifluous talker who uses unctuous flattery and hypocritical blarney. (2) A person of Irish descent.

flapjaw, *n.* A very talkative person.

flasher, *n.* An exhibitionist.

flash in the pan, *idiom.* A person who shines briefly and then returns to his mediocre status. ["After one year in the majors, the flash in the pan was sent down to the minors."]

flashy, *adj.* Gaudy, flamboyant, pretentious, garish, tawdry, ostentatious, bedizened, vulgar. [" 'What the public wants' is being translated into the flashy, the gadgety, the spectacular"—Raymond Loewy.] *Idioms*: flashy as a Chinky's horse, flashy as a rat with a gold tooth, meretriciously showy, tricked out.

flat, *adj.* Insipid, dull, vapid, dead. ["How weary, stale, flat and unprofitable, seem to me all the uses of this world" —William Shakespeare *Hamlet* I ii.]

flatophile, *n.* A fart lover.

flat tire, *n.* A man who is sexually impotent.

flatulent, *adj.* Pretentiously windy and overblown. ["... enthusiasts who read into him all sorts of flatulent bombast"—H. L. Mencken.]

flavor, *n.* A woman viewed as a sexual object.

flaw, *n.* A defect. ["We most enjoy, as a spectacle, the downfall of a good man, when the fall is justified by some flaw in his being"—Albert Léon Guerard, *Testimony of a Liberal.*] *Syn.:* blemish, blot, smudge, stain, blotch, crack.

flea, *n.* An insignificant person.

fleece-hunter, *n.* A whoremonger, a womanizer. [From *fleece* = pubic hair.]

flesh fly, *n.* A lecher. *Syn.:* flesh maggot.

fleshpot, *n.* A woman viewed as a sex object.

flesh-presser or **palm-presser,** *n.* An insincere politician. ["The only time you saw that flesh-presser in the district was during election time."]

flicking, *adj.* A disguise for the word *fucking*.

flimflam, *n.* (1) A phony line used to cheat someone out of money. (2) Pretentious nonsense.

fling the bull, *v.* To boast, to lie.

Flip, *n.* A Filipino.

flip-flap, *n.* A flighty, giddy woman.

flip-lipped, *adj.* Glibbly loquacious.

flip-out, *n.* An eccentric person.

flipped out, *adj.* Out of touch with reality.

flipper, *n.* A wanton, young woman.

flit, *n.* An effeminate man. ["He was Queen of the Flits of Hoboken"—G. Legman, *The Limerick.*]

floozie, *n.* A sexually promiscuous woman, a woman of easy morals. ["Flat foot Floogie with the Floy-Floy"—Song of the 1940s.] *Syn.*: floogie, floosie.

flop, *n.* A failure. *Syn.*: dud, Edsel, fiasco, floppola, flopp-eroo, disaster, lemon, loser, stiff, turkey, washout.

flopocrat, *n.* A member of a government that bounces from one grotesque fiasco to another, a foolocrat.

floppy disk, *n.* A student who studies too much.

flop sweat, *n.* Anxiety due to the fear of failure.

flossed up, *adj.* Referring to a woman made up like a tart. *Syn.*: tarted up.

flubdub, *n.* An incompetent or klutzy person.

fluff, *n.* A frivolous young woman, or a sexually passive lesbian.

fluffie, *n.* A conventional male-dependent woman.

fluff-off, *n.* A person who shirks work.

flummoxed, *adj.* Confused or baffled.

flunky, *n.* A low-level subordinate, a gofer, a loser who has reached his potential.

fluter, *n.* A fellator. *Syn.*: flute, one-holed flute, living flute, silent flute.

fluzz dyke, *n.* A sexually passive lesbian.

fly, *n.* An insignificant person.

fly ball, *n.* (1) A male homosexual. (2) An oddball.

fly-by-night, *n.* A dubious, dishonest operator.

flychick, *n.* A pleasure-loving young woman.

flying fuck, *n.* Someone totally worthless.

fly in the milk, *idiom.* The offspring of white and black parents. *Syn.*: milk and molasses.

flyspeck, *n.* An unimportant person.

F.O., *n.* A worthless do-nothing. [From *fuck-off.*]

F.O., *interj.* Get out of here, you make me sick, stay away from me. [From *fuck off.*]

F.O.B., *n.* A newly arrived immigrant. [From "fresh off the boat."]

fogo, *n.* A disgusting, despicable person. [From *fogo* = a bad stink.]

fogram or **fogrum,** *n.* A stuffed shirt, or a fussy elderly man.

fogy, *n.* An out-of-date person. *Syn.*: antediluvian, alter kacker, antique, dodo, fogram, fossil, fuddy-duddy, geezer, mossback, square. *Idiom*: stick-in-the-mud.

fomper, *n.* One who plays around sexually.

fonky or **funky,** *adj.* Bad-smelling.

fool, *n.* A person lacking in judgment. ["First Law of Debate: Never argue with a fool—people might not know the difference"—Arthur Block, *Murphy's Law.*]

foolhardy, *adj.* Brash, rash, reckless, headstrong, incautious, impulsive, impetuous, imprudent, madcap, harebrained, heedless, careless, thoughtless. ["... the perfectly foolhardy feat of swiming the flood"—Sinclair Lewis.]

foot-in-mouth disease, *idiom.* Continual embarrassing verbal gaffes. ["Ronald Reagan is the Fred Astaire of foot-in-mouth disease"—Jeff Davis.]

foozle, *n.* A conservative, a dodo.

fop, *n.* An elegantly, overly dressed man; a dandy. ["I might have taken him for a fop, for he wore white lace at throat and wrists"—Kenneth Roberts.] *Syn.*: Beau Brummel, coxcomb, dude, gallant, lounge lizard, macaroni, popinjay, prettyboy, princock, silk stocking, strut-noddy.

fopdoodle, *n.* A mediocre, insignificant man.

fork and knife, *n.* One's own wife. [British rhyming slang.] *Syn.*: duchess of fife, trouble and strife.

forking, *adj.* Euphemism for the intensifier *fucking*.

for the birds, *idiom.* Inferior, of little worth. *Syn.*: shit for the birds.

fossil, *n.* An elderly person or an old-fashioned person of any age.

foul, *adj.* Offensive to one's physical or moral senses. ["Much of this tedious book is foul, lewd, and revolting"—Hartley Shawcross.]

foul ball, *n.* An oddball. [From baseball, a ball that falls outside the foul lines.]

foulmouth, *n.* A person who uses excessive profanity.

foul-up, *n.* A hopeless situation. [Sometimes used as a euphemism for *fuck-up*.]

four-eyes, *n.* (1) A person who wears glasses. ["But I wouldn't be 'Four Eyes' or 'Chicken Chest' anymore, I'd be beautiful..." Darryl Pinckney, *High Cotton* (1992).] *Syn.*: glass-eyes, specs. (2) An egghead, a double-dome.

four-flusher, *n.* A bluffer, a faker, a cheat, or a swindler.

four-horned billy goat, like a, *idiom.* A blatant show-off.

four-letter man, *n.* A detestable man, a real bastard. [From the four letters of *shit*.]

fox, *n.* (1) A crafty man. ["A fox is a wolf who sends flowers"—Ruth Weston, *New York Post*.] (2) An attractive, sexy woman. ["... a crazy sex scene, laying in bed for a weekend with two steaming foxes"—Albert Goldman, *Ladies and Gentlemen, Lenny Bruce* (1974).]

fox-hunter, *n.* A man on the prowl for women.

foxy, *adj.* (1) Sexy, very attractive. ["Young foxy looking chick; Mr. Walker say (*sic*) she lays by the swimming pool without her top on"—Elmore Leonard, *The Switch*.] (2) Stinking with perspiration odor. (3) Tricky, devious, shifty, sneaky, slippery, serpentine.

fractious, *adj.* Churlish, bitchy, contentious, shrewish.

frail, *n.* A woman. [Probably from the concept of "the weak sex". "Wit and woman are two frail things"—Thomas Overbury, *Characters*.] *Syn.*: frail eel, frail job.

frame, *n.* (1) A heterosexual man attractive to homosexuals. (2) A male or female figure admired by either sex.

framis, *n.* Comic double-talk.

franion, *n.* (1) A woman-chaser. (2) A sexually easy woman.

frapping, *adj.* Accursed, dammed.

frass, *n.* A good-for-nothing, a lowlife. [From the word for the dung of insect larvae.]

freak, *n.* (1) An odd, unconventional person. (2) A person who engages in unusual or deviant sexual activities. ["They wanted to go down to Greenwich Village and see the freaks"—Lawrence Sanders, *The Third Deadly Sin* (1981).] (2) A person addicted to a particular thing or cause; e.g., acid freak, phone freak, ecofreak. (4) A person with a physical abnormality. (5) A weird-looking, weird-acting person. (6) A slut, a nymphomaniac.

freaking, *adj.* Euphemism for the intensifier *fucking.*

freaky, *adj.* Odd, bizarre, unnerving, strange, eccentric, unusual, kinky, far out, way out.

free-baser, *n.* A person who heats and sniffs cocaine.

freebie, *n.* A sexually available woman. *Syn.*: free-for-all, free ride.

freelancer, *n.* A successful seducer. *Syn.*: wolf, fast worker, make-out artist.

freeloader, *n.* One who eats and never pays, a parasite, a moocher.

freemartin, *n.* A person whose sexual identity is ambivalent, a hermaphrodite.

freep, *n.* An older homosexual man [A blend of *freak* + *creep.*]

free-rider, *n.* A nonunion worker who benefits from union gains without paying dues.

French abortion, *n.* A totally despicable and disgusting person. [From slang for the act of spitting out semen after fellation.]

frencher, *n.* A fellator.

French-fried fuck, *n.* A contemptible jerk, a nonentity.

French fries, *n.* French-Canadians. *Syn.:* frites.

fresh bit, *n.* A virgin, or a relatively sexually inexperienced woman.

freshman, *n.* A first-time drug user.

freshwater trout, *n.* A good-looking woman.

fresser, *n.* One who performs oral sex. [From the Yiddish *fress* = eat.]

fribble, *n.* A piece of nothing, a silly jerk, an effeminate or homosexual male, a foppish nitwit. ["William gives his sex to a fribble." T. E. Lawrence, *letter* (1932).]

fricking or **frigging,** *adj.* Euphemism for the intensifier *fuck-ing.*

frigid, *adj.* (1) Deficient in passion. *Syn.:* stiff, unresponsive, aloof, prim, straitlaced. (2) Unable to reach orgasm or respond sexually. ["Men always fall for frigid women because they put on the best show"—Fanny Brice.]

Frigidaire, *n.* A sexually unresponsive woman.

frill, *n.* A young woman.

frilly blouse, *n.* A busty, good-looking woman.

frip, *n.* A weak, ineffective person. [A blend of *freak* + *drip*.]

frisker, *n.* A promiscuous female. *Syn.:* hayride, tumbler, romp, romp in the hay.

frit, *n.* A gay male. [A blend of *fruit* + *flit*.]

fritzer, *n.* A false or phony act.

frog, *n.* A French person. *Syn.:* frog-eater, froggie, frog-lander.

frogging, *adj.* Euphemism for the intensifier *fucking.*

froggy, *adj.* Belligerent, overly aggressive.

frosty, *n.* A black who prefers to act as a white.

frosty, *adj.* Sexually unresponsive, frigid.

froufrou, *n.* A flashy wanton.

frowsy, *n.* A sloppy, unkempt woman.

fruit, *n.* A male homosexual. *Syn.*: fruiter, fruit plate, radish, finocchio.

fruitcake, *n.* An eccentric person. ["God knows they've got their share of armed fruitcakes"—Lyall, *The Crocus List* (1985).] *Idiom:* nutty as a fruitcake.

fruit fly, *n.* A straight woman who associates primarily with male homosexuals.

fruiting, *n.* Acting in a promiscuous manner.

fruit-picker, *n.* A man who is heterosexual in his public life, but who privately looks for homosexual partners.

fruity, *adj.* (1) Gay. (2) Eccentric, oddball, nutty.

frump, *n.* A dowdy, unpleasant person.

fuant or **fiant,** *n.* A nauseating, disgusting person. [From the word for the dung of vermin.]

fubsy, *adj.* Short and obese.

fuck, *n.* (1) A rotten person. (2) A woman or man considered as a sexual object. ["An aborted marriage to a favorite fuck." S. Greenlee, *Spook who sat at the Door* (1969).]

fuck, *v.* To mess someone up.

fuck, *interj.* An exclamation of anger.

fuck a duck, *interj.* Damn! Hell! Oh shit! Oh Hell! *Syn.*: Fuck a dog!

fuck around, *v.* To waste time.

fuckbrained, *adj.* (1) Mindless. (2) Obsessed with sex.

fuck-bunny, *n.* A woman who loves sex.

fucked, *adj.* Messed up, ruined, confused. ["To be human is to be fucked. To know that you're fucked right off the bat"—Murray Shisgal, *Playboy* (1975).] *Syn.*: fucked up. *Idioms*: diddled by the dirty digit of destiny, fucked by the fickle finger of fate.

fuck 'em all, *interj.* To hell with all of them!

fucker, *n.* (1) A willing woman. (2) A rotten person. ["Send the fucker home/Till he's gone we'll bitch and moan" —Protesters at a Republican Presidential primary rally for Patrick Buchanan in New Hampshire, *New York Review of Books* (1992).]

fuck freak, *n.* A person obsessed with sex.

fuckhead, *n.* A mentally confused or emotionally unstable person.

fucking or **fuckin',** *adj.* Dirty, rotten, stinking, damned, bloody. [Used as an intensifier. "I'll break the fucking neck of any fucking bugger who says a word against my king"—James Joyce, *Ulysses* (1922).]

fucking ada, *interj.* You're full of shit! I don't believe you, you lying bastard!

fuck it, *interj.* To hell with it! Forget it! *Idioms*: fuck it all, damn it, damn it all, fuck all.

fuck me gently, *idiom.* Cheat me in a genteel way. *Idioms*: kiss me while you screw me, fuck me pink.

fuck me hard, *interj.* I'm screwed!

fuck-off, *n.* An unreliable person, one who doesn't meet his commitments, a shirker, a goof-off.

fuck off, *interj.* Get the hell out of here! Scram! ["She wants to know if you're the one in charge! Fuck off! said Lemuel." S. Beckett, *Molloy* (1955).]

fuck over, *v.* To exploit or to hurt someone. ["Women got tired of being fucked over—on the job, at home—and now they're doing their share of fucking over."]

fuck-pig, *n.* Someone low enough to have sex with a pig.

fuck someone's mind, *v.* To confuse someone, to coerce one.

fuck someone over, *v.* To give one a hard time, to abuse one.

fuckster, *n.* A lecher, a woman-chaser.

fuckstress, *n.* A woman who is sexually willing. ["A talented fuckstress . . . renowned for her fine paroxysm"—G. Legman, *The Limerick.*]

fuck that noise, *interj.* Forget it!

fuck the dog, *v.* To waste time, to fool around.

fuck-up, *n.* A chronic bungler, one who messes up everything. *Syn.:* bobbler, blunderer, bonehead, dub, foozler, fumblefist, goof, goofball, goofer, goof-up, goofus, screw-up, slob.

fuck-wit, *n.* A contemptible, despised person. ["You've all been coining it for years. All you fuckwits in the City" —Caryl Churchill, *Serious Money.*]

fuck with, *v.* To tease, to meddle with.

fuck you, *interj.* Go to hell! ["If you had a million years to do it, you couldn't rub out even half of the 'Fuck You' signs in the world. It's impossible"—J. D. Salinger, *The Catcher in the Rye.*] *Syn.:* fuck you, Charlie; f you; fuck you, Jack, I'm all right; chuck you, Farley, and your whole damn family; eff you; fork you; fuck you and the horse you rode in on; take a flying fuck at a rolling doughnut; take a flying fuck at a rubber duck.

fuddy-duddy, *n.* A fussy, old-fashioned, conservative fogy. *Syn.:* fuddy-dud, fudbucket, fud.

fudge, *n.* Balderdash, nonsense.

fudge, *v.* To finagle figures or facts in order to deceive or cheat.

fudge one's pants, *v.* To become scared.

Fudgsicle, *n.* A black person who adopts middle-class white values.

fug, *n. & v.* Euphemism for *fuck.* [From Norman Mailer's *The Naked and the Dead.*]

fugazi, *n.* A despicable person. ["Anyway we inherit this fog-leaf major—a real fugazi . . ."—William Diehl, *Thai Horse* (1987).]

fugitive from a daisy chain gang, *idiom.* A male homosexual.

fugly, *adj.* Very ugly. [Blend of *fucking* + *ugly.*]

full-flavored, *adj.* Really dirty or obscene.

full hank, *n.* A nerd.

full-mooner, *n.* A nutty or very eccentric person. [From the folklore notion that eccentric behavior increases during the full moon.]

full of beans, *idiom.* Very wrong, lying, mistaken. *Syn.*: dead wrong, full of hops, full of baloney, full of crap, full of hot air, full of it, full of prunes, full of shit, as full of shit as a Christmas goose.

fulsome, *adj.* Insincere and exaggerated. ["He could never be made ridiculous, for he was always ready to laugh at himself and to prick the bladder of fulsome praise"—Sir John Buchan.] *Syn.*: oily, oleaginous, slick, smarmy, soft-soaping, soapy, unctuous.

fumble-fingered, *adj.* Clumsy.

fumbler, *n.* An impotent or sexually clumsy man.

fumet, *n.* A despicable, repulsive person. [From the word for deer dung.]

fumunda cheese, *n.* A totally repulsive and disgusting person. [From the allusion to smegma, a foul secretion that collects around the genital organs.]

fungusface, *n.* A bearded man. *Syn.*: fuzzface.

fungus-faced, *adj.* Repulsive-looking.

funk, *n.* (1) Fear, cowardice. (2) A person who thinks he is cool, but is definitely self-deluded.

funker, *n.* A coward.

funky, *adj.* (1) Smelly, obnoxious, unkempt. ["Funk was a bad smell"—James Baldwin, *Tell Me How Long the Train's Been Gone.*] (2) Old-fashioned, quaint. (3) Odd, kinky. *Syn.*: funkybutt, funkyass, fonky.

funny, *adj.* Homosexual, or effeminate.

furburger or **fur pie,** *n.* A woman viewed as an object of oral sex.

furrowbutt or **craterbutt,** *n.* A promiscuous woman.

fussbudget, *n.* A person who becomes upset over trifles. *Syn.*: fusser, fusspot, granny, old lady.

fussocks, *n.* A lazy, obese woman.

fussy, *adj.* Persnickety, picky, finicky, hypercritical. ["I am fastidious, you are fussy, he's an old woman"—*New Statesman.*]

fustian, *n.* Pompous overblown speech or writing. ["... romantic fustian; which may be defined as the enormous disproportion between emotion and the outer object of incident on which it expends itself. Victor Hugo abounds in fustian of this kind"—Irving Babbitt.]

fustilarian, *n.* A scoundrel.

futz around, *idiom.* To waste time.

futzed-up, *adj.* A euphemism for *fucked-up.*

fuzz bumper, *n.* A lesbian. [From *fuzz* = pubic hair.]

fuzz-nutted, *adj.* Inexperienced. [Said of one who has only a light fuzz on his genitals.]

fuzzy-wuzzy, *n.* A dark-skinned person with kinky hair. [From the colonial name of a people of the Sudan.]

G

gabacho, *n.* A white American. [From the Spanish.]

gabber *n.* A windbag ["He's such a gabber. The only part of his body that he exercises is his tongue."] *Syn.*: gasbag, motormouth, bigmouth, flapjaw, gimbaljaw, gabbleguts.

gaff, *v.* To cheat, swindle, to fool, to shortchange.

gaffer, *n.* An old man. [Bernard Baruch, a gaffer at the age of eighty-five, used to say: "To me old age is always fifteen years older than I am."]

gaga, *n.* An inexperienced homosexual.

gagger, *n.* (1) A disgusting person or object. (2) A pimp for one's own wife.

gag me with a spoon, *idiom.* That makes me vomit! ["Like this flake was so totally skanky, OK, like he has yukky green stuff on his braces and he doesn't even know it, like gag me with a spoon!"—Corey and Westermark, *Fer Shurr! How to Be a Valley Girl—Totally* (1982).]

gal-boy, *n.* A mannish woman.

gall, *n.* Arrogant self-assurance, cheek, brass.

galley wench, *n.* A promiscuous woman or a whore. *Syn.:* capercock, chubcheeker, rawhide.

galley-west, *adj.* Confused, upset. ["News of the bankruptcy knocked the investors galley-west"]

galumphing, *adj.* Graceless, awkward, heavy.

game, *v.* To be dishonest, untruthful, defensive, to con, to bluff.

ganymede, *n.* A pederast or sodomite. [In Greek mythology, Ganymedes was the cupbearer to Zeus.]

gar, *n.* A black person. [Short for *nigger.*]

garbage, *n.* A worthless or meaningless person or thing. ["All writing is garbage"—Antonin Artaud.]

garbage can, *n.* A dirty, unkempt hooker; a common sewer, drain, or scupper.

garbagehead, *n.* An addict who will take any drug or combination of drugs.

garbagemouth, *n.* An obsessive user of obscene language. *Syn.:* foulmouth, foultongue, pottymouth, blackmouth, bucketmouth, cudcaster, sewermouth, toiletmouth.

garbo, *n.* A snob. [After Greta Garbo, who made a fetish of her privacy.]

gargoyle, *n.* An ugly person. ["Who gives a rat's ass, you puke-faced gargoyle"—*National Lampoon* (1984).]

gasconade, *n.* Extremely boastful speech. ["... an enlightened statesman and not a gasconading militarist"—Claude G. Bowers.]

gash, *n.* A woman viewed as a sexual object; hence, gash-hound = a lecher, a womanizer. [From *gash = vulva.*]

gash-greaser, *n.* A woman who masturbates. *Syn.*: beaver-beater, clit-clapper, poodle-petter, stump-jumper.

gassy, *adj.* Pretentiously talkative.

gaubshite or **gobshite,** *n.* A slovenly, unkempt man.

gaudy, *adj.* Garish, flashy, loud, showy, cheap, vulgar, worthless, tasteless, tawdry, meretricious. ["... another attendant, gaudy with jingling chains and brass buttons, led us along a corridor"—Kenneth Roberts.]

gawky, *adj.* Lacking skill or grace. *Syn.*: awkward, ungainly, clumsy, left-handed, cumbersome, lubberly, klutzy, bungling, fumbling, blundering, ham-fisted, all thumbs, graceless, maladroit, lumpish.

gay, *n.* A male homosexual. *Syn.*: angel, capon, daisy, fag, faggot, fairy, fegelah, femme, flaming fruitbar, flit, flower, flute, fluter, freak, frit, fruit, fruitcake, gay-boy, homo, jocker, limp-wrist, maricon, nancy, nelly, pansy, punk, queen, queer, sissy, swish, three-letter man.

gay as pink ink, *idiom.* Obviously homosexual.

gay dog, *n.* A philanderer.

gazooney or **gazoonie,** *n.* (1) A bully or strong-arm man. (2) A pederast or catamite.

gearbox or **gearhead,** *n.* A dimwit.

geck, *n.* A simpleton.

geech, *n.* An unattractive person.

geechee or **geechie,** *n.* A Southern rural black person.

geek or **geekoid,** *n.* A revolting, disgusting person. [From circus slang for a man whose act consists of biting off the head of a live chicken.]

geezer, *n.* An odd, old man.

gender bender, *n.* An androgynous or transsexual person.

generic, *adj.* Out of it.

geri, *n.* An old person. [From the abbreviation of *geriatric.*]

get a hair up one's ass, *idiom.* To be angry.

get a job, *interj.* Get away! Don't bother me!

get a life, *interj.* Do something useful! Stop being such a jerk! Improve your social life!

get down dirty (or **shitty**)**,** *idiom.* To become abusive, to make trouble.

get it in the neck, *idiom.* To be severely chastised or punished. ["You keep goofing off and you're going to get it in the neck."] *Syn.:* be shot down, be wiped out, get clobbered, get one's lumps, get cut off at the knees, get the business.

get off my case, *interj.* Leave me alone! Stop bothering me! *Idioms:* give me some slack, lighten up.

get off one's high horse, *idiom.* Stop being so high and mighty.

get off your ass, *idiom.* Get cracking, get moving.

get off my back, *idiom.* Stop nagging! *Idiom:* back off, get off my neck, let me breathe, get off my wick.

get on one's high horse, *idiom.* To become arrogant.

get on one's tits, *idiom.* To irritate, to annoy.

get one's ass in a sling, *idiom.* To get in deep trouble.

get one's ass in gear, *idiom.* To get moving, stop loafing and fooling around, change one's ways.

get one's finger out of one's ass, *idiom.* To stop dawdling and start doing something.

get one's head out of one's ass, *idiom.* To pay attention, be alert, know what's happening.

get one's shit together, *idiom.* To get straightened out. *Syn.:* have one's ducks in a row.

get out of here, *interj.* Shut up! You're lying! You don't mean it!

get out of my face, *interj.* Stop bothering me!

get stuffed, *interj.* Fuck you!

get the business, *idiom.* To be punished, rebuked, or victimized.

get the lead out, *interj.* Hurry up! Stop dawdling! Start moving!

get the red ass, *idiom.* To become irritated, to hold a grievance.

get the shaft, *idiom.* To be abused. *Idiom:* screwed, blued, and tattooed.

get under someone's skin, *idiom.* To bug.

get up someone's nose, *idiom.* To provoke someone.

get weaving, *interj.* Stop wasting time!

get your bowels in an uproar, don't, *idiom.* Don't get too excited, don't get bent out of shape.

gfy, *n.* A total loser. [From *general fuck-up*.]

ghoul, *n.* An ugly, unattractive woman.

ghoulish, *adj.* Macabre, ghastly [From *ghoul* = an evil spirit that robs graves.] *Syn.:* weird, eerie, sinister, diabolic, hellish, infernal, satanic, grisly, fiendish, monstrous, demonic, horrifying, ogreish, necrophilic, zombielike.

gibber or **gibber-gabber,** *n.* Gossipy nonsense. ["... listened to gibber about our present form or methods of government"—*The Nation*.]

gibberish, *n.* Gobbledegook, drivel, gabble, twaddle, flap-doodle, double-talk, doublespeak, mumbo-jumbo. ["I've endured just about enough gibberish about the modern woman, how she complicated her life, has sacrificed her femininity and competes in a man's world"—Mike McAuliffe, *The Irish Digest*]

gidget, *n.* A saucy young woman.

giftbox, *n.* A promiscuous woman, a joy girl.

gigolo, *n.* A man who services women sexually, usually for money; a boy toy, a toy boy.

gimp, *n.* (1) A lame person. (2) A person with major personality defects.

gin and fuck it, *n.* A female tourist who can be seduced for the price of a drink.

ginch, *n.* A sexually loose woman.

gink, *n.* A useless mediocrity.

ginny or **ginzo,** *n.* A person of Italian descent.

girl, *n.* (1) A male homosexual. (2) A woman. [For a woman to be called a girl "is not so offensive on the surface as to be called a pig, yet the harm may be deeper and longer lasting"—Eve Merriam, in *A Feminist Dictionary* (1985).]

girl-trap, *n.* A woman-chaser.

give a flying fuck, *idiom.* To care. ["I don't give a flying fuck whether you stay or go."]

give it to someone, *idiom.* To punish or rebuke.

give one a grease job, *idiom.* To flatter.

give one a pain in the ass, *idiom.* To be a pest, to bug someone. *Idioms:* frost one's ass, get in one's hair, put one's nose out of joint.

give one grief, *idiom.* To hassle.

give one hell, *idiom.* To reprimand someone severely. ["I never give them hell; I just tell them the truth and they think it is hell"—Harry S. Truman.]

give one hemorrhoids, *idiom.* To annoy or pester.

give one's ass a chance, *interj.* Stop talking! ["Why don't you shut up and give your ass a chance?"]

give one the business, *idiom.* To treat someone roughly, punish, rebuke.

give one the double cross, *idiom.* To betray or cheat one's own friends or associates.

give one the fish-eye, *idiom.* To stare at one in a cold or menacing way. *Idioms:* give the beady eye, give the hairy eyeball.

give one the fluff, *idiom.* To brush someone off.

give one the needle, *idiom.* To nag someone, criticize continually, to hassle.

give one the works, *idiom.* To maltreat or beat severely. *Idiom:* work someone over.

glabrous, *adj.* Bald.

glacial, *adj.* As cold as an iceberg or glacier. *Syn.:* frigid, polar, arctic, icy, numbing, cutting, piercing, biting, hostile, antagonistic, disdainful, cold as a witch's tit.

gladhander, *n.* A person who displays insincere warmth. *Syn.:* flesh-presser, handshaker, mitt-glommer, phony.

gleep, *n.* A jerk.

glitterbag, *n.* A flashy, coarse female. ["Did you see that glitterbag sashay into the club on those four-inch spikes?"]

glitzy, *adj.* Gaudy, Day-Glo, flashy, flossy, loud, splashy.

glob, *n.* An insignificant person. [From *glob* = a mass of gooey matter.] *Syn.:* blob, gob.

gloomy Gus, *idiom.* A morose person. *Syn.:* crepe-hanger, grinch, killjoy, party pooper, prophet of doom and gloom, turn off, pessimist, wet blanket.

gluey, *adj.* Maudlin, corny, glutinous, schmaltzy.

glutton, *n.* One who eats to excess or is very eager for something. *Syn.*: trencherman, gorger, stuffer, pig, belly-slave, chowhound.

glutz, *n.* A sluttish woman.

gnarly, *adj.* Gross.

gnat's piss, *n.* A despicable person.

gnof, *n.* A crank or a boor.

go and take a running jump at yourself, *idiom.* Get lost! *Syn.*: go and take a flying fuck.

go around the bend, *idiom.* Freak out.

goat, *n.* (1) A lecherous man. ["Did you see that old goat trying to pick up that filly?"] (2) A scapegoat. (3) A politician's constituent. ["Let's see what's in the goats' mail today."]

goat-fuck, *idiom.* A confused operation. ["The Bay of Pigs was one big goat-fuck."]

goat-smelling, *adj.* Stinking. ["Get that goat-smelling armpit away from me."]

go away and play with yourself, *interj.* Scram! *Syn.*: go home and jerk off, go piss up a rope, go shit in a pot and duck your head, go shit in your hat and pull it down over your ears and call it curlies, go beat your meat, go pump your pickle.

go bananas, *idiom.* To become completely irrational. *Syn.*: freak out, go ape, go bughouse.

gobbledygook, *n.* Language obscured deliberately by insiders, scholars, or politicians. ["I don't get all this real estate gobbledygook: twenty-seven to five, five down, exclusive development, unspoiled area..."—Steve McNeil.] *Syn.*: nonsense, officialese, government jargon, gibberish, bafflegab, federalese, Greek, babble, doubletalk, barnacular, bumblery, bureaucrap, jungle English, mumblespeak, mushmouth, polluted English, verbocrap.

gobble-prick, *n.* A lewd woman.

gobbler or **gobler,** *n.* A fellator.

go boil your head, *interj.* Go to hell!

gobslotch, *n.* A greedy fool.

go chase yourself, *interj.* Get lost! Beat it! Go away! Go fry an egg!

go down in flames, *idiom.* Be completely defeated. ["You keep that up and you're going down in flames."]

go down the tube or **go down the chute,** *idiom.* Lose everything, or fail.

goer, *n.* A woman who will go to bed with anyone just for the hell of it. ["She used to be a well-known goer, but now she has her future security to think of"—Martin Amis, *Money* (1984).]

gofer or **go-for,** *n.* A low-level employee who caters to others. *Syn.:* bench warmer, best boy, doormat, gal Friday, guy Friday, lackey, flunky, hired help, lightweight, little shot, munchkin, man Friday, peon, scrub, spear-carrier, stooge, third-stringer, low man on the totem pole.

go fly a kite, *idiom.* Go away now! Go to hell! Get lost!

go fuck yourself, *interj.* Go to hell! *Idioms:* go fuck a dead horse, go fuck yourself with a rubber weenie, go fuck yourself in the ass and give yourself some brains.

goldberg, *n.* A Jewish person, especially one who has a store in a black neighborhood.

goldbrick or **goldbricker,** *n.* A shirker. ["He got his M.A. in goldbricking in the army, and his Ph.D. working as an inspector for the city."] *Syn.:* goof-off, loafer, dawdler, dillydallyer.

golden shower boy, *n.* A gay male who gets his jollies from being urinated on, a shower queen.

goldilocks, *n.* A pretty blonde woman.

golliwog, *n.* (1) A nonwhite person. (2) A dark-skinned Italian, Spaniard, or Portuguese.

gomer, *n.* A stupid social outcast. [From the TV show "Gomer Pyle."]

goniff or **gonef,** *n.* A thief, a cheat, an unethical business-person.

gonsel or **gonzel,** *n.* (1) A slob or fool. (2) A catamite.

gonzo, *n.* An empty-headed fool.

goober or **goob,** *n.* A stupid and peculiar person, a weirdo. [From *goob* = *pimple.*]

goodman-turd, *n.* A contemptible guy.

goody-goody, *n.* An excessively and ostentatiously virtuous person. *Syn.:* bluenose, goody, prude, prig, goody two-shoes, holier-than-thou, nice Nelly, old maid.

gooey, *n.* A girlfriend.

goof or **goofus,** *n.* A stupid person. *Syn.:* goofball, oaf, jerk, goofer, goopus, fool, dumb ox, boob, klutz.

goofed-up, *adj.* Disoriented.

goof off, *v.* To avoid work, shirk duty. *Syn.:* bunny fuck, coast, conk off, dog it, dope off, drag ass, drag tail, fake off, featherbed, float, flub, flub the dub, fluff off, fuck off, goldbrick, goof around, jerk off, lollygag, screw off, screw the pooch, skate, slack, sluff snurge, soldier. *Idioms:* drag one's tail, fuck the dog, hump the hound, lie on one's oars, sit on one's ass, spin one's wheels, whip the dog.

goof-up, *n.* A mess-up.

goofy, *adj.* Silly, inept.

go off half-cocked, *idiom.* To respond angrily, without thinking.

goo-goo, *n.* A liberal political reformer. [From *good government.*]

gook, *n.* (1) An Asian, most often a Vietnamese. ["To the G. I. the Vietnamese is a 'gook', 'dink', 'slope', or 'slant'." *Time* (1969).] *Syn.:* dink, goo-goo, gu-gu, Luke the Gook, slant-eye, gooner, slope, slopie, zip. (2) A dull, stupid, foolish person.

goombah or **goombar,** *n.* (1) An Italian. (2) A thug, a gangster.

goon, *n.* (1) A paid thug. *Syn.:* ape, bad baby, biff guy, big tuna, bimbo, bozo, bruiser, cowboy, enforcer, goombah, gorilla, hard-boiled egg, hard case, heavy, heavy man, hood, hoodlum, hooligan, jaboney, knuckle-dragger, lobo, muscle, muscle man, plug-ugly, pretty boy, pug, rough customer, roughneck, shtarker, sidewinder, strong-arm man, tough, tough baby, tough mug, ugly customer, yegg. (2) A disliked person. *Syn.:* jerk, pill. (3) A violent strikebreaker.

goophead, *n.* A despicable person. [From *goophead* = purple zit.]

gooseberry pudding, *n.* A morally lose woman.

gooser, *n.* A pederast.

goosy or **goosey,** *adj.* Touchy, overly sensitive.

go over like a lead balloon, *idiom.* Flop, to fall flat on one's face. ["His proposal for a new health policy went over like a lead balloon."]

go piss up a rope, *interj.* Get lost!

gorgon, *n.* A terrifying person, applied mostly to women. ["The president's wife was a real gorgon."]

gork, *n.* A person whose brain no longer functions.

gormless, *adj.* Dumb, slow-witted, or unattractive.

go spare, *idiom.* To blow up, to act crazily.

gospel-shooter, *n.* An evangelical preacher. *Syn.:* gospel-grinder, gospel-pusher, gospel-shark, gospel-sharp, gospel-shouter, gospel-whanger.

gotch-eyed, *adj.* Having bulging eyes.

gotchgut, *adj.* Potbellied.

goth, *n.* A despoiler of art and culture. [After the ancient Germanic tribe.]

go to blazes, *interj.* Fuck off! Lay off! Stop bothering me!

go to hell in a hand basket, *idiom.* To fall apart suddenly, to degenerate. *Syn.:* go to hell in a bucket, go to pot, go to the dogs, go downhill.

gouger, *n.* A cheat.

goulash, *n.* A Hungarian.

go up in the air, *idiom.* To miss a cue, to fluff one's lines.

go up the wall, *idiom.* To blow one's stack.

gourd, *n.* A stupid, inane student.

goy, *n.* A Gentile, a heathen, or a non-Jew.

grade-grubber, *n.* A student who butters up a teacher for a higher grade.

grammatist, *n.* A hairsplitter over points of grammar.

grandstander, *n.* A persistent show-off. *Syn.:* glory-grabber, grandstand player, gunner, hot dog, showboat.

grape-stomper, *n.* A European of Latin extraction (French, Spanish, Italian, Romanian, Portuguese.)

grasping, *adj.* Excessively acquisitive. ["People who are hard, grasping . . . and always ready to take advantage of their neighbors, become very rich"—George Bernard Shaw.] *Syn.:* greedy, avaricious, rapacious, covetous, selfish, venal, wolfish, hoggish.

grassback, *n.* A promiscuous woman. [From one who spends a lot of time on her back.]

grass-eater, *n.* A corrupt police officer who accepts graft but doesn't demand it. ["Between the grass-eaters and the meat-eaters you can starve."]

grave-dancer, *n.* Someone who profits from others' misfortunes.

graveolent, *adj.* Fetid, heavily odoriferous.

gray, *n.* A white person.

greaseball or **greaser,** *n*. (1) An Italian, Greek, Spaniard, Puerto Rican, or Latin-American. (2) A rough and aggressive male. [From long, greased-down hair.] (3) A sycophant or toady.

great white father, *n*. Any powerful, authoritarian white man. [From Native American usage of Great White Father to mean the president of the United States.]

Greek, *n*. An Irishman.

green-ass, *adj*. Callow, green.

greenhorn, *n*. An inexperienced person. *Syn.:* neophyte, boot, buckwheater, greenhead, cheechako, greeny, jaboney, rookie, rube, tenderfoot.

greldge, *n*. A nasty and yucky object.

greldge, *interj*. Nuts!

grey, *adj*. Boring, hardworking.

grifter, *n*. A con man, a minor criminal.

grimalkin, *n*. A bossy old woman.

grimgribberer, *n*. A person who uses legal gobbledygook.

grind, *n*. A serious student. *Syn.:* bone, dexter, dweeb, eager beaver, gradehound, grunt, gweebo, poler, sunshine girl, throat, tool, ween, wonk.

gringo, *n*. A white U.S. citizen, a Yankee, or a European.

gripe one's ass, *idiom*. To be extremely annoying or objectionable. ["His constant mooching of money gripes my ass."] *Idioms:* gripe one's balls, gripe one's cookies, gripe one's left nut, gripe one's middle kidney.

grit, *n*. A Southerner. [Allusion to the food grits.]

gritch, *n*. A complainer.

grod, *n*. A big male slob.

groddess, *n*. A slobby woman.

grody or **grotty,** *adj.* Disgusting, nauseating, gross. ["Omigod, Mom, like that's totally beige ... I mean grody to the max, just gruesome. Gimme a royal break"—*New York Times* (1982).] *Syn.:* grungy, scuzzy, grody to the max.

groid, *n.* A black person.

groovy, *adj.* Stodgy, old-fashioned.

groper, *n.* A blind man.

gross, *adj.* (1) Crude, vulgar, uncouth, offensive, lewd, lascivious, lecherous, carnal, smutty, foul-mouthed, ribald, obscene, licentious. ["Like Joan's Marlene's entire range of expression was pretty much limited to 'far out,' 'super' and 'gross' "—Cyra McFadden, *The Serial.*] (2) Obese, huge, monstrous, gigantic, massive, titanic, gargantuan.

gross-out, *n.* A particularly disgusting action or event.

grossed out, *adj.* Revolted.

ground ape, *n.* An American black.

groupie, *n.* A young woman who follows and offers herself sexually to celebrities. ["Then there were these telephone calls from. . . . groupies. . . . They'd phone up and say 'Hi Jeff (Beck), how's your 'amton wick?' Ridiculous" —Jimmy Page, *Oz Magazine* (1969).]

grubber, *n.* A filthy person.

grubby, *adj.* Dirty, grimy, slovenly, unkempt, seedy, frowzy, filthy, squalid, foul, shoddy, shabby, frumpy, bedraggled, sordid.

grunge or **grunch,** *n.* A dull nerd, or a nasty person.

grungy or **gungy,** *adj.* Shabby, smelly, dirty.

grunt, *n.* (1) A low-ranking person. [From *grunt* = infantryman.] (2) A hardworking student disliked by his peers.

grunter, *n.* An older person who dislikes young people.

gubbish, *n.* Useless information. [A blend of *garbage* + *rubbish.*]

gucky, *adj.* Likely to make one vomit, yucky.

guff, *n.* Lies, nonsense, twaddle, backtalk.

guidette, *n.* A silly, overdressed woman who uses much hair spray to keep her hair piled high; a glitterbug.

guido, *n.* A man with slick hair, gold jewelry, an exposed hairy chest, acid-washed jeans, and a fondness for loud music.

guinea, *n.* An Italian.

gull, *n.* A simple, credulous fellow.

gully bum, *n.* A promiscuous woman, or a prostitute.

gully-raker, *n.* A lecher, a womanizer.

gum-beater, *n.* A braggart.

gumby, *n.* A dull, out-of-date person.

gummixed, *adj.* Confused, chaotic.

gummy, *n.* A bumbler.

gummy, *adj.* Inferior or maudlin.

gumsucker, *n.* A dope.

gundiguts or **gundyguts,** *n.* A fat person or a sloppy eater.

gunge, *n.* A despicable, disgusting, repugnant person. [From a skin irritation in the groin.]

gunzelbutt, *n.* A strange-looking man.

guru you, *interj.* Screw you!

gusset, *n.* A woman viewed as a sexual target.

gussie, *n.* An effeminate man.

gutbucket, *n.* A fat, pompous person.

gut-butcher, *n.* One who practices anal sex. *Syn.:* gut-fucker, gut-reamer, gut-scraper, gut-sticker, gut-stretcher, gut-stuffer.

gutless wonder, *n.* A spineless person.

gutter slut, *n.* A hooker who is slovenly and unkempt.

guttersnipe or **gutterpup,** *n.* A person of vulgar habits. ["... this bloody guttersnipe"—Winston Churchill speaking about Adolf Hitler.]

gweebo, *n.* A dull, contemptible person. [A variant of *dweeb.*]

gynephobe, *n.* One who has fear of or hatred for women.

gyp, *n.* A swindler, a cheater, or a fraudulent act or event. *Syn.:* fraud, trick, deception, hoax, cheat, con game, rip-off, scam.

hab, *n.* A French-Canadian.

hack *n.* (1) A writer who grinds out second-rate, commercial material. ["He's just a hack out for a quick buck."] (2) A white person.

hackneyed, *adj.* Pertaining to obvious, much-used expressions or ideas. ["If I hear another one of your hackneyed ideas, I'll vomit."] *Syn.:* stale, trite, banal, inane, insipid, stereotyped, clichéd, pedestrian, worn-out, shopworn, platitudinous, bromidic, moth-eaten.

had it up to here, *idiom.* To be exasperated. ["I've had it up to here with you."]

hag, *n.* An ugly, often older, woman. ["They're nothing but exasperating, irritating/Vacillating, calculating, agitating/Maddening and infuriating hags!"—Lerner and Lowe, *My Fair Lady* (1956).] *Syn.:* harridan, crone, harpy.

hagseed, *n.* An offspring of a witch or an ugly old woman.

hag-mouth, *v.* To bitch, to nag. ["Stop hag-mouthing me, you hagseed."]

hair, *n.* A woman considered as a sexual object; hence, hair-monger: a woman-chaser, a lecher.

hairsplitting, *adj.* Carping, quibbling, niggling, caviling, nitpicking, overcritical.

hairy-assed, *adj.* Aggressively masculine.

half-assed, *adj.* Deficient, defective, inadequate, insufficient, half-baked, hit-or-miss, skewgee, slapdash, sloppy, sorry-ass, incompetent. ["He's a half-assed worker who by all rights should be fired."]

half-breed, or **breed**, *n.* A person of mixed parentage (usually native American and caucasian). *Syn.*: half-and-half, half-caste.

half-cocked, *adv.* Prematurely, or unprepared. ["Keep your shirt on. I don't want to see you go off half-cocked as you usually do."]

half-cracked, *adj.* Stupid, at half-mast.

half-hipped, *adj.* Unsophisticated.

half-pint, *n.* A small or ineffectual person.

half-wit, *n.* A fool. ["We are setting it aside till we think of a way of half-witting halfwit Hages and his region of Decency." F. Scott Fitzgerald, *letter*, (1938).] *Syn.*: dunce, dummy, dolt, ninny, nitwit, nincompoop, dimwit, dumb-dumb, moron, imbecile, idiot, simpleton, mental defective, dullard.

halitotic, *adj.* Having bad breath.

hallelujah-peddler, *n.* An evangelist. ["He is just another hallelujah-peddler like what's-her-name's husband. You know, the TV guy who skimmed all those millions."]

ham fat, *n.* A mediocre person or object.

ham-handed, *adj.* Awkward, clumsy, all thumbs, butterfingered, ham-fisted, klutzy.

hammer, *n.* A woman viewed as a sexual object.

hammerhead, *n.* A very stupid or hardheaded person.

hampton, *n.* A contemptible person. [British rhyming slang hampton wick = prick.]

hand-galloper, *n.* A masturbator.

handkerchief-head, *n.* An Uncle Tom or Aunt Jemima. ["A 'handkerchief-head' is an old-fashioned Negro who doesn't know his rights," Stephen Longstreet, *Real Jazz* (1956).]

handshaker or **gladhander,** *n.* A person who gets by through being amiable, pleasing superiors.

hangdog, *adj.* Abject, defeated, humiliated, browbeaten, wretched, hopeless, embarrassed, guilty-looking, shame-faced. ["Get that hangdog look off your face."]

hanky-panky, *n.* Dishonesty, cuckolding, crookedness, cheating, monkey business. ["He's playing hanky-panky with his secretary."]

happa, *n.* A person who is of mixed Asian descent. [Hawaiian usage.]

hard-ass(ed), *adj.* Stern, unforgiving, cruel. ["Stop being such a hard-assed bastard and have a little charity in your heart."]

hard-boiled, *adj.* Mean and tough. ["He thinks he's hard-boiled, but he's mush inside."]

hard case, *n.* A tough, ruthless person, or a person who causes problems continuously.

hard-core, *adj.* Fanatic, uncompromising. ["Neither candidate can please his hard-core constituents."]

hard hat, *n.* A conservative, a right-winger. ["A 'Hard Hat' is a construction worker, but his helmet symbolizes all those beefy blue-collar workers who have suddenly become the knuckleduster on the strong right arm of President Nixon's silent majority." *Sunday Mail* (1970).]

hardhead, *n.* (1) An obstinate person. (2) A black person. (3) A white person.

hardleg, *n.* An ugly woman.

hard-liner, *n.* A person with a strict or unyielding position on an issue. ["The hard-liners in Russia went down the drain."]

hard-nosed, *adj.* Hardheaded, tough, stubborn, unyielding, inflexible, uncompromising, rigid, hard-line, unbending, tough, severe, pugnacious.

hard-off, *n.* A sexless male or unappealing woman. [The opposite of *hard-on.*]

hard-on for someone, to have a, *idiom.* To dislike a person strongly, to seek to create problems for someone.

hard-rock, *adj.* Severe, pugnacious.

hard-shell, *adj.* Strict, conservative, inveterate, bred-in-the-bone, deep-dyed, deep-rooted, deep-seated, dyed-in-the-wool, entrenched, hard-core, sworn.

hard-tonguer, *n.* A fellatrice, or a prostitute.

harebrain, *n.* A complete idiot. ["A foolish harebrain. This is not she"—Richard Burton.]

harp, *n.* An Irish person, or an Irish immigrant to the United States. ["The foreman was a big loudmouthed harp." John Dos Passos, *Big Money* (1936).] *Syn.*: bark, bog-hopper, bog-lander, bog-trotter, boiled dinner, chaw, chawmouth, cheap shanty mick, mick, mike, narrowback, paddy, pat, saltwater turkey, sham, shamrock, shanty Irish, spud, turf-cutter.

harpy, *n.* A shrew.

harridan, *n.* A vicious old woman.

harum-scarum, *adj.* Disorganized, undependable, unreliable, erratic, careless, foolish, scatterbrained, featherbrained, flighty, absentminded, confused, bewildered.

hat, *n.* (1) A promiscuous woman [From the idea that a hat is frequently felt.] (2) A gay man.

hatchet man, *n.* (1) A political spokesperson who handles dirty and vicious attacks on opponents. ["... the cat's-paw of corrupt functionaries and the henchman of ambitious humbugs"—George Bernard Shaw.] (2) A person who handles distasteful tasks for superiors. ["He gave the job of firing the negligent secretary to his hatchet man."] (3) A hit man, an assassin.

hatchet-thrower, *n.* A Hispanic.

haul (or rake) someone over the coals, *idiom.* To rebuke someone nastily. *Syn.*: castigate, chew out.

hausfrau, *n.* A woman whose main interest is in her home and family. ["Women in West Germany appear to have taken a tremendous leap forward from *hausfrau* to high executive positions." *Punch* (1962).]

have a bellyful of, *idiom.* To become angered by someone's repeated irritating or stupid actions.

have a brass neck, *idiom.* To be impudent.

have a bug up one's ass, *idiom.* To be very touchy, to be feisty. ["Don't go near her today. She has a bug up her ass."] *Idioms:* have a hair up one's ass, have a hair up one's nose, have a bug up one's nose.

have a case of dumbass, *idiom.* To make very stupid mistakes. ["What's the matter? You got another one of your cases of dumbass!"]

have a hole in one's head, *idiom.* To be stupid. "Lawyers can't walk and fart at the same time." *Idioms:* be a quart low, be overdosed on dumb pills, have a few buttons missing, have a hole in one's wig, have a loose shingle, have a screw loose, have shit for brains, can't find one's way to first base, not have all one's switches on, not have both oars in the water, not have brain one, not know one's ass from third base, not playing with a full deck.

have a mind like a sieve, *idiom.* To be forgetful. ["Can't you ever remember anything I tell you? You have a mind like a sieve."]

have (or **cop**) **an attitude,** *idiom.* To be arrogant, angry, or haughty.

have a shit fit, *idiom.* To become very angry. *Idioms:* shit a brick, shit green.

have a stick up one's ass, *idiom.* To be incorrigibly boring.

have a yellow streak down one's back, *idiom.* To be a coward.

have a wild hair up one's ass, *idiom.* (1) To be hyperactive. (2) To be obsessed with an offbeat idea.

have bats in one's belfry, *idiom.* To be loco.

have brass balls, *idiom.* To be brave or foolhardy. *Syn.*: have cast-iron balls.

have egg on one's face, *idiom.* To be caught in an embarrassing position.

have lead in one's pants or **have lead in one's ass,** *idiom.* To move or work slowly, be dull and unresponsive.

have one by the balls, *idiom.* To have someone firmly in a dangerous and painful position. ["When you have 'em by the balls, they sure answer to your roll call."] *Idioms:* have one by the short hairs, have one by the curlies, have one by the wool, have one by the nuts, have one where the hair is short.

have one foot in the grave, *idiom.* Almost dead, unresponsive. ["I can't marry you. You've got one foot in the grave."]

have one's ass, *idiom.* To punish someone or retaliate.

have one's ass in a crack, *idiom.* To be in an awkward posture.

have one's ass in a sling, *idiom.* To be in deep trouble.

have one's cock caught in a zipper, *idiom.* To be in deep trouble.

have one's glasses on, *idiom.* To be uptight.

have one's guts for garters, *idiom.* To hurt badly.

have one's head up one's ass, *idiom.* To be completely unaware or stupid.

have one's number, *idiom.* To know the inside, true story about another, particularly negative information.

have shit for brains, *idiom.* To be extremely stupid. ["Boy, you've got shit for brains. How could you have ever thought of saying that to her?"]

have some buttons missing, *idiom.* To be a bit mad. *Idioms:* have some marbles missing, be off the wall.

hawk, *n.* An advocate of reliance on military strength to resolve international conflicts.

hay-eater, *n.* A white person.

hayseed, *n.* A rural bumpkin.

haywire, *adj.* Crazy, mixed-up.

head, *n.* A drug addict. *Syn.:* acidhead, a-head, cokehead, cubehead, drughead, gowhead, hophead, methhead, pill-head, pinhead.

head case, *n.* An insane or eccentric person.

head-cheese, *n.* A despicable person. [From a foul-smelling material (smegma) that builds up in the male foreskin.]

head-chick, *n.* A woman adept at fellatio.

head-fucker, *n.* A person who deliberately disorients others.

-headed, *suffix.* Having some type of mental deficiency.

headhunter, *n.* A lecher who zeroes in on virgins.

head nigger in charge, *idiom.* A high-level black in government. ["The one who acts like he makes the decisions, but is only doing what the man says"—Andrews and Owens, *Black Language.*] *Syn.:* nigger in charge, H.N.I.C., N.I.C.

heat merchant, *n.* A constant critic.

heavy cake, *n.* A ladies' man.

heavy cream, *n.* An obese person.

hebe or **heeb,** *n.* A Jew. [Short for *Hebrew.*] ["He should've been a nigger or a hebe instead of Irish." James T. Farrell *Studs Lonigan* (1936).]

hebess, *n.* A Jewish woman.

heel, *n.* A louse, a bastard, a bounder, a cad, a double-crosser. ["Time wounds all heels"—Jane Ace, in "The Fine Art of Hypochondria" by Goodman Ace.]

heifer, *n.* (1) A young and pretty woman. ["I've been a mighty good bull cow, oh Lordy, but I got to go/ I found me a pigmeat heifer, I can tell by the way she lows" —"Lowing Heifer," blues song.] (2) An unattractive, obese woman.

hein, *n.* A person who is ugly and unpleasant.

heinie, *n.* A German. ["It's not the Russians we should be congratulating ... but the Heinies. Sure we got Von Braun, but the Russians grabbed all the rest of the German rocket guys." *Listener* (1961).]

hellcat, *n.* A volatile, furious, or mischievous woman.

hellhag, *n.* An extremely unpleasant old woman.

hellion, *n.* A scold.

heliumhead, *n.* An airhead.

hell of a way to run a railroad, *idiom.* A botched operation.

hellpig, *n.* An obese girl.

hell-raiser, *n.* A troublemaker, an overly defiant person.

hell's bells and buckets of blood, *idiom.* Exclamation of distress and anger. *Idioms:* hell's fire and damnation, shit fire and damnation.

hemipygic, *adj.* Foolish, inane, half-assed.

hemorrhoid, *n.* Person who is painful to spend time with.

hen, *n.* (1) A woman over thirty. (2) A fussy and gossipy woman.

henpecked, *adj.* Wife-ridden, submissive, pussywhipped, docile, meek, dominated, unassertive, browbeaten, bullied, obedient. ["But—Oh! ye lords of ladies intellectual/Inform us truly, have they not henpeck'd you all?" —George Gordon Byron, *Don Juan.*]

herbie or **Herbert,** *n.* A very conventional part of the establishment.

heretic, *n.* A dissenter, an apostate. *Syn.:* skeptic, pantheist, nonconformist, recusant, deviationist, freethinker, backslider, recreant.

herkel, *n.* A drip.

herky-jerky, *adj.* Jerky, spasmodic.

herring-choker, *n.* A Scandinavian, or a Nova Scotian.

hesh, *n.* A he-she, an effeminate male or gay male.

he-she, *n.* A gay man. *Syn.:* him-her, himmer.

Hessian, *n.* A hireling, a boor.

hick, *n.* (1) A naive person. (2) An ignorant rural person. ["Hicks Nix Pix in Sticks"—famous *Variety* headline.] *Syn.:* apple-knocker, Arkie, brush ape, chaw-bacon, Clem, clodhopper, clover-kicker, provincial, gully-jumper, boor, hayseed, peasant, Herkimer Jerkimer, hillbilly, honyock, hoosier, jaspar, jay, John farmer, joskin, local yokel, Okie, plow jockey, pumpkin-roller, redneck, rube, rustic, shit-kicker, SK, sodbuster, stump-jumper, yap, yokel.

hicksville, *adj.* Dull, corny, passé.

hicky, *adj.* Rural, poor, and mean.

high-and-goodbye, *adj.* Unreliable.

high-binder, *n.* A corrupt politician or jobholder.

highbrow, *n.* Intellectual, thinker, Brahmin, mandarin, elitist, snot, pundit, egghead, brain, double-dome. ["A highbrow is a person educated beyond his intelligence" —J. Brander Matthews: Epigram.]

high cockalorum, *n.* A pompous person.

highfalutin' or **hifalutin,** *adj.* Pompous, pretentious ["When all the high falutin' and magical jargon of diplomacy is removed, you'll find the diplomats like a group of children aged about three or four," *Manchester Guardian Weekly* (1948).] *Syn.:* arrogant, uppity, grandiose, proud, self-important, lordly, presumptuous, pretentious, bombastic, inflated, florid, sententious, exaggerated, flamboyant.

high-hat, *v.* To act in a superior manner.

high-mucky-muck or **high-muck-a-muck,** *n.* An arrogant self-important, high-ranking person. *Syn.:* high-monkey-monk, big shot, higher-up, muckie-muck, top dog, big noise, big cheese.

high-pooped, *adj.* Big-assed.

high-siding, *v.* Showing off through an ostentatious display of jewelry, flashy clothes, and cars. *Syn.*: high-steppin'.

high yaller or **high yella,** *n.* A light-skinned African-American woman. ["High yeller, She'll kick you, that ain't all/ When you step out at night, 'nother mule in your stall" —"Brownskin Woman," blues song. "And in some colored families I know personally down south, you can hardly tell high yellows from white"—Langston Hughes, *Simple Speaks His Mind.*] *Syn.*: mellow yellow, melted butter, mulat.

himbo, *n.* A male bimbo. ["Sex was commonplace, from a Melanie Griffith look-alike stuffed into her gown like salami in Spandex to the macho himbo . . . wearing a 16-foot python like a stole around his shoulders"—*Washington Post* (1988).]

hincty, *adj.* Stuck-up, seditty, uppity. [Often used about blacks who identify with white values.]

hinkty, *n.* (1) A snob, or a white person. *Syn.*: hinkty-ass, hankty.

hind, *n.* An ass.

hinky, *adj.* Suspicious.

hipflipper, *n.* (1) A streetwalker, or a promiscuous woman.

hippie or **hippy,** *n.* Someone who rejects conventional society, leads an unconventional life, and shares antiestablishment values and beliefs. ["Yippies, hippies, yahoos, Black Panthers, lions and tigers alike—I would swap the whole damn zoo for the kind of young Americans I saw in Vietnam"—Spiro Agnew.]

hippie witch, *n.* A woman who wears black sixties-style clothing.

hipshooter, *n.* An impulsive, hot-tempered person; a hothead.

hireling, *n.* A low-level employee.

his nibs or **himself,** *n.* A high-level executive whose ego demands deferential treatment from his subordinates. ["Shall I bring the coffee to his nibs now?"]

hitchy, *adj.* Nervous.

hit him where he lives, *idiom.* To hurt or insult one badly. [Reference to a man's testicles. "Lloyd George couldn't see a belt without hitting below it"—Margot Asquith, quoted in *The Autobiography of Herbert Asquith.*]

hit the roof or **hit the ceiling,** *v.* To explode, to blow up.

ho or **hoe,** *n.* A hooker, or a slut. [Short for *whore.*]

hobby horse, *n.* A sexually loose woman. [From the idea of one who is ridden.]

hocky or **hockey,** *n.* Empty and pretentious trickery. [From the word for dog feces.]

hocus-pocus, *n.* Nonsensical words, mumbo-jumbo. [From words used in magic or conjuring. "The potency of movies depends upon the quality of their dramatic articulation, not upon the working of hocus-pocus on the eyes" —Bosley Crowther.]

hodad, *n.* A cretin, a clown, a wimp, a phony.

ho-daddy, *n.* (1) A braggart, a wiseguy. (2) A hanger-on who seeks the company of celebrities. (3) An obnoxious phony.

ho-ho, *n.* A young, fat woman. *Syn.:* thunder thighs.

hoi polloi, *n.* The common people. ["The boss's wife is too proud to rub shoulders with the hoi polloi."] *Syn.:* the plebs, the proles, the masses, the mob, the herd, the lower classes, pawns, riffraff, rabble, canaille, cogs.

hoitch, *n.* An unpleasant woman.

hoity-toity, *n.* Pretentious, arrogant, haughty.

hokey, *adj.* Fake, contrived, phony.

hold no weight, *idiom.* To lack credibility, or to impress no one. ["You hold no weight with me, buster."]

hold one's feet to the fire, *idiom.* To punish severely, to crucify. *Idioms:* let turn slowly in the wind, nail to the cross, nail to the wall.

hold your horses or **hold your water,** *interj.* Wait a minute! Don't get excited!

hole, *n.* A person seen merely as a sex object.

holer, *n.* (1) A hooker. (2) A woman-chaser.

hollow men, *n.* People who are shallow, lacking in idealism. ["We are the hollow men./We are the stuffed men,/ Leaning together/Headspiece filled with straw./Alas 1" —T. S. Eliot, "The Waste Land" (1925).]

holly-golly or **hully-gully,** *n.* Nonsense, hogwash.

holy dog shit or **holy dog crap,** *interj.* An exclamation of surprise or anger.

Holy Roller, *n.* A fire-and-brimstone preacher or church member.

holy shit, *interj.* An oath of surprise or anger.

home boy, *n.* A black man.

hommocks, *n.* An overgrown, sloppy girl.

homo, *n.* A homosexual man or woman. ["I'm the last of Britain's stately homos"—Quentin Crisp.] *Syn.:* con, fag, faggot, fairy, flit, fruit, he-she, homie, invert, joto, lesbian, maricon, nellie fag, punk, queen, queer, sissy, uranian, uranist.

homo sap, *n.* A dumbbell, a sap. [Short for *Homo sapiens.*] *Syn.:* Boobus Americanus, Homo Boobus.

homosexual, *adj.* Displaying sexual interest in a person of the same sex. *Syn.:* fay, gay, sweet.

honker, *n.* A strange person.

honky or **honkey,** *n.* A white person. *Syn.:* hunky, beast, ofay.

hoo-ha, *n.* Nonsense, twaddle, a lot of noise for nothing.

hook or **hooknose,** *n.* A Jewish person.

hoople, *n.* A white person.

hophead, *n.* A drug addict. *Syn.:* hop fiend, hop fighter.

hopper-arsed, *adj.* Double-assed, fat-assed, shuttle-butted, hopper-hipped.

hopping Jesus, *n.* A lame person.

horndog, *n.* A dedicated woman-chaser and fornicator.

horse, *n.* A big, ugly man.

horse apple, *n.* Pretentious trash [From the word for horse-shit balls.] *Syn.:* horse hockey, horseradish, horsh.

horse-godmother, *n.* A big, masculine virago.

the horselaugh, *idiom.* A loud, nasty laugh of dismissal and ridicule.

horse's ass, *n.* An idiot. ["Why are there more horses' asses than there are horses?"—American proverb.] *Syn.:* horse's hangdown.

horseshit, *n.* Rubbish, nonsense, bullshit.

horseshit and gunsmoke, *idiom.* Great excitement, confusion, and chaos.

hose, *n.* A woman who sleeps with many men. [From *hose* = copulate.] *Syn.:* hosebag, hose monster.

hoser, *n.* (1) A person who deceives and cheats. (2) A simple Canadian.

hot air, *n.* Pompous nonsense. ["The balloon with the most hot air makes the loudest noise when it bursts"—American proverb.]

hot and bothered, *idiom.* Very angry.

hot-assed, *adj.* Sexually aroused.

hot baby, *n.* A wild, sexy young woman. *Syn.:* hot bot, hot meat, hot beef, hot mutton, hot number, hot pants, hot patootie, hotpot, hot stuff, hot tamale, hot tomato.

hot chocolate, *n.* A sexually appealing black woman.

hot dog or **hotdogger,** *n.* A show-off, an athlete who turns a routine play into a dazzling exhibition of his abilities. *Syn.:* grandstand player, showboat.

hot-gospeler, *n.* A rabid ideologue or ardent puritan.

hot nuts, *n.* A horny man.

hot shit, *n.* An aggressive, conceited man. *Syn.:* hot poo, hot-shot Charlie, hot stuff.

Hottentot, *n.* A dumb, uncivilized person.

hot tongue, *n.* A sexually aroused woman or a lecherous man.

hot under the collar, *idiom.* Very indignant, steamed up. ["The senator got hot under the collar every time someone mentioned S & Ls."]

hot water, in, *idiom.* To be in great trouble.

hound dog, *n.* A skirt-chaser.

house nigger, *n.* A servile black; sometimes abbreviated hn or HN. [Refers to a class of black slaves assigned to the master's house rather than to the field. "There's something new on the scene today . . . Blacks in government as—what? Servants—civil servants. In olden times, they would say house niggers"—Louis Farrakhan, address to Blacks in Government Conference (1989).]

huckleberry, *n.* A jerk.

huckster, *n.* A person who sells or peddles junk.

hully, *n.* A fat person.

humbug, *n.* (1) Deception, double-dealing. *Syn.:* imposture, dodge, sham, make-believe, spoof, hoax, deceit, trickery, fraud, flimflam, swindle, gyp. (2) A person involved in the above practices. *Syn.:* fraud, quack, faker, impostor, charlatan, mountebank, swindler, cheat, cheater, sharper, trickster, hummer, liar, fibber, perjurer, hypocrite.

hump, *n.* A person who will readily engage in sex.

hung like a chicken, *idiom.* A man with tiny genitals.

hun, *n.* A brutal person.

hung up, *idiom.* Held back by social pressures, or obsessed with an idea.

hunk, *n.* A man viewed primarily as a sex object. *Syn.*: Adonis, beefcake, caveman, collar ad, dreamboat, glamour puss, Greek god, he-man, hunk of beef, hunk of meat, macho, pin-up boy, sexpot.

hunkey or **hunky,** *n.* An immigrant from Central Europe. *Syn.*: bohunk, ginz, hunk, hunks.

hunk of cheese, *n.* An obnoxious person.

hurtin' for certain, *idiom.* Extremely ugly.

husker, *n.* A masturbator.

hustler, *n.* (1) A male or female prostitute. (2) Any person who runs a "game," such as a con artist, a thief, a pimp. ["The hustlers sold phony knock-offs of expensive watches."]

hyena, *n.* A despicable person.

hype, *n.* A deception.

hyperdrive whore, *n.* A very sleazy, unattractive girl.

I

iceberg, *n.* A cold, unemotional person.

iceberg slim *n.* An exploiter.

iceman *n.* A hired killer. [From *ice* = to kill.]

ice queen *n.* A cold and haughty woman, often frigid. ["That ice queen looks as though butter would not melt in her mouth or any part of her" —adapted from Elsa Lanchester, *The Filmgoer's Book of Quotes.*] *Syn.*: ice maiden, ice wagon.

ick, *n.* A person who is generally disliked.

icky, *adj.* Sickly sweet, sticky, gooey, gucky, tacky.

ideologue, *n.* A holder of rigid and uncompromising political views, left or right. ["If the ideologues take over, you better head for the hills."]

idleheaded, *adj.* Stupid, foolish.

ig man or **ignant,** *n.* An ignorant man. ["The ignorant man always adores what he cannot understand"—Cesare Lombroso, *The Man of Genius.*]

ignatz, *n.* A stupid person.

ignoble, *adj.* Unworthy, base, dishonorable, mean. ["... to see how those he has converted distort and debase and make ignoble parodies of his teaching"—Aldous Huxley.] *Syn.*: despicable, infamous, contemptible, nefarious, vile, dastardly.

ignoramus, *n.* A know-nothing, a grossly uninformed person. ["A filthy story-teller, despot, liar, braggart, buffoon, usurper, monster, ignoramus, old scoundrel, purjurer, robber, swindler, tyrant, field-butcher and land-pirate" —*Harper's Weekly* on Abraham Lincoln.]

illiberal, *adj.* Bigoted, intolerant, narrow-minded, biased, prejudiced, hidebound, brassbound, small-minded, short-sighted.

illin' or **un-chillin',** *adj.* Stupid.

imbecile, *n.* An extremely foolish person. ["Man is a clever animal who behaves like an imbecile"—Albert Schweitzer, *On Politics.*] *Syn.*: ament, cretin, idiot, nitwit, ass, jerk, dumbbell, dummy, simpleton, moron, feeb, dunce, nincompoop, ninny, colt, dingbat.

immature, *adj.* Childlike, not fully developed mentally. ["Basically my wife was immature. I'd be at home in the bath and she'd come in and sink my boats"—Woody Allen, quoted in the *Daily Mirror* (1964).]

immerd, *n.* To cover with feces. [From French *merde* = shit.]

immoral, *adj.* Evil, wrong. ["Is it really true that the best things to do in life are immoral, illegal, or fattening?"] *Syn.*: unethical, unprincipled, corrupt, vicious, wicked, iniquitous, sinful, nefarious, heinous, profligate, unchaste, dissipated, dissolute.

impassive, *adj.* Apathetic, phlegmatic, stolid, unresponsive. ["Did you ever see such an impassive character in your whole life?"]

impenitent, *adj.* Remorseless, unashamed, unrepentant, regretless, uncontrite, unapologetic.

imperious, *adj.* Domineering, overbearing. ["He was an imperious, bossy husband who wasn't above an occasional session of wife-bashing."] *Syn.:* dictatorial, lordly, despotic, bossy, autocratic, tyrannical, peremptory, high-handed.

impertinent, *adj.* Fresh, impudent. ["Keep that impertinent snotnose out of my office."] *Syn.:* intrusive, unmannerly, disrespectful, insolent, impudent, presumptuous, meddlesome, fresh, smarty.

impious, *adj.* Irreverent, sacrilegious, blasphemous, profane, ungodly, irreligious, godless, unholy, disrespectful.

implacable, *adj.* Irreconcilable, unappeasable. ["He (an African god) is utterly and absolutely implacable; no prayers, no human sacrifices can ever for one moment appease his cold, malignant rage"—L. P. Smith.] *Syn.:* inexorable, unamenable, inflexible, unflinching, intractable, ruthless, unrelenting.

impostor, *n.* Fake, faker, fraud, humbug, phony. ["The more gross the fraud, the more glibly will it go down and the more greedily will it be swallowed, since folly will always find faith wherever impostors will find impudence"—Christian Nestell Bovee.]

impotent, *adj.* Ineffective, powerless, feeble, weak, helpless, feckless, hapless, nonfunctional. ["A woman is a woman until the day she dies, but a man's a man only as long as he can"—Moms Mabley.]

in a funk, *idiom.* Depressed or frightened.

in a hole, *idiom.* In terrible difficulty or trouble. *Syn.:* up shit creek, in a jam, in deep shit, in deep water.

in a huff, *idiom.* Petulant, grumpy, upset. *Idioms:* in a lather, in a sweat, in a stew, in a tizzy.

in a mucksweat, *idiom.* Frightened, flustered, alarmed, in a panic.

in-and-outer, *n.* An erratic, eccentric performer.

inaniloquent, *adj.* Talking stupidly, babbling.

in a pig's ass, *interj.* Impossible! No way! *Idioms:* in a pig's ear, in a pig's cunt, in a pig's eye.

inarticulate, *adj.* Dumb, incomprehensible, unintelligible.

in a tizzy, *idiom.* Very upset, in a state.

in cement, *idiom.* Immovable, intractable, uncompromising, unyielding.

indecisive, *adj.* Irresolute, vacillating, blowing hot and cold. ["Once I make up my mind, I'm full of indecision" —Oscar Levant.] *Syn.:* mercurial, shilly-shallying, half-hearted, uncertain, wishy-washy.

indecorous, *adj.* In bad taste. ["A generation of critical circles has maintained an indecorous silence, not so much discreet as unbecoming, concerning John Masefield" —Isidore Salomon.] *Syn.:* improper, indecent, malodorous, ridiculous, rough, unbecoming, ungodly, unseemly, untoward.

Indian giver, *n.* A person who demands the return of a gift.

indorser, *n.* A sadist.

infelicitous, *adj.* Awkward, graceless, ill-chosen, inept.

infernal, *adj.* Damnable, hellish. ["... the most abhorred fiend in the infernal regions is sent to torment me"—Sir Walter Scott.] *Syn.:* devilish, horrible, fiendish, diabolical, demoniacal, flagitious, accursed, nefarious, abominable, monstrous, iniquitous.

influence peddler, *n.* A person who seeks special privileges from government for his clients. ["(The Committee) which is inquiring into the activities of the 'five percenters' and the 'influence peddlers' has discovered that selling influence may be unethical but it is not always illegal," *New York Times* (1949).]

ingle, *n.* A catamite. ["(He) called them whoresons, ingle's accidents, sons of a bitch. ..." T. E. Lawrence, *Seven Pillars of Wisdom* (1926).]

injun, *n.* A Native American. [Colloquial and dialect form of Indian.]

ink, *n.* A black person. *Syn.*: inkface, inky-dink.

in over one's head, *idiom.* To be helpless.

insane, *adj.* Crazy. ["... the insane ambition and insatiable appetite which have caused this vast war"—Winston Churchill.] *Syn.*: brainsick, unhinged, psychotic, manic, schizophrenic, paranoiac. *Idioms*: bats in the belfry, mad as a hatter, mad as a March hare, mentally disordered, off one's chump, potty [British usage], off one's rocker.

in shit order, *idiom.* Very messy, or dirty.

insipid, *adj.* Characterless, wearisome, bland, trite, vapid, wishy-washy, namby-pamby. ["Happiness is a wine of the rarest vintage, and seems insipid to a vulgar taste"—L. P. Smith.]

insolent, *adj.* Arrogant, impudent. ["The insolence of the vulgar is in proportion to their ignorance: they treat everything with contempt which they do not understand"—William Hazlitt, *Characteristics*.] *Syn.*: bumptious, outrageous, nervy, overbearing, haughty, supercilious.

inspector of manholes, *idiom.* A pederast.

intellectual, *n.* A well-read person interested in ideas and culture who is considered impractical and wooly-headed. ["To the man-in-the-street who, I'm sorry to say/ Is a keen observer of life,/ The word Intellectual suggests straight away/ A man who's untrue to his wife"—W. H. Auden, "New Year Letter."]

in the dumper or **in the tub,** *n.* Bankrupt, insolvent.

in the life, *idiom.* Engaged in a socially unapproved way of living.

in the red, *idiom.* In debt, insolvent.

in the shit, *idiom.* In real trouble.

intimidate, *v.* Browbeat, bulldoze, bullyrag, hector, strong-arm.

intolerant, *adj.* Bigoted, prejudiced, narrow-minded, closed-minded, xenophobic, chauvinistic.

invective, *n.* Abusive or denunciatory language. ["John Bull stopped at nothing in the way of insult; but its blazing audacity of invective never degenerated into dull abuse"—Agnes Repplier.]

iracund, *adj.* Easily angered.

irascible, *adj.* Choleric, cranky, cross, grouchy, grumpy, ireful, quick-tempered, ratty, splenetic, stomachy, testy, tetchy. ["... the irascible but kindhearted deity who indulges in copious curses to ease his feelings"—Morris Cohen.]

Irishman's fart, like an, *idiom.* Making a lot of noise and raising a stink.

irksome, *adj.* Boring, tedious, tiresome. ["He laid down his irksome editorial duties and spent the next fifteen years in farming"—F. H. Chase.]

it-shay, *n.* A despicable person. [From the Pig Latin.]

ivory-dome, *n.* A pretentious intellectual.

it will be someone's ass, *idiom.* Someone is going to get it, but good!

I wouldn't stick my walking stick where you put your prick, *idiom.* Your choice of women is for the birds! *Syn.*: I wouldn't do it even with someone else's.

izod, *n.* A preppy guy or girl. [After the manufacturer of the sport shirt with the alligator logo.]

izzatso, *interj.* Balls! Bullshit! Hooey! *Idioms*: don't give me that shit, says who, tell it to the marines, the hell you say, who you kidding, you wouldn't shit me, you're full of shit.

jabber, *n.* Idle talk. ["When the eagles are silent the parrots begin to jabber"—Winston Churchill.] *Syn.:* prate, gibber, gibberish, drivel, ranting, prattle, blabber, hot air, jabberjack

jackal *n.* A henchman who does another's dirty work. ["This whipped jackal, who to save his own skin, has made Italy a vassal state . . ."—Winston Churchill, referring to Benito Mussolini, who treacherously attacked France in 1940.]

jackanapes, *n.* An impertinent person.

jack around, *v.* To screw around, to waste time.

jackass, *n.* A stupid person, a fool. ["Any jackass can make money; it takes a wise man to keep it"—American saying.]

jackdaw, *n.* A person who talks too much, a prattler.

Jack Nasty, *n.* An unpleasant man.

jack-off, *n.* A masturbator, a jerk. ["You're not really dating him. I can't believe it. He's a complete jack-off."] *Syn.:* jag-off, jerk-off.

jacksauce, *n.* A rude person.

jack shit, *n.* (1) Absolutely nothing. [Always used with a qualifying negative verb. "He doesn't know jack shit about what has to be done."] (2) A worthless person.

jacksie, up your, *idiom.* Up yours! [From *jacksie* = anus.]

jade, *adj.* A promiscuous woman, a minx.

jail bait, *n.* A sexually attractive or flirtatious girl below the legal age of sexual consent, copulation with whom constitutes statutory rape.

jaisy, *n.* An effeminate man or a gay man.

jam, *n.* An attractive female or a heterosexual man.

janus, *n.* A two-faced person.

Jap, *n.* A person of Japanese nationality or descent. *Syn.*: jeep, jerkenese, little yellow bastard, Nip, skibby.

JAP, *n.* A spoiled young Jewish person who acts haughty. [Acronym for *J*ewish *A*merican *P*rincess, or *J*ewish *A*merican *P*rince. "What do the Pope and a JAP have in common? They both spend millions on travel and fancy gowns and won't let you have sex"—*Maledicta, IX.*]

jape, *v.* To cheat or deceive.

jarhead, *n.* A black man.

jaspar, *n.* (1) A lesbian. ["Get a look at that jaspar at the bar smoking a big, fat cigar."] (2) A hick.

jay, *n.* An easily duped fool or hick.

jay bird or **J-bird,** *n.* A Jewish person.

jazz, *n.* Women considered as sexual objects.

jazz baby, *n.* A woman of easy morals.

jazzbo, *n.* A black man.

J.B. or **jaybee,** *n.* A very dark black person. [From shortening *jet black.*]

J.D., *n.* A young hoodlum. [From *juvenile delinquent.*]

Jebby, *n.* A Jesuit.

jeff, *n.* (1) A white person. [Allusion to Jefferson Davis, president of the Confederacy during the American Civil War.] (2) A tedious person, a square. (3) A black man who plays up to to a white man.

jel, *n.* A person with minimal intelligence. [Short for *Jell-O-brain.*]

jelly, *n.* An attractive woman. ["It must be jelly for jam don't shake like that"—American folk saying.] *Syn.*: jelly-on-springs, jelly roll.

jellybelly, *n.* (1) A fat person. (2) A coward.

jellyfish, *n.* A weak, cowardly person.

jelly roll, *n.* A man obsessed with lechery, a woman-chaser. [From *jelly roll* = sex. "Jelly roll killed ma pappy, drove ma momma stone blind"—"Jellyroll Blues."]

jerk, *n.* (1) A fool, a person of absolutely no importance, a worthless and ineffectual person. ["You know perfectly well that the jerk-offs do all the talking at meetings," William Sheed, *People Will Always Be Kind* (1973).] *Syn.*: ass, bimbo, boob, bozo, chump, clown, corn dog, creep, dildo, dill, dingbat, dipshit, dolf, dork, drip, drizzle, drool, dud, dumdum, dweeb, eightball, fathead, fishball, foul ball, fuckhead, funk, fuzznuts, geek, gink, goobatron, goober, goof, grind, groover, grunch, gug, gumby, gump, gweebo, Herkimer Jerkimer, hoakie, ho-dad, huckleberry, jack-off, jag-off, Jerk McGhee, jerk-off, joker, kink, klutz, lame, lummox, lunk, lunkhead, meatball, Melvin, mutt, nebbish, nerd, numbnuts, ook, outz, pill, pinhead, pogue, poop, poor slob, poot, pud, punk, ringtail, sad apple, sap, scag, schlemiel, schlep, schmo, schnook, schtoonk, shitass, simp, skag, slob, snarf, stick, stiff, twit, weenie, wonk, worm, yap, yo-yo, zhlub, zod. (2) A masturbator. ["A woman is a quite serviceable substitute for masturbation. It takes an abundance of imagination, to be sure"—Kare Kraus. *Aphorisms and more Aphorisms*] *Syn.*: jerk-off, jag-off, shank-cranker, pipe-greaser, chicken-milker, sword-polisher, flounder-pounder, poker-stroker, pickle-tickler, pump-thumper, pole-varnisher, wanker, whack-off.

jerk around, *v.* To waste time.

jerk one around, *idiom.* To victimize, to annoy, to harass. *Syn.*: jerk one's chain, yank one's chain.

Jerkenese, *n.* The Japanese people or a Japanese person.

jerk off, *idiom.* To idle about.

jerkwater, *adj.* Insignificant, trivial. ["What a jerkwater dump this town turned out to be."]

Jersey side of snatch play, *idiom.* To be over forty.

Jesuit, *n.* A sodomite or a practitioner of aberrant sexual practices.

Jesus screamer or **Jesus freak,** *n.* (1) An evangelical or Pentacostal Christian. (2) A clergyman.

jew, *n.* (1) A cheater. (2) Any well-to-do person regardless of race or religion. ["I determine who is a Jew" —Hermann Göring.]

jew or **jew down,** *v.* (1) To haggle or bargain. (2) To cheat or defraud.

jewboy or **jewie,** *n.* A Jewish boy or man.

Jewess, *n.* A Jewish woman or girl. ["Virgin Mary is a Jewess"—American graffito, collected by Alan Walker Read, in *Maledicta X.*]

Jewish American Prince, *n.* A pampered and usually well-to-do young man of any ethnic background who feels he deserves special treatment.

Jewish mother, *n.* An all-embracing, hovering, overfeeding, oversolicitous mother of any ethnic background who suffocates her child with too much TLC, chicken noodle soup, sexual and moral restrictions. ["... we can't take it anymore! Because you Jewish mothers are too fucking much"—Philip Roth, *Portnoy's Complaint* (1969).]

jezebel, *n.* A shrew or a whore. [After Jezebel, wife of Ahab, who introduced the worship of the fertility god Baal, as mentioned in the Bible.]

jibone or **jabone,** *n.* (1) A greenhorn, an innocent, a newly arrived immigrant. (2) A heavy, a thug, a muscleman.

jig, *n.* A black person. ["Newark is dago vigilantes hunting jigs with tire irons"—Philip Roth, *Zuckerman Unbound.*] *Syn.*: jibagoo, jigaboo, jiga, jit, zig, zigaboo.

jig-lover, *n.* A white person who is concerned with the welfare of blacks.

jingoist, *n.* A person who feels the way to settle international disputes, when push comes to shove, is by military might. ["We don't want to fight,/But, by Jingo, if we do,/We've got the ships, we've got the men,/We've got the money too"—W. G. Hunt, "We Don't Want to Fight" (1878).]

jive, *n.* Glibly deceptive language, insincere talk, mendacity, nonsense, bull, bullshit, garbage.

jive around, *v.* To talk nonsense, to deceive, to confound.

jive or **jive-ass,** *adj.* Phony, deceitful, fake, undependable, boastful, insignificant. [A general negative intensifier.]

jive turkey, *n.* One who jives.

joanie, *adj.* Antiquated, strictly passé, out-of-date, paleolithic.

joanin, *v.* To insult publicly.

jock, *v.* To cheat or deceive.

jocker or **jockey,** *n.* A pederast.

jock-gagger or **jack-gagger,** *n.* A man who lives off his wife's prostitution.

jody, *n.* A backdoor lover of a married woman or a soldier's girlfriend. [Jody was the traditional 4F who was rejected for the army and remained at home. "Ain't no use in writing home/Jody's got your gal and gone./Ain't no use in feeling blue/Jody's got your Cadillac too"—World War II army song.]

Joe Cunt, *n.* A nickname for any jerk. *Syn.*: Joe Hunt, Joe Erk.

Joe Schmoe, *n.* A sad nonentity.

john, *n.* (1) A hooker's customer, or a male who is easily exploited by women. (2) An older homosexual who supports a young one.

John Chinaman, *n.* A Chinese person. *Syn.*: canary, chinamang, chinee, chink, chow, coosie, dink, gook, john, mustard, pigtail, pong, ricebelly, riceman, slope, yellowbelly, yellow boy.

joker, *n.* A man, a clown, a wiseguy.

Jonah, *n.* One who puts a curse or whammy on others, a jinx.

joyrider, *n.* An occasional drug user. *Syn.*: chipper, joy popper.

Judas, *n.* A particularly despicable traitor.

Judy with the big booty, *idiom.* A fat woman.

juggins or **jiggins,** *n.* A dupe, a patsy.

juice dealer, *n.* A person who lends money at usurious interest rates. ["That mob made most of its money as juice dealer to garment companies."] *Syn.*: loan shark, shylock.

juice freak or **juicehead,** *n.* Someone who chooses alcohol over drugs.

juicer, *n.* A steroid user.

juking and jiving, *idiom.* Frivolity, triviality, and dishonesty.

jungle bunny, *n.* An American black.

junglemouth, *n.* A person with bad breath.

junior flip, *n.* A teenager, a teenybopper.

junkie, *n.* A narcotics user or addict. *Syn.*: acidhead, bagster, channel swimmer, coke friend, cokehead, cokey, cubehead, dip, doper, dopester, dreamer, druggie, drughead, feeblo, fiend, flier, freak, glassy-eye, goof, gowhead, grasshopper, hashhead, head, hog, hophead, hop merchant, hype-shooter, jabber, junker, junkhound, junk man, liner, mainliner, meth, freak, narco, needle fiend, needle-pusher, needle-rusher, pillhead, pill-popper, pinhead, pin-jabber, pothead, reefer, sleighrider, smack freak, smackhead, smecker, snowbird, space cadet, speedball, student, unkjay, vein-shooter, weed-eater, weedhead, zone.

just another pretty face, *n.* Someone of no particular achievement, a so-so person. ["Will you start taking me seriously? What do think I am, just another pretty face?"]

J.W., *n.* A flirtatious, sex-seeking young man. [Abbreviation of *junior wolf.*]

kakistocrat, *n.* A participant in kakistocracy. [From *kakistocracy* = government by the worst people.]

kaput *adj.* Dead, finished, done, washed-up. ["You're kaput. Pack up and get out."]

kedgebelly, *n.* A glutton, a fat-bellied person.

keek, *n.* A voyeur.

kelt or **keltch,** *n.* (1) A white person. (2) A light-skinned black person who passes as white. ["Then he met a high-yellah gal, a three-quarter belt from down Harlem way." Chester Himes, *Black on Black* (1973).]

Ken, *n.* A conformist. [From the male doll partner of the Barbie doll.]

keptie, *n.* A mistress. ["A mistress is someone between a master and a mattress."]

kern, *n.* A rude peasant.

key-swinger, *n.* A boaster.

khazerei, *n.* Odious and useless matter, crap, shit. [From the Yiddish word that means pig food.]

kibitzer, *n.* A giver of unwanted advice, a backseat driver. ["Keep your eyes closed to the kibitzers or wiseguys." Jack Dempsey, *Championship Fighting* (1950).] *Syn.:* buttinsky, meddler, nosey Parker, Paul Pry, snoop, yenta.

kick ass., *idiom.* To punish, to assert authority. *Idioms:* climb one's frame, crack down on, give hell, jump all over, kick ass and take numbers, kick booty, lower the boom, put the wood to, settle one's hash, skin alive.

kicking can, *idiom.* A regular target or victim. *Syn.:* whipping boy.

kick freak, *n.* A nonaddicted drug user.

kick in the ass, *idiom.* A surprising and upsetting setback or rebuff, a slap in the face. ["What you need is a swift kick in the ass."] *Syn.:* kick in the butt, kick in the pants, kick in the rear.

kick some ass (around), *idiom.* To raise hell, to show someone who's the boss.

kicksy-wicksy, *n.* A woman.

kid-simple, *adj.* A pederast who prefers young boys.

kid-stretcher, *n.* A lecher who likes young prostitutes.

kike, *n.* A Jewish man or woman. [From the Yiddish *kikel* = *circle,* the symbol that was used by Jewish immigrants when they entered the country in place of a cross (*X*) for their signature. "N.Y. is to me a scream—a kyke's dream of ghetto. The lost tribe has taken the island"—Theodore Dreiser, letter to H.L. Mencken (1922).] *Syn.:* clipped dick, eagle-beak, Goldberg, hebe, hooknose, Ike, Ikey, mockie, sheeny, Yid, zip top.

kiki, *adj.* Bisexual.

kinabra, *n.* A person who smells to high heaven. [From the Greek word for the stink of a goat.]

king grod, *n.* A very offensive man.

king of clubs, *n.* A woman-chaser, a womanizer. [From *club* = penis.]

kingshit nigger, *n.* A successful black, especially one in authority.

kink or **kinko,** *n.* (1) A person with bizarre sexual tastes. ["Porno photos, various drugs and birds for kinkies at Oxford." A. Diment, *Dolly Dolly Spy* (1967).] (2) A black person. *Syn.:* burrhead, kinkyhead, kinkynob, nap, nappy, nappyhead, woolyhead.

kinky, *adj.* Preferring deviant or perverse behavior. ["And you should have said last night he was 'that kind' ... funny, kinky"—Bogarde, *Voices in the Garden* (1981).] *Syn.:* aberrant, abnormal, bent, bizarre, flaky, freaky, funky, funny, oddball, offbeat, perverted, queer, rat fuck, strangioso, twisted, weird.

kipper, *n.* An English person. [From the name of one of the staple foods of England.]

kissass or **kissbutt,** *n.* (1) One who tries to impress by being obsequious. (2) Flattery or nonsense.

kiss my ass, *interj.* Go fuck yourself! *Syn.:* kiss my tail, kiss my tuna.

kiss-off, *n.* A rude dismissal. *Syn.:* brush off, royal kiss-off, California kiss-off, New York kiss-off.

kiss your ass goodbye, *idiom.* You're going to get it in the neck!

kiss one's ass, *idiom.* To kowtow, to be obsequious.

kitchen-cleaner, *n.* One who does anilingus.

kitschy, *adj.* Having pretentious bad taste, especially in the arts. ["He was a kitschy culture vulture who knew absolutely nothing about art."]

kleptocrat, *n.* A participant in kleptocracy. [From *kleptocracy* = government by thieves.]

klooch, *n.* A woman.

klutz, *n.* A stupid-acting, clumsy, bungling person. ["As the incidents repeated themselves, Ms. Reagan told her fellow workers and friends that she was a 'klutz' who kept banging into doors and falling down stairs"—*Guardian* (1989).]

knave, *n.* A scoundrel, villain, blackguard. ["Abhor a knave and pity a fool in your heart, but let neither of them unnecessarily see that you do so"—Lord Chesterfield.]

knee-bender, *n.* A religious churchgoer or self-righteous person.

knee-deep in shit, *idiom.* In very bad trouble.

knobber, *n.* A male transvestite hustler.

knock, *n.* An easily available young woman.

knock one's block off, *idiom*. To hit someone very hard, to clobber. *Idioms:* knock one for a row of ashcans, knock one into the middle of next week, knock the shit out of someone.

knocker, *n*. (Pronounced "nock-er.") (1) A carping critic, a detractor (2) A womanizer.

knocker, *n*. (Pronounced "knah-ker.") A self-important person, a big shot, a macher. ["He's a big knocker in the movie business."]

know from nothing, *idiom*. To be extremely ignorant. ["Just be quiet! You know from nothing about this."]

know shit, you don't, *idiom*. You're all wet!

know what one can do with something, *idiom*. Take your idea and shove it! *Idiom:* know where one can stick it or shove it.

knuff, *n*. A person who is boorish.

kook, *n*. (1) An eccentric person, a screwball. (2) A person with extreme views, whether left or right.

kosher cutie, *n*. A Jewish woman.

kraut, *n*. A German. ["Maybe . . . he should have been in a war, Japs in trees, krauts in Tiger tanks." Tipynchon, *Crying of Lot 49*, 1966.] *Syn.:* Boche, cabbagehead, Dutchie, Dutchman, Fritz, Fritzie, Heinie, Hun, Jerry, krauthead, squarehead.

Ku Kluxer, *n*. A believer in white supremacy. [From the racist white supremacist organization, the Ku Klux Klan.]

kurva, *n*. A promiscuous woman, or a prostitute.

kvetch, *n*. A constant complainer or whiner.

kweefer, *n*. A slovenly, unkempt woman [From *queff* = a vaginal fart.]

lackey, *n.* A servile subordinate. ["In those days the Kremlin called him a lackey for the imperialists."] *Syn.*: flunky, stooge, toady, minion.

lacy, *adj.* Effeminate, gay.

la-di-da, *adj.* (1) Stuck-up, arrogant. (2) Effeminate, sissified, superrefined.

lad-lass, *n.* An effeminate man or gay man.

lady-bird, *n.* A lewd woman.

lady-dog, *n.* A shrew. [A polite term for *bitch.*]

lady-killer, *n.* A wolf or a dandy. ["He thinks he is a real lady-killer."]

lady-lover, *n.* A female homosexual.

laid, relaid, and parlayed, *adj.* Badly cheated, completely screwed. ["They took me for everything I had. I was laid, relaid, and parlayed."] *Syn.*: screwed, blued, and tattooed.

lamb, *n.* An easy victim, a patsy, a sucker.

lame, *n.* A conventional person. ["Essentially the lame—whether a 'wannabe' or a 'never was'—is out of step with his or her peers"—Edith Folb, in *Runnin' Down Some Lines* (1980).] *Syn.*: square, straight, laine, lane.

lame, *adj.* Stupid, socially inept, halfhearted, lamebrained. ["If your children found out how lame you really are, they'd kill you in your sleep"—Frank Zappa.]

lapdog, *n.* Someone with a fierce bark and no bite.

lapper, *n.* A performer of oral sex.

lardbag, *n.* A very overweight, lazy person. ["... brutish, dumpy, boorish lardbags in cardboard double-breasted suits"—P. J. O'Rourke, *National Lampoon* (1976).] *Syn.*: lardball, lardass, lardbucket, lardo, tub of lard.

latrine lawyer, *n.* An amateur lawyer, an argumentative soldier or other spokesperson who has mastered rules and regulations to some degree. *Syn.*: barracks room lawyer, clubhouse lawyer, forecastle lawyer, guardhouse lawyer, jailhouse lawyer, sea lawyer.

latrine lips, *n.* A user of dirty language.

laughingstock, *n.* An object of ridicule. ["He was the laughingstock of the entire platoon."] *Syn.*: butt, jest, joke, mock, pilgarlic, sport, target, goat.

lay, *n.* A woman as a sexual target or conquest. *Syn.*: baloney, band, bed-bunny, biffa, bike, bimbo, bummerkeh, cake, cuddle-bunny, dirtyleg, easy meat, easy rider, flapper, free-for-all, gash, goober-grabber, graduate, groupie, highflyer, hot pants, hot stuff, hot tomato, hump, jazz baby, mutton, openass, pig, playgirl, poke, pushover, quiff, roundheels, scupper, sleaze, slotted job, snatch, split-tail, trollop, town punch, tube, wanton, yes-girl.

lay it on, *idiom.* To exaggerate, to bullshit.

lazybones, *n.* A lazy person.

lean on (one), *idiom.* To ridicule or pressure.

lease piece, *n.* A hooker. *Syn.*: vent-renter, meat vendor, peddlesnatch.

leather, *n.* A sadistic gay male.

lecher, *n.* A lewd man who chases after women. *Syn.*: alley cat, animal, bed-presser, belly-bumper, bird's nester, bum-fiddler, Casanova, chimney sweep, chippy-chaser, cock-hound, cocksman, Corinthian, D.O.M., crotchhound, Don Juan, fishmonger, fleece-hunter, fox-hunter, fuckster, gap-stopper, gashhound, goat, hairmonger, horseman, hot nuts, hot pants, kid-stretcher, lech, letch, leg-lifter, make-out artist, meathound, parish bull, peach-orchard boar, pinch-ass, pinch-bottom, pinch-buttock, pinch-cunt, quail-hunter, quim-sticker, rider, rooster, rump-splitter, smell-smock, stallion, stud, swinger, tomcat, town bull, town stallion, tummy-tickler, twat-faker, wencher, whisker-splitter, whorehopper, whorehound, wolf, woodman, yentzer.

leech, *n.* A clinging, exploitative deadbeat. ["Every time I went to lunch at Sardi's the leech was never far behind."] *Syn.:* sponge, parasite, mooch.

left-handed, *adj.* Homosexual.

left-handed wife, *n.* A common-law wife.

lefty or leftie, *n.* A radical. ["Leftwingers are incapable of conspiring because they are all egomaniacs"—Norman Mailer.]

leg, *n.* (1) A woman deemed a sexual target. (2) A promiscuous woman, or a prostitute.

lemon-sucker, *n.* An Englishman. *Syn.:* lemon-eater, limey, lime-juicer.

leper, *n.* An outcast.

les or lez, *n.* A lesbian. ["She would not screw. I often wondered if she was a closet lez"—Sanders, *The Tangent Objective* (1977).] *Syn.:* Amy-John, B.D., bluff, boondagger, bull, bulldagger, bull dike, bulldiker, butch, diesel dyke, dike, duff, fairy, fairy lady, fem, fluff, fluzz dyke, gal-boy, jasper, lady-lover, lesbine, lesbo, leso, lezbo, lesbyterian, leslie, lezo, lover under the lap, man, marge, mary, mason, mintie, queen, ruffle, sapphic love, screaming queen, sergeant, sucker, third-sexer, top sergeant.

lewd, *adj.* Preoccupied with sex, obscene. ["Certain lewd fellows of the baser sort"—Acts 17:5] *Syn.:* lascivious, bestial, bucksome, crackish, dissolute, fescennine, free-fucking, goatish, lenocinant, libidinous, perve, radgy, ribald, tentiginous, unchaste, x-rated.

L.F., *n.* A poor sexual performer. [From the abbreviation for *lousy fuck*.]

libber, *n.* A member of a liberation movement, especially the women's lib movement. [In English dialect, *libber* = a castrator of pigs.]

liberal, *n.* A believer in gradual reform, individual liberty, and a government role to aid the helpless and poor. ["A liberal is someone who leaves the room when the fight begins"—Heywood Broun.]

libertine, *adj.* Dissolute, not bound by traditional morality. ["By merely living together a couple is practicing libertine love—and the mere repetition doesn't, in some mysterious way, make it legal"—Stone.]

libidinous, *adj.* Lustful, lewd. ["A lewd youth . . . advances by degrees into a libidinous old man"—Joseph Addison.]

licentious, *adj.* Sexually and morally uninhibited. [". . . an irreligious and licentious age had abetted depravity"—Ellen Glasgow.] *Syn.:* fast, lascivious, lecherous, lewd, libertine, libidinous, lustful, randy, salacious, satyric, profligate, dissolute.

lick-box or **lick-twat,** *n.* A person who carries out oral sex with a woman.

lick me, *imper.* Shut up! You make me sick! Kiss my ass! Fuck you! *Idiom:* Lick my love pump!

lick-penny, *n.* A greedy person.

lick-spigot, *n.* (1) A vicious parasite. (2) A fellator or fellatrice, a mouth-whore.

lick-spittle, *n.* An extreme sycophant. *Syn.:* lick-spit, lick-dish.

lift-skirts, *n.* A promiscuous woman.

lightfoot, *n.* A minor or untrustworthy person.

light-footed, *adj.* Homosexual.

light-heeled, *adj.* Wanton.

lightheels, *n.* A streetwalker. *Syn.:* gutter-flopper, puddletrotter, shortheels.

lightweight, *n.* An unimportant person. ["There's no point of inviting him to the meeting. He's a lightweight who can add nothing."] *Syn.:* busher, bush-leaguer, dud, eightball, featherweight, half-pint, limp-dick, little shot, loser, nebbish, nobody, nonentity, nonstarter, peanut, pipsqueak, pissant, poor fish, punk, sad sack, schlemazel, second-stringer, slob, small potatoes, small-timer, third-rater, tinhorn. *Idioms:* man with a paper ass, no prize package.

like a bump on a log, *idiom.* Uselessly, helplessly.

like a wooden Indian, *idiom.* Stolidly, silently.

like death warmed over, *idiom.* To look horrible, deathlike. ["You look like death warmed over."]

like fuck, *interj.* Exclamation of disbelief. *Idioms:* like hell, the hell you say, in a pig's ass, like fun, like shit.

like it or lump it, *idiom.* Take what we give you and don't protest.

lily, *n.* (1) A white person. (2) An effeminate or gay man.

lily-liver, *n.* A coward.

limberger, *n.* A German.

limousine liberal, *n.* A wealthy liberal.

limp-dick or **limp-noodle,** *n.* An impotent man. [From *dick* = penis.]

limp dishrag or **dishrag,** *idiom.* An ineffectual or spiritless person.

limping Jesus, *n.* A lame person.

limp wrist, *idiom.* A gay man or a person with latent homosexual tendencies.

line one's pockets, *idiom.* To make money in a venal or crooked fashion.

lip, *n.* (1) Impertinent retorts. ["Don't give me any of your lip!"] (2) An attorney. ["I'm going to get a good lip before going before the grand jury."]

lip-mover, *n.* A dull, stupid person.

lippie chaser, *n.* A black man who seeks out white women.

lippy, *adj.* Insolent or talkative.

lisper or **lithper,** *n.* An effeminate male.

Lit, *n.* A Lithuanian.

little Eva, *n.* A loudmouthed white girl.

little lady, *n.* A gay man.

little mama, *n.* An attractive black girl.

little Miss Roundheels, *n.* A promiscuous woman.

little shit, *n.* A stupid, unimportant person.

the little woman, *n.* One's wife. ["I'd love to play poker with you guys, if only I could get away from the little woman."] *Syn.*: ball-and-chain, missus, the Mrs., old lady, old woman, rib, squaw.

little yellow bastard or **little yellow man,** *idiom.* A Japanese person or other Asian.

Litvak, *n.* A Lithuanian.

Liza, *n.* A young black woman.

lizzie or **lizzie-boy,** *n.* An effeminate man.

loaded, *adj.* Very rich, affluent. *Syn.*: bloated, dirty, fat filthy, lousy rich, nigger rich, oofy, six feet up a bull's ass, stinking rich.

loaf, *n.* A fat person.

loan shark, *n.* A usurer. ["There are 350 varieties of shark, not counting loan and pool"—L. M. Boyd.] *Syn.*: juice dealer, shy, shylock.

local yokel, *n.* A small town or rural resident.

lock assholes or **tangle assholes,** *v.* To fight. ["If you keep running off at the mouth, we're going to lock assholes."]

loco or **plumb loco,** *adj.* Crazy, nuts.

L.O.L, *n.* A prudish person. [Acronym for *l*ittle *o*ld *l*ady.]

lollapalooza, *n.* A whopping lie.

lollygag, *v.* To do nothing, to fuck off.

long drink of water, *idiom.* A tall, thin person.

longhair, *n.* (1) A highbrow, an egghead. (2) A hippie or beatnik.

long in the tooth, *idiom.* Aged, old.

loogan, *n.* (1) An incompetent person. (2) A goon, a hood, a thug.

look like a drowned rat, *idiom*. To look like hell. *Syn*.: look like something the cat dragged in.

look like ten pounds of shit in a five-pound bag, *idiom*. To be sloppily dressed, to look lousy, or to be obese.

look who's talking, *interj*. You're just as guilty! You're just as much at fault!

loon, *n*. A demented person. ["The devil damn thee black thou cream-faced loon"—William Shakespeare, *Macbeth*.] *Syn*.: loony-tune, loony-tunes, crazy as a loon.

loop, *n*. A fool, an eccentric.

loose cannon, *n*. An extremely irresponsible, unpredictable, harmful person. ["Mr. Wallach was a loose cannon, which is why Mr. Meese should have watched him closely"—*New York Times* (1988).]

loose in the beam, *idiom*. Nutty. *Syn*.: loose in the upper story.

loose in the rump, *idiom*. Wanton. *Syn*.: loose-bodied, loose-ended, loose-legged.

lord muck, *n*. A snobbish, contemptuous person.

lose one's gourd, *idiom*. To lose one's mind, to go crazy, go ape, freak out.

lose all one's marbles, *v*. To become crazy.

losenger, *n*. A flatterer or liar.

lose one's wig, *idiom*. To lose one's mind.

loser, *n*. An incompetent person. ["Show me a good and gracious loser and I'll show you a failure"—Knute Rockne.] *Syn*.: bust, dud, lemon, born loser, also-ran, clinker, dog, eightball, foul ball, never-was, nonstarter, poor slob, sad sack, schlemiel, schmendrick, schmo, schnook, slob, turkey, wipeout.

lose your cool, *idiom*. Lose your control.

Lothario, *n*. A womanizer. ["Is this that Haughty, Gallant, Gay Lothario?"—Nicholas Rowe, *The Fair Penitent* (1703).] *Syn*.: ladies' man, Casanova, lover-boy, stud.

louse up, *idiom.* To fail, or to ruin something. *Syn.:* botch, bollix up, screw up.

lout, *n.* A clumsy or stupid man. *Syn.:* bumpkin, galoot.

lovely, *n.* an attractive woman.

lover under the lap, *idiom.* A lesbian.

lowbrow, *n.* A uneducated, uncultured person.

low-down, *adj.* Dishonest, vile. ["No one thought he could be low-down enough to steal a nickel from a blind beggar's cup."]

low-downer, *n.* A poor white.

lower than spots on a snake's ass, *idiom.* Immoral. *Idioms:* so low he can kiss a tumblebug's gillie winkle without bending his knees, can look up a snake's ass and think it is the North Star, lower than whaleshit—and that's at the bottom of the ocean.

lowgap or **flapgap,** *n.* A promiscuous woman.

low rent, *n.* An easy woman.

low-res or **lo-res,** *adj.* weak or unpleasant. [From *low resolution* in a cathode tube computer terminal.]

lug or **lughead,** *n.* A big, clumsy, dumb man.

lugan, *n.* A Lithuanian.

lump, *n.* A stolid, stupid man.

lunatic fringe, *n.* Extremist members of any social or political movement. ["The foolish fanatics always to be found in such a movement and always discrediting it—the men who form the lunatic fringe in all reform movements" —Theodore Roosevelt, *Autobiography* (1913).]

lunchbox, *n.* A simpleton.

lunchy, *adj.* Dull, absentminded, unfashionable [From *out to lunch.*]

lunger, *n.* A despicable, dirty person. [From *lunger* = a gob of mucus.]

lunk or **lunkhead,** *n.* A curmudgeon, or a fool.

lush, *n.* A heavy drinker, an inebriate. *Syn.*: bar fly, booze-fighter, boozehound, boozer, bottle man, dipso, tippler, bibber, drunk, elbow-bender, ginhound, guzzler, hooch-hound, juicehead, lusher, rumhound, rummy, shikker, soak, sot, souse, sponge, stewbum, wino.

lustful, *adj.* Excited, most often sexually. ["She took the greatest care of his health and comfort, and was faithful to him, not being naturally lustful except of power" —Robert Graves.]

 macaroni, *n.* (1) An Italian. ["Cut the throats of the macaronis," Madame Absalom said. She disliked Italians slightly more than the rest of the human race"—E. Paul, *Narrow Street* (1942).] (2) An affected dandy.

mac, *n.* (1) A pimp. [Short for *mackerel.*] (2) An Irish person.

macho, *n.* An aggressively masculine man. ["Macho is not mucho"—Zsa Zsa Gabor.]

mackerel-snapper, *n.* A Roman Catholic. [From the allusion to eating fish on Friday.]

mad as a wet hen, *idiom.* Extremely angry, infuriated, pissed off. *Syn.*: mad as a cut snake.

madbrain, *n.* A hothead.

mad dog, *n.* A mentally imbalanced wild man, a killer.

mafioso, *n.* A member of a small, powerful, highly organized clique of insiders in a large corporation or organizations. [From *mafia* = the organized crime institution. "He said 'Mafia' in the loose but not ubiquitous sense of black marketeering, a way of life swooping across the city (Moscow) like a vulturous harbinger of the long-awaited free market"—*New York Times* (1991).]

maggot, *n.* (1) A vile person who feeds off others. (2) A white person.

maggot-brained, *adj.* Idiotic. [From the idea of what occurs when maggots get into one's brain.]

magoozlum, *n.* Kitsch, rubbish, trash. [From the movie use of *magoo,* meaning the gooey stuff in custard pies.]

mahogany, *n.* A light-skinned black.

main saw on the hitch, *n.* One's wife. [—M. Mezzerow, *Really the Blues* (1946).]

main squeeze, *n.* One's wife or girlfriend.

make, *n.* A person regarded merely as a sex partner.

make hamburger out of, *idiom.* To clobber or trounce someone. *Idioms:* make mincemeat out of, make hash out of.

make my day, *idiom.* Go ahead and do it and your ass belongs to me!

make-out artist, *n.* A successful woman-chaser.

malapert, *adj.* Insolent, impudent.

malarkey, *n.* Glib, bombastic talk; nonsense; bullshit. *Syn.:* marmalade.

male chauvinist pig or **MCP,** *n.* A man who believes in the superiority of men over women. ["He'd ordered a Heineken from a waitress who was a real throwback, an MCP's delight"—Cyra McFadden, *The Serial.*] *Syn.:* sexist porker, pig.

mall crawler, *n.* An empty-headed teenager whose principal purpose in life is shopping.

malodorous, *adj.* Having a foul odor. *Syn.:* fetid, funky, fusty, gamy, mephitic, musty, nidorous, noisome, olid, putrid, rancid, reeking, smelly, stale, stenchful, stinking, stinky, whiffy.

mama, *n.* (1) A woman, especially if sexually attractive or available. (2) A lesbian who takes the passive role. (3) One's wife or girlfriend. ["I says I'm beggin' you, mama/ Yeah mama, why don't you quit your ways?"—"Baby, Quit Your Lowdown Ways," blues song.]

mama's boy, *n.* An effeminate boy or man. ["He was a mama's boy, and if you don't know the kind of trouble mama's boy tourists go looking for when they're loose on the shores of the Mediterranean, you just haven't travelled." M. Stein, *Executioner's Rest* (1967).] *Syn.*: mammy's boy, maama's boyu (Caribbean usage.)

man, *n.* A lesbian who takes the masculine role.

man, the, *n.* Any white viewed as being in a position of authority over blacks. *Idiom:* working on the plantation.

maneater, *n.* (1) A person who performs fellatio. (2) A woman actively hunting for a husband.

mantanblack, *n.* A black who acts like an Uncle Tom.

man with a paper ass, *idiom.* A person who is all talk and no action.

man with the fuzzy balls, *idiom.* A white man.

marble-dome, *n.* A stupid person. [From the allusion to one's head as hard as stone.]

marblehead, *n.* A Greek person. [Allusion to ancient Greek sculpture.]

mare, *n.* A woman or a wife. [Allusion to *ride* = copulation.]

maricon, *n.* A gay male. [Spanish usage.]

marshmallow, *n.* (1) A white person. (2) A weak, useless person.

Mary, *n.* (1) A gay man who takes the feminine role (2) A lesbian. (3) An aborigine woman. [Common in the Pidgin language of the Pacific.]

masher, *n.* A man who makes repeated sexual approaches to women, a wolf.

mason, *n.* (1) A pederast. (2) A lesbian who takes the masculine role. [Both definitions refer to the one who does the "laying."]

mat, *n.* A woman, or one's wife.

mattoid, *n.* A partly mad man.

mau mau, *n.* A black militant. [Allusion to the military resistance movement against the British in Kenya in the 1950s.]

McCarthyite, *n.* One who impugns another's political integrity or loyalty by unfair, malicious allegations in order to squelch opposition. [After Joseph R. McCarthy, U.S. Senator in the late 1940s and early 1950s. "Ideological sins have lost their bite, but there's a growing fear of moral McCarthyism"—*Newsweek* (1989).]

meacock, *n.* An effeminate man.

meadow dressing, *n.* Euphemism for bullshit, cow slop.

meally-mouth, *n.* One who speaks with a forked tongue.

mean white, *n.* A poor, low-class white person. [Probably from *menial white.*]

meat, *n.* A person of either sex considered as a sex object. ["One man's meat is another man's poison"—Oswald Dykes, *English Proverbs* (1709).]

meatball, *n.* A foolish, obnoxious, distasteful person.

meat-cooker, *n.* A promiscuous woman. [From *meat* = penis.] *Syn.*: meat-grinder, pipe-cleaner, sausage-grinder, prickpocket, stump-thumper.

meat-eater, *n.* A corrupt policeman who aggressively solicits bribes.

meat-flasher, *n.* (1) A man who exposes his penis in public. (2) A woman who displays her body to entice men.

meathead or **beefhead,** *n.* One who has meat where he should have brains. ["But I have a feeling that a bunch of Born-again Assholes and scataphagous Moron Minority Meatheads will curse me for studying the cursing in the Bible"—Reinhold Aman, *Maledicta V.*]

meathound or **meatmonger,** *n.* A person always seeking sexual partners.

mediocrity, *n.* A person of so-so ability. ["Some men are born mediocre, some men achieve mediocrity, and some men have mediocrity thrust upon them" Joseph Heller.]

megadork, *n.* A very, very stupid person. [From *mega* = extremely huge; thus *huge* + *dork* = penis.]

megillah, *n.* A long, involved explanation or excuse.

melonbelly or **melon,** *n.* A person with a potbelly.

melted butter, *n.* An attractive woman viewed as a sexual object.

Melvin, *n.* A dull, unattractive person; a nerd; a dweeb.

mendaciloquencer, *n.* A person who has developed lying into a fine art.

mental or **mental midget,** *n.* A person who is mentally below par.

mental job, *idiom.* A neurotic person.

merdivorous, *adj.* Feces-eating.

Merkin, *n.* A nerd, a dork, a dweeb. [From Merkin Miffley, a character played by Peter Sellers in Stanley Kubrick's movie *Dr. Strangelove* (1964); Lyndon B. Johnson often addressed the American people as "My fellow 'merkins." In the 17th and 18th centuries a merkin was a pubic wig.]

meshuggna, *n.* A person who is obsessed, weird, insane; a nut.

mess, *n.* A hopeless, mixed-up person. ["You're a complete mess. Why don't you start by cleaning up the mess inside?"]

mess someone around, *idiom.* To exploit or maltreat.

metalmouth, *n.* A person with braces on his or her teeth.

methhead or **meth freak,** *n.* A habitual user of methamphetamine.

Mex, *n.* A Mexican, a Mexican-American, a Chicano. *Syn.*: bracero, bravo, brown, dino, greaseball, greasegut, greaser, hombre, Mexicano, Mexie, never-sweat, oiler, paisano, peon, pepper, shuck, spic, spig, sun-grinner, wetback.

M.F., *n.* A person who is extremely rotten. [Abbreviation of *motherfucker*.] *Syn.*: Marilyn Farmer, Mister Franklin

mick, *n.* (1) An Irish person. ["Fortunately it was a Mick regiment, so we needn't worry over who was killed." P. L. Ford, *Hon. Peter Sterling* (1894).] *Syn.*: bog-hopper, bog-trotter, harp, mickey, Mike, Mulligan, Paddy. (2) A Roman Catholic (not necessarily of Irish descent). "[Religious rivalries from Salvationists to Plymouth Brethren—united in hatred of the 'Mickeys' or Catholics." *Times* (1960).] *Syn.*: Mickey (3) A citizen of Mexico.

mickey-fickey, *n.* A motherfucker. [Korean-American usage in Spike Lee's movie *Do the Right Thing*.]

mickey mouse, *adj.* Sentimental, insincere, inane, mindless, shoddy, inferior, lousy, worthless.

micrologist, *n.* A nitpicking person who pays excessive attention to minor differences.

middlebrow, *n.* A person of so-so taste. *Syn.*: vanilla, white bread.

midnight or **midnight the cat,** *n.* A very dark-complexioned black person. [From the blackness of midnight.]

midnight cowboy, *n.* A gay male hustler.

milker or **milkman,** *n.* A masturbator. [From *milk* = semen.]

milksop, *n.* A weak, effeminate male, a jellyfish. ["... don't girls like a rake better than a milksop?"—William M Thackeray, *Vanity Fair*.]

milkwoman, *n.* A woman who masturbates men.

miller, *n.* A woman-chaser. [Allusion to *grind* = copulate.]

mince, *n.* (1) A boring person, a drip. (2) A gay man.

mincy, *adj.* Dainty, finicky, fussy, squeamish.

mindfuck(er), *n.* A manipulative person who disorients another's thinking.

mind-fuck, *v.* To deceive or to mess with someone's mind.

minge bag, *n.* An extremely unpleasant woman. [From *minge* = vagina.]

mingy, *adj.* Tight-fisted, miserly, mean. [Blend of *mean* = stingy.] ["I called you a mingy and coprologous oxford poetaster." Rupert Brooke, *Letter* (1912).]

minion, *n.* A subordinate or a stooge.

mink, *n.* An attractive, sexy young woman, often considered to be promiscuous. ["She screws like a mink."]

minor-league, *adj.* Dinky, small-fry, small-time.

mintie or **minty,** *n.* (1) A homosexual man. (2) A masculine lesbian.

minx, *n.* A flirtatious girl or woman. ["Damn her, lewd minx, O damn her, damn her"—William Shakespeare, *Hamlet.*] *Syn.:* hussy, jade, malapert, saucebox, slut, snip.

misandrist, *n.* A man-hater. ["Should not be confused with misanthropy, a hatred of men and women, and misogyny, women hating, a widely accepted social attitude in a sexist world"—*A Feminist Dictionary* (1985).]

misanthrope, *n.* One who hates both men and women. ["I love mankind, it's people I can't stand"—Charles M. Schulz, *Go Fly a Kite, Charlie Brown.*]

miscreant, *n.* A rascal.

mishmash or **mishmosh,** *n.* A confused mixture.

misogynist, *n.* A hater of women. ["Includes the beliefs that women are stupid, petty, manipulative, dishonest, silly, gossipy, irrational, incompetent, undependable, narcissistic, castrating, dirty, overemotional, unable to make altruistic or moral judgments, oversexed, undersexed . . ."—Sheila Roth, in *A Feminist Dictionary* (1985).]

misologist, *n.* A person who hates reasonable or logical discussion.

missionary man, *n.* A man who is a boring sexual partner. [Allusion to the missionary or poppa/momma position in coition.]

Miss Ann, *n.* A white woman. ["Those were the fine houses of Mr. Charlie and Miss Ann . . ." Darryl Pinckney, *High Cotton* (1992).] *Syn.:* Miss Amy, Miss Lillian.

Miss Nancy, *n.* An effeminate man, or a gay man.

Mister Tom, *n.* A middle-class black man who has been assimilated into the white middle-class culture.

mitt man, *n.* A religious impostor.

mo, *n.* A homosexual man. [Short for *homo*.]

mockie or **mockey,** *n.* A Jewish person. ["Love thy neighbor if he's not . . . a mockie or a slicked–up greaseball from the Argentine." Ira Wolfert, *Tucker's People* (1943).]

moke, *n.* (1) A black person. *Syn.:* blue-gum moke, fem-moke. (2) A Filipino.

moldy fig, *n.* A prude, an old-fashioned person, a square.

mollycoddle, *n.* A pampered weakling or an effeminate male. ["Look here, mother dear; I'm as well as ever I was, and I'm not going to be mollycoddled anymore"—Braddon.]

mollyfock, *n.* A motherfucker.

momist, *n.* One who blames all his misfortunes on his mother's role in his upbringing. ["Everything is all Mom's fault with her domineering unfeminine ways"—Marlene Dixon and Joreen, in *A Feminist Dictionary* (1985).]

mo-mo, *n.* A moron.

momser or **momzer,** *n.* A devious, untrustworthy person. [Literally, a bastard in Yiddish.]

moneybags, *n.* A filthy-rich person. ["The wealthy curled darlings of our nation"—Shakespeare, *Othello*.] *Syn.:* bloated plute, Daddy Warbucks, deeppockets, fat cat, lord of creation, Mister Moneybags, plute.

money grubber, *n.* A stingy person, a miser.

monk, *n.* A Chinese person.

monkey, *n.* (1) A white person. (2) A black person.

monkey-chaser, *n.* A black person from the West Indies.

monkey-fart, *v.* To waste time, to goof off. *Syn.:* fiddle-fart, monkey around.

monkey-Jesus, *n.* An ugly person. [Caribbean usage.]

moo, *n.* A silly woman. [From *moo* = a cow.]

mooch or **moocher,** *n.* A parasitical borrower living off other people. *Syn.:* bum, bummer, cadger, deadbeat, deadhead, freeloader, drone, panhandler, schnorrer, scrounger, spiv (British usage), sponge.

mooncalf, *n.* A daydreamer, or a foolish person. *Syn.:* moon-head, moonling, moonraker.

mooner, *n.* An eccentric person who is hyperactive during the full moon. [From the folklore that the full moon brings out the crazies.]

moose, *n.* A Japanese girlfriend or woman. [From the Japanese *musume* = girl. Brought into English during the American occupation of Japan after World War II.]

mopsy, *n.* A unkempt young woman.

more pricks than a secondhand dart board, to have, *idiom.* To be promiscuous.

Mormon, *n.* A womanizer, a whoremonger, a lecher. [From the former practice of polygamy by the Mormons in the 19th century.] ["Because a few of the inmates of the Hollywood film colony have 'married from time to time,' they are less to be censured as Mormons than pitied as morons." *Literary Digest* (1922).]

moron, *n.* A stupid person. ["It is possible that while we are governed by high-grade 'morons' there will be no practical recognition of the dangers which threaten us." W.R. Inge in *Edinburgh Review* (1922).]

morphadite, *n.* A person who has both male and female sex organs. *Syn.* ambosexous, androgyne, bisexual, epicene, gynandrous, transie, John-and-Joan, morf, morpho, panatrope, scrate, will-jill.

mose, *n.* A black man.

moshky, *n.* A user of marijuana. *Syn.:* motter, M. U., mugglehead, muggles.

moss or **mosshead,** *n.* A black person. [Allusion to hair texture.]

mossback, *n.* An extremely conservative person. [From the word for a turtle that has been submerged so long that moss is growing on its back.] *Syn.:* fogy, old square, stick-in-the-mud, stuffed shirt, back number.

mother, *n.* (1) An effeminate or homosexual male. (2) The mentor of younger homosexuals. (3) A despicable person. [Short for *motherfucker.*]

mother, your, *interj.* An insulting, derogatory curse.

motherfucker, *n.* A despicable person. [Hardly ever taken literally. "Oedipus was a motherfucker"—English graffito.] *Syn.:* ma'fa, ma, motha, mother, M.F., mother-dangler, mother-eater, motheree, motherferyer, mother-flunker, mother-fouler, mother-grabber, mother-hugger, mother-humper, mother-hugger, mother-jiver, mother-jumper, mother-kisser, mother-lover, mother-nudger, mother-rammer, mother-raper, mother-rucker, mother superior, mother-sucker, mother-ugly, motorscooter, muthafucka, mutheree, mutherfucker, granny-jazzer, momma-hopper, poppa-lopper. *Note: mama, mammy, momma,* or *muther* often replaces *mother.*

motherfucking, *adj.* Low, rotten, despicable, detestable, disgusting, nasty, accursed, god-damn. [Used as an intensifier. "I'll stick ma shank in your motherfuggin' heart just to watch yoh die"—Ray Johnson, "Walking East on 125th Street" (Spring 1959).] *Syn.:* mothering.

mother-ugly, *adj.* Extremely ugly.

motorcycle, *n.* A woman considered as an object of sex. [The implication is that both are to be ridden.] *Syn.:* bike, bicycle, motorbike, mount.

motormouth, *n.* An excessively talkative, indiscreet person.

mouse, *n.* One's wife or girlfriend. ["Tempt you again to bed; pinch wanton your cheek; call you his mouse"—William Shakespeare, *Hamlet.*]

mouser, *n.* A fellator. [From the allusion to nibbling as a mouse nibbles on cheese.]

mouth-breather, *n.* An idiot, a person who acts stupidly.

mouth whore, *n.* One who performs fellatio, a cannibal, a gobble-prick, a vacuum cleaner.

mouthy, *adj.* Boastful, cocky.

Mr. Cracker, *n.* A Southern white male. *Syn.:* Mr. Peanut.

Mr. Groin, *n.* A make-out artist, a cocksman. *Syn.:* Mr. Horner.

Mr. Money, *n.* A wealthy plutocrat. ["... nothing will last forever, not Mr. Money nor Mrs. Cunt, nobody and nothing. I find it healthy"—Thomas Berger, *Killing Time.*]

Mr. Thomas, *n.* A black person who has taken on white middle-class values.

Mrs. Grundy, *n.* A straitlaced, prudish, censorious, language purist. [From a character in Thomas Morton's play *Speed the Plough* (1798).]

muck-heap, *n.* A filthy, slovenly person. [From *muck* = dirt, mud, feces.] *Syn.:* muck-scutcheon, muck-suckle.

mucking, *adj.* Euphemism for fucking. ["I'll miss the silly little mucker ... Poor old Bob. Went down with his mucking duffle," *Penguin New Writing* (1942).]

muck something up, *idiom.* To mess something up, to ruin something.

muckworm, *n.* A miser, a skinflint.

mudcrusher, *n.* A tough bully.

mudkicker, *n.* A ho who walks the streets. ["She was a stomp down mudkicker"—"Pimping Sam," a well-known black toast.]

mudsnoot, *n.* A person who is disliked or despised.

muff, *n.* Woman viewed as a sexual object. [From *muff* = pubic hair.]

muff-diver, *n.* One who performs oral sex on a woman. *Syn.:* diver, clit-licker, skin-diver, pearl-diver.

mufugly, *adj.* Very ugly [From "motherfucking ugly."]

muhfuh, *n.* A motherfucker.

mulatto meat, *n.* A light-skinned black woman considered for sexual purposes.

mule, *n.* (1) A hard-headed, stupid person. *Syn.:* bitter-ender, bulldog, bullethead, bullhead, diehard, donkey, hammerhead, hardnose, hard nut to crack, pighead, stiff-neck. (2) An unattractive female. (3) A person who smuggles drugs, a burro. (4) A white male.

mullipuff, *n.* A twit.

mumbler, *n.* One who doesn't talk clearly. ["He mumbles so much, most of the time he sounds like he has a mouth full of wet toilet paper"—Rex Reed, referring to an actor.]

mumbo-jumbo, *n.* Meaningless nonsense. [From a voodoo fetish. "Mumbo-Jumbo will hoodoo you"—Vachel Lindsey, "The Congo" (1913).]

muncher or **muncher-boy,** *n.* A person who fellates men.

mundo-, *prefix.* Used for emphasis. [Hence, *mundo-bizarro* = very strange.]

mundungus, *n.* A vile-smelling person. [From the word for the stink of dung and odoriferous garbage, and later the stench of tobacco.]

mung, *n.* Filth or dirt of any kind. *Syn.:* crap, glop, grunch, grunge, muck, prut, scrunge, scunge, scuzz, scuzzo.

mungshit, *n.* A filthy, dirty, worthless person.

muscle moll, *n.* A masculine woman.

mush, *n.* Sickly sentimental, meaningless talk. ["Two-thirds mush and one-third Eleanor"—Alice Roosevelt Longworth about Franklin Delano Roosevelt.]

mushmouth, *n.* A person who talks indistinctly. ["Take the shit out of your mouth, mushmouth, I can't understand you!"]

mushroom-picker, *n.* A person of Czechoslovakian descent.

mustard, *n.* A Chinese person. [From the yellow color of mustard.]

mustard, can't cut the, *idiom.* To be impotent, or to be unable to perform a job satisfactorily.

mustard-pot, *n.* One who indulges in anal sex. [Allusion to the color of feces.]

mutant, *n.* An antisocial delinquent or criminal.

mutt, *n.* A homely woman, a dog.

mutton, *n.* Women considered as sexual objects.

mutton dressed as lamb, *idiom.* A middle-aged or elderly woman wearing clothes much too young for her. ["Youthful excess is one thing, but mutton dressed as lamb is another"—Sharpe, *Porterhouse Blue* (1974).] *Syn.:* baroness, countess, dutchess, old auntie, old queen, overripe fruit, elderberry, geriatrick.

muzzfucker, *n.* A motherfucker. ["So watch out for D.J. muzzfuckers"—Norman Mailer, *Why Are We in Vietnam?* (1967).]

muzzy, *adj.* Befuddled.

my ass, *interj.* An exclamation of strong disagreement. *Syn.:* in a pig's eye, my foot.

myxoid, *adj.* Snotty. [From the word for *mucus.*]

nabob, *n.* A self-important person. [". . . nattering nabobs of negativism." Spiro Agnew.] *Syn.:* nawob, pooh-bah.

naff off *interj.* Fuck off!

nag, *v.* To find fault incessantly ["Nagging is constructive criticism too frequently repeated"—Percy Cudlipp.] *Syn.:* carp at, fuss, henpeck, peck at.

nailhead, *n.* An unattractive female with short nappy hair.

namby-pamby, *adj.* Sentimental, insipid, wishy-washy, undecided. ["The hottest places in Hell are reserved for those who in time of great moral crises maintain their neutrality"—Dante Alighieri.]

nance, *n.* A passive male homosexual. *Syn.:* Nancy, nancy-boy, na-boy, tickle-my-fancy, willie-boy.

nap, *n.* A black person. [Allusion to kinky hair.] *Syn.:* nappy, nappy black.

narrowback, *n.* An Irish person who refuses to work. [From the idea that he was unfit for hard work because his back was narrow and not broad.]

nasal on that, *interj.* Forget that!

nasty, *adj.* Disgusting, filthy, smutty, indecent. [From *do the nasty* = to copulate. ". . . squandered all their virile energy on greasy slave girls and nasty Asiatic-Greek prostitutes"—Robert Graves.]

nationalist, *n.* A believer in the primary interests of one's nation, even at the expense of other nations. ["Born in iniquity and conceived in sin, the spirit of nationalism has never ceased to bend human institutions to the service of dissension and distress"—Thorstein Veblen.]

nause someone out, *idiom.* To nauseate

neanderthal, *n.* (1) A boorish, ugly man. (2) An old-fashioned, reactionary person. ["The neanderthal men of the military and industrial establishments." *Guardian* (1970).]

nebbish or **nebekh,** *n.* A dull, pitiful, awkward, hapless person. ["When a nebekh leaves the room, you feel as if someone came in."]

needle dick or **pencil dick,** *n.* A worthless male. [An allusion to small penis size.]

negress, *n.* A black woman. [A double insult: sexist *and* racist.]

negro, *n.* An Uncle Tom. ["... (they) often tangled with Dr. Harleston, accusing the President, who is black, of being a 'Negro apologist' ..."—*New York Times* (1992).]
Note: While black and African-American are terms of choice (in 1992) Negro was applied in much of the 19th and 20th centuries to people of African ancestry. In the past twenty years it has taken on a pejorative meaning to many.

nellie or **nelly,** *adj.* Homosexual or effeminate. *Syn.:* overfastidious, finicky, schoolmarmish.

nellie fag, *n.* A gay male with campy walk, gestures, and speech.

neo-con, *n.* A conservative who was formerly a progressive. ["A neo-con is a liberal who has been mugged."]

neo-Nazi, *n.* A fascist, a racist. [From the acronym for the Nationalist Socialist German Workers' Party, led by Adolf Hitler.]

nerd or **nurd,** *n.* A dull, witless, repulsive person who is socially unacceptable. ["And the jock shall dwell with the nerd and the cheerleader lie down with the wimp and there will be peace upon the campus"—*Observer* (1988).]

nervous Nellie, *n.* A nervous person.

nesh, *adj.* Delicate, prissy.

never-sweat, *n.* A Mexican.

never-was, *n.* A total loser from way back. ["The age when physcians were divided in Has-beens and neverwozzers." *Psyche* (1929).]

nibbler, *n.* A male fellator.

nice Nellie, *n.* (1) A prudish man or woman. (2) An effeminate male.

nic frog, *n.* A Dutch person.

nickle-dime, *adj.* Small-time or insignificant.

nifty, *n.* A sexually attractive woman ["His six blonde nifties on their spike heels"—Jerome Weidman.]

nigger or **nigga,** *n.* (1) A black person. ["... here you have explanations—/psychological, cultural, sociological/epistemological, cosmological, political/economic, aesthetic, religious, dialectical/existential/jive-ass explanations for being niggas"—Welton Smith, "Special Section for the Niggas on the Lower Eastside or: Invert the Divisor and Multiply."] *Syn.*: nig, nigra, niggra, nig-nog. (2) A member of any group that is the object of discrimination. ["... a typical minority-group stereotype—woman as nigger—if she knows her place (home), she is really quite a lovable, loving creature, happy and childlike"—Naomi Weisstein, "Woman as Nigger," *Psychology Today* (1969).]

nigger gal, or **nigger wench,** *n.* A black woman.

nigger-lover, *n.* A white person who supports causes favorable to blacks.

nigger-rich, *idiom.* Suddenly flushed with money.

nigger's nigger, *n.* A subservient black person. ["You're a nigger's nigger/A white man in the head"—James Danner, "My Brother."]

nightbag or **ragbag,** *n.* A promiscuous woman.

nightmare, *n.* An ugly person.

NIGYYSOB, *interj.* Now I've got you, you son of a bitch!

ninety-day wonder, *n.* A person with minimal training. [From World War II when officers were commissioned after only 90 days training.]

Nip, *n.* A Japanese or East Asian person. ["A few little nips popping away with cameras." John Osborne, *West of Suez* (1971).]

nipcheese, *n.* A cheapskate, a skinflint.

nisty, *adj.* Extremely ugly.

nit, *n.* An insignificant person.

no-account or **no-count,** *adj.* Shiftless, worthless, mediocre.

a nobody, *n.* An insignificant person.

nobody home, *idiom.* Stupid, feebleminded, out to lunch.

nobody loves a smartass, *idiom.* You're too smart for your own good! Don't be a wiseguy!

no bullfighter, *idiom.* A sissified man.

N.O.C.D. or **N.O.C.K.,** *n.* A person who is not a member of the upper middle class or the very rich. [The acronyms for "*n*ot *o*ur *c*lass, *d*ear" and "*n*ot *o*ur *c*lass, *k*id." "There are only two classes—first class and no class"—David O. Selznick.]

no great shakes, *idiom.* Mediocre, nothing to write home about.

nola, *n.* A homosexual man.

non, *n.* An awkward person. *Syn.*: cripple.

non compos, *idiom.* Out of one's mind. ["Barron's non compos. Lear controls him completely"—Kenneth Roberts.]

no-neck, *idiom.* A stupid, brutish, bigoted person.

nonentity, *n.* An insignificant person. ["I'm tired of dealing with those nonentities in City Hall."] *Syn.*: cipher, rushlight, whiffet, whippersnapper, whipster, zero, zilch.

nonstarter, *n.* A total incompetent.

noodle or **noodlehead,** *n.* A melonhead.

nookie or **nooky,** *n.* A woman considered as a sexual partner.

noove or **nouveau,** *n.* A member of the newly rich who lacks taste and breeding, one who is vulgar and showy. [From the French *nouveau riche* = an upstart.]

no prize package, *idiom.* A worthless person.

Norski, *n.* A Swedish person, a Scandinavian.

nose-lunger, *n.* A disgusting, nauseating person [From the word for a glob of nasal mucus.]

nose-picker, *n.* A gross person or a little pipsqueak. ["Go back to reform school, you little nose-picker"—W. C. Fields.]

no spring chicken, *idiom.* An older woman.

notch, *n.* A woman considered as a sex object. [From *notch* = vulva.]

not count for spit, *idiom.* To be insignificant. [From *spit* = shit.] *Syn.:* nothing to write home about.

not dry behind the ears, *idiom.* Immature, inexperienced.

not give a damn, *idiom.* To be indifferent to or contemptuous of. *Syn.:* not give a fuck for nothing, not give a flying fuck, not give a rat's ass.

not have a hair on one's ass, *idiom.* To lack courage, even when dared.

not have all one's switches on, *idiom.* To be weird, eccentric, nutty. *Syn.:* not have brain one, not have the foggiest.

a nothing, *n.* A person who lacks talent, charm, or ability. ["The trouble with some women is that they get all excited about nothing—and then marry him"—Cher.]

nothing, *adj.* Inane, lacking talent, worthless. ["He's a nothing guy."]

not know shit from Shinola, *idiom.* To be very stupid, to be ignorant. *Idioms:* know from nothing, not know one's ass from one's elbow, not know one's ass from a hole in the ground, not know zilch.

not have both oars in the water, *idiom.* Slightly crazy, weird, eccentric.

not worth a damn, *idiom.* Worthless. *Idioms:* not worth a bucket of warm spit, not worth a fart in a noisemaker, not worth a pisshole in the snow.

nougat or **nugget,** *n.* A sappy person.

no way, José, *idiom.* Absolutely not! You must be joking!

nowhere, *n.* An undesirable person.

nubian, *n.* A socially unacceptable person.

nudge, *n.* A nagger, a constant complainer.

nudnik, *n.* An annoying, obnoxious pest.

number, *n.* A sexually attractive girl. ["She's a cute little number."]

numbnuts, *n.* A despicable male.

nut, *n.* A crazy, stupid, odd, strange, or very eccentric person. *Syn.:* nutball, nutbar, nutcake, nut case, nut roll, nutso, nutter.

nutcracker, *n.* (1) A promiscuous woman or a prostitute. *Syn.:* spread eagle, pillowgut, fleshpot. (2) An aggressive, castrating woman; a ballbreaker.

nut-crunching, *adj.* Pertaining to the sapping of masculinity. [From *nut* = testicle. "She's a nut-crunching spitfire."]

nympho, *n.* A woman thought to be sexually insatiable. ["There once was a nympho named White/Who insists on a dozen each night./A fellow named Fedder/Had the brashness to wed 'er./His chances of survival are slight" —American limerick.] *Syn.:* nymphomaniac, nymph.

oaf, *n.* A stupid, clumsy fellow.

obdurate, *adj.* Stubborn, hard-hearted. ["The obdurate philistine materialism of bourgeois society"—Connolly.]

obfuscator, *n.* One who makes things deliberately obscure or who uses unnecessarily complex language.

objugatrix, *n.* A scolding woman.

objurgate, *v.* To rebuke. ["Violently had he objurgated that wretch of a groom"—Vaughan.]

obloquy, *n.* Verbal abuse. ["Those who . . . stood by me in the teeth of obloquy, taunt, and open sneer"—Oscar Wilde.]

obscene, *adj.* Using language or taking action that is immoral or offensive; lewd.

obscurantist, *n.* One who limits the spread of knowledge by using excessive jargon or high-sounding words.

obtuse, *adj*. Dumb, insensitive, dull-witted. ["An obtuse insensibility to the rich and subtle variety of human relations"—Morris Raphael Cohen.]

oddball, *n*. An eccentric person, a strange one. ["A phlegmatic oddball in a world of make-believe." Wallis and Blair, *Thunder Above* (1959).] *Syn.*: character, creep, cueball, dilly, ding-a-ling, dingbat, misfit, flake, freak, fruitcake, goof, kook, nut, odd bird, odd fish, queer duck, queer fish, screwball, screw-loose, space cadet, space-out, spastic, spazz, spook, wack, weirdo, zod, zombie, zone.

odious, *adj*. Repulsive, hateful. ["It was an odious face—crafty, vicious, malignant, with shifty, light gray eyes"—Sir Arthur Doyle.]

ofay, *n*. A white person. ["Nice integrated neighbourhood, ofays, Arabs, Chaldeans, a few colored folks. Ethnic man"—Elmore Leonard, *The Switch*.] *Syn.*: fay, ofaginzy, oofay, peckawood.

offal-eater, *n*. A Dutchman.

off artist, *n*. A thief.

off one's bean, *idiom*. Insane, eccentric. *Idioms*: off one's cake, off one's chump, off one's noodle, off one's nut, off one's onion, off one's rocker, off one's trolley.

oil or **banana oil,** *n*. Unctuous talk, baloney, bunk.

oiler, *n*. An Hispanic person.

oily, *adj*. Cunning and unctuous. ["A little, round, fat, oily man of God"—James Thomson, *The Castle of Indolence*.]

okey-doke, *n*. (1) White values. (2) A con game.

okie, *n*. A hillbilly, a rustic. [From Oklahoma, many of whose people had to leave the state for urban centers during the Great Depression of the 1930s. "Okie used to mean that you was from Oklahoma. Now it means you are scum. Don't mean nothing in itself, it's the way they say it"—John Steinbeck, *The Grapes of Wrath* (1939).]

old bag, *n*. An old woman. ["Get a look at that old bag coming on to that hunk."] *Syn.*: no spring chicken, old bat, old battle-ax, old broad, old girl, old heifer, old hen.

old bat, *n.* An old, gossipy, shrewish woman.

old cocker, *n.* A silly or senile old man. ["... Twas Roger, the lodger,/The dirty old codger,/The bugger, the bastard, the sod"—English limerick.] *Syn.:* codger, alter kacker, old coot, old fart, old gaffer, crock, dodo, duffer, fogy, fossil, gaffer, geezer, old bird, relic, old buzzard, old duffer, old fogy, old futz, old poop, oldster, old-timer, pappy.

old goat, *n.* A dirty, lecherous old man.

old maid, *n.* An elderly spinster, a fusspot. ["Old maids lead apes in hell"—16th-century English proverb.]

old massa, *n.* A white man. [From a form of addressing a white slaveholder.]

old saw, *n.* A cliché, a platitude.

old woman, *n.* One's wife or mother, or a fussbudget. ["He's acting just like an old woman."]

on the rag, *idiom.* Testy, snappy. [From *The Official Preppy Handbook.*]

on the chopping block, *idiom.* In a bad or dangerous position. ["One more goof like that and your head is on the chopping block."]

on the pad or **on the take,** *idiom.* Taking bribes.

on your bike, *interj.* Go away! Be off with you!

one-a-day man, *idiom.* A man continually engaged in sexual activity. ["He was a one-a-day man who regarded women as receptacles for his poisons"—Albert Goldman, *Ladies and Gentlemen, Mr. Lenny Bruce* (1974).]

one-shot, *n.* A woman who goes for a one-night stand.

oofus, *n.* A goofy person.

oomph girl, *n.* A sexually appealing young woman. [After Ann Sheridan, a movie actress in the 1930s.]

opportunist, *n.* One who sells out his principles for immediate gain.

Oreo, *n.* A black person who emulates white values. [From the idea of appearing black on the outside but being white on the inside, like the cookie of the same name.] *Syn.:* Afro-Saxon, Aunt Jane, chalker, cookie, fade, faded boogie, frosty.

organ-grinder, *n.* An Italian.

ort, *n.* A despicable, disgusting person. [From *orts* = mouse droppings.]

Oscar, *n.* A narrow-minded man. [M. Mezzerow, in glossary, *Really the Blues* (1946).]

ostrich, *n.* An unrealistic person.

out of one's head, *idiom.* Crazy, out to lunch.

out of it, *idiom.* No longer in the running, not coherent.

out of one's tree, *idiom.* Nuts, ape.

out of shape, *idiom.* Disturbed and irrational. *Syn.:* bent, bent out of shape, pushed out of shape.

out of the box, *idiom.* Out of contention. *Syn.:* ruined, finished, kaput.

out on one's ass, *idiom.* Discharged, rejected, done for, history. ["After thirty years, they threw me out on my ass."]

outrageous, *adj.* Barbarous, unchristian, uncivilized, unconscionable, unholy, wicked.

over my dead body, *idiom.* Not if I can help it.

over the hill, *idiom.* (1) Ineffective, impotent. ["I'm thinking of divorcing Jack. He's over the hill."] (2) Middle-aged or older.

owlshit, *n.* Anything tedious or distressful. ["The boss just dropped another load of owlshit on my desk."]

ox, or **dumb ox,** *n.* A big, strong, dumb, awkward person.

oyster, *n.* A person who is uncommunicative.

ozone or **zone,** *n.* One who is on a psychedelic high.

P

pablum, *n.* Mindless, shallow drivel or pap. ["Boy, that prof sure spoons out the pablum."]

pachuco, *n.* A young, tough Mexican-American gang member. ["The fathers of today's pachucos were called zootsuiters."] *Syn.:* cholo.

packer *n.* A gay male.

Paddy or **Paddywood,** *n.* (1) A white person. ["(He) ... had run with 'Paddy' (white), 'Chicano' (Mexican), and 'Blood' (Negro) sets since the age of twelve." *Trans-Action* (1967).] (2) An Irish person or one of Irish descent.

pain in the ass, *idiom.* An annoying or difficult person or situation. ["You give me a pain in the ass"—John O'Hara, *Appointment in Samara* (1934).]

paki or **pakkie,** *n.* An immigrant from Pakistan.

paleface, *n.* A white person. ["Whitey, the latest word of contempt for a white person superseding *ofay* ... and pale face." *New York Times Magazine* (1964).]

paleface nigger, *n.* A despised white person.

palindrome, *n.* (1) A bisexual. (2) One who takes part in mutual oral sex. [From the original definition: a word or sentence that reads the same forward or backward.]

palm something off, *idiom.* To try to pass off an inferior item or person as being of good quality. ["Did you see how he tried to palm himself off as a Harvard graduate?"] *Syn.:* foist, fob off.

palm oil, *n.* A bribe. ["A little palm oil goes a great way in City Hall."]

palm-presser or **flesh-presser,** *n.* A politician who tries to win votes by shaking hands with anyone he meets. ["He's a good palm-presser but a lousy legislator."]

palooka, *n.* A big, inept, and stupid man. ["This big palooka has been trying to get me pregnant every which way but lopsided"—*The Boss's Wife,* U.S film (1986).]

pancake, *n.* An Uncle Tom or any servile person.

pansified, *adj.* Effeminate or homosexual.

pansy, *n.* (1) A gay male who assumes the female role. (2) A weak or effeminate man.

pantywaist, *n.* A sissy or coward. ["He was a panty waist . . . very *dainty* about things." H. A. Smith, *View from Chivo* (1971).]

pap, *n.* Empty, simplistic ideas, arguments, or materials.

paper asshole, have a, *idiom.* To be full of hot air. ["You're talking like a man with a paper asshole."]

paperbelly, *n.* A person who can't take his liquor straight.

paper-pusher or **paper-shuffler,** *n.* An unimportant office worker or executive.

paper tiger, *n.* A person who can't deliver on his threats. ["Comrade Mao Tse Tung . . . expressed his famous viewpoint that all reactionaries are paper tigers." *Peking Review* (1958).]

papist, *n.* A Roman Catholic.

papmouth, *n.* An effeminate man.

pappy guy, *n.* An elderly, relatively helpless man.

papuliferous, *adj.* Pimply.

parakeet, *n.* A Puerto Rican.

paranoid, *n.* A person who has delusions of persecution. ["I am a kind of paranoiac in reverse. I suspect people of plotting to make me happy"—J. D. Salinger.]

parasite, *n.* A person who lives at the expense of others. *Syn.:* bloodsucker, freeloader, hanger-on, leech, spiv, sponge, drone, sucker.

parlor pink or **pinko,** *n.* A socialist who talks big but does very little. [From the idea that pink is a watered-down version of red.]

parolist, *n.* A pretentious person.

party pooper, *n.* A person whose unpleasant behavior spoils others' fun at social occasions. *Syn.:* spoilsport, killjoy.

pashy-petter, *n.* A sexually willing and passionate female.

pat or **patlander,** *n.* An Irish person.

pato, *n.* A gay man. [From the Spanish.]

patsy, *n.* A person who is easily deceived or victimized. ["She's a patsy for anyone with a Mercedes."] *Syn.:* dupe, Alvin, boob, chump, cousin, doormat, douchie, dumb-john, easy make, easy mark, fall guy, gork, lamb, prune, pushover, schnook, setup, sitting duck, sucker, yold.

patty, *n.* A white person.

pawn, *n.* A person who is exploited by another. *Syn.:* lackey, cat's-paw, stooge.

peacenik, *n.* A peace advocate. *Syn.:* pacifist, antiwar activist, peacemonger.

peacock, *n.* A blatantly vain, strutting man.

peanut, *n.* An insignificant person or object.

pea-souper, *n.* A French-Canadian.

pebble on the beach, *idiom.* A relatively unimportant person, just one of the crowd.

peckerwood or **peckawood,** *n.* A white person, especially a rural Southerner. ["When I tried to get into the black caucus, they said, 'No peckerwoods allowed in here, Sonny." *New York Times* (1967).] *Syn.:* ballface, beast, blue-eyed devil, bright-skin, buckra, Charlie, Chuck, cracker, dog, face, fade, fay, frosty, wood, good ol' boy, gray, gray boy, hay-eater, hinkty, honky, Jeff, keltch, lily-white, long-knife, marshmallow, mean white, Mister Charlie, monkey, ule, ofay, Paddy, Patty, paleface, peck, pecker, peckerhead, peek-a-woods, pink, redneck, ridgerunner, round-eye, silk, snake, the man, white meat, white paddy, whitey.

pecksniff, *n.* An oily hypocrite. [From a character in Dickens's *Martin Chuzzlewit.*]

peddle your papers, *imper.* Leave me alone! Take off!

pederast, *n.* A man who copulates anally with males. *Syn.*: angel, ass-fucker, birdie, backdoor-bandit, backdoor worker, back-scuttler, backgammoner, bird-taker, brown-hatter, brownie, brown-holer, browning king, brush-dauber, bugger, bung-holer, butt-fucker, bugger, bunker, burglar, capon, dung-puncher, eye doctor, eye-opener, father-fucker, fudgepot-dipper, gentleman of the back door, gooser, Greek, ingler, Jesuit, jocker, kiester-stabber, pig-sticker, reamer, ring-snatcher, sod, sodomist, stir-shit, stuffer, turk, usher, vert, wolf.

pedomorphic, *adj.* Childlike.

Pedro, *n.* Any Spanish-speaking person.

P.E.E.P., *n.* A woman viewed as a prime candidate for oral sex. [Acronym for "*p*erfectly *e*legant, *e*ating *p*ussy."]

peer-queer, *n.* A gay man who likes to watch others' sexual activities.

peewee, *n.* A short person.

peg boy, *n.* One who submits to anal sex.

pelican, *n.* (1) A glutton. (2) A tough woman or prostitute.

pencil-pusher, *n.* A lower-level office worker. *Syn.*: pencil-driver, pencil-shover, desk jockey.

pendejo, *n.* A truly stupid, useless person. [In Spanish *pendejo* = a pubic hair.]

penguin, *n.* A nun.

penis breath, *n.* A disgusting, despicable man.

penis wrinkle, *n.* A dorky male.

penny-ante, *adj.* Insignificant, petty. *Syn.*: miserly, tight-fisted.

peo, *n.* A fart.

peola, *n.* A light-skinned African-American woman. ["An older word for someone mellow and yellow"—Andrews and Owen, *Black Language* (1973).]

peon, *n.* (1) An unimportant person. ["He (Elvis Presley) periodically tossed a sweat-stained scarf to the peons below." *Time* (1977).] (2) A Mexican.

pepperbelly, *n.* A Mexican. *Syn.*: chillibelly, peppergut.

pepper-kissing, *adj.* A negative intensifier meaning "no good."

Pepsi, *n.* A French-Canadian.

Percy, *n.* An effeminate man. *Syn.*: Percy boy, Percy pants.

period, *interj.* And that's final!

perv or **perve,** *n.* A person with out-of-the-ordinary sexual pursuits. [Shortening of *pervert.* "Once, a philosopher; twice, a pervert"—Voltaire.]

pessimist, *n.* One who expects the worst. ["A pessimist is a man who thinks all women are bad. An optimist is a man who hopes they are"—Chauncey Depew.] *Syn.*: calamity howler, Cassandra, crapehanger, worrywart, wet blanket.

peter-pansy, *n.* A gay male who practices fellatio.

petticoat, *n.* A woman viewed as a sex object.

petticoat merchant, *n.* A pimp or a hooker.

pettifogger, *n.* (1) A dishonest lawyer. *Syn.*: jackleg lawyer, shyster, ambulance chaser. (2) A quibbler, a hairsplitter, a nitpicker.

pharisee, *n.* A sanctimonious hypocrite.

phedinkus, *n.* Nonsense, crap.

philistine, *n.* A conformist, a person with little interest in culture. ["Philistine: a term of contempt applied by prigs to the rest of their species"—Sir Leslie Stephen.] *Syn.*: babbitt, boeotian, middlebrow.

philodox, *n.* One in love with his own views.

phony, *n.* A person who pretends to be something he isn't. ["This simple test—a way of telling the phonies from the truly committed." *New Yorker* (1977).] *Syn.*: poseur, impostor, actor, bluffer, boogerboo, fakeroo, ringer, four-flusher, fraud, humbug, pseud, quack, charlatan, phonus balonus.

phooey or **pfui,** *interj.* It stinks! To hell with it! *Syn.*: ugh, feh.

phrasemonger, *n.* A heavy user of clichés and secondhand expressions.

picayune, *adj.* Of little importance. *Syn.*: petty, trifling, paltry, insignificant, no great shakes.

piccolo player, *n.* A person who performs oral sex on males. [From *piccolo* = penis.] *Syn.*: blow-boy, cannibal, cock-sucker, dick-sucker, dicky-licker, lapper, lick-spigot, mouth whore, nibbler, peter-eater, pink pants, punk, skin-diver, smoker, spigot-sucker, suckster, suckstress.

picker, *n.* Someone who likes to view others' sexual or other private actions, a voyeur.

piddle around, *v.* To waste time working aimlessly.

piddling or **piddly,** *adj.* Beneath consideration. *Syn.*: trivial, paltry, chickenshit, five-and-dime, half-assed, measly, mickey mouse, niggardly, penny-ante, rinky-dink, small-beer, small-change, small-potato, two-bit.

piece of ass or **piece of rump,** *n.* A female sex partner. ["I was day after day with this choice piece of rump, not so much as touching her, let alone squeezing or grappling"—Fraser, *Flashman in the Game* (1975).] *Syn.*: hunk of ass, hunk of tail, piece of mutton, piece of snatch, piece of stray, piece of stuff, piece of tail.

piece of chickenshit, *n.* A coward, a wimp.

piece of dark meat, *n.* A black woman when targeted sexually.

pie card, *n.* A labor union bureaucrat.

piff, *n.* An insignificant person.

piffle, *n.* Nonsense.

pig, *n.* (1) A woman, especially a sloppy, loose, or ugly one. ["... a pig he had picked up once. She was too lousy and scummy to take a chance on." James T. Farrell, in *Story* (1932).] (2) A police officer. ["When you got a problem with swine, you've got to call in the pigs"—S. I. Hayakawa.] (3) A man, particularly a male chauvinist.

pig brother, *n.* A black informer. ["Pig brothers, Tom 'o Lees, jus' black people tommin' fo' d'white folks"—Edith Folb, in *Runnin' Down Some Lines* (1980).]

pigeon, *n.* (1) A stool pigeon. (2) A sucker, an easy mark.

pigging, *adj.* An intensifier, a euphemism for *fucking.*

pighead, *n.* A stubborn, stupid person. ["I am firm. You are obstinate. He is a pigheaded fool"—Katharine Whitehorn.]

pig-ignorant, *adj.* Very stupid.

pig meat or **pig poke,** *n.* An older, loose woman, or a prostitute. ["Perhaps words like *pig, pig-meat,* or *dog* are inspired by the sadness which follows unsatisfactory sex." Germaine Greer, *The Female Eunuch* (1970).]

pigmouth or **pigger,** *n.* A very obese woman.

pig's ass, *interj.* Exclamation of anger or surprise. *Syn.*: in a pig's eye.

pigshit, *n.* Rubbish, nonsense. ["All writing is pigshit" —Antonin Artaud.]

pigtail, *n.* A Chinese person.

pi-jaw, *n.* Pious hypocrisy.

pile of shit, *n.* A worthless person or object.

pilgarlic, *n.* A self-pitying person who wants everyone else to pity him.

pill, *n.* An obnoxious person, a weakling, a bore.

pillhead, *n.* Someone who takes illegal drugs in tablets or capsules.

pillock, *n.* An idiot.

pilpul, *n.* Subtle analysis and conflicts, often over seemingly trivial details. [From the Hebrew word.] ["Let's get down to cases. What you have been spouting for the past half-hour is nothing but a pilpul."]

pimp, *n.* A man who lives off prostitutes. *Syn.*: ass-peddler, butt-peddler, crack salesman, eastman, easy rider, fancy man, fishmonger, flesh-peddler, honey man, hustler, pander, pee-eye, p.i., procurer, stable boss.

pinchbelly, *n.* A miser.

pinch-bottom, *n.* A womanizer. *Syn.*: pinch-buttock, pinch-cunt.

pinch-fart or **pinch-gut,** *n.* A miserly man. [From the idea that he is so stingy that he tries to retain his intestinal gas.]

pink or **pink boy,** *n.* A white male.

pink-chaser, *n.* A black man who seeks out white women.

pinkie or **pinky,** *n.* A white person, or a light-skinned black who is believed to be white.

pink pants, *n.* A gay man.

pinktoes, *n.* A white woman. ["When ... even the great Mamie Mason had lost her own black Joe to a young Pinktoe, the same panic prevailed among the black ladies of Harlem as had previously struck the white ladies downtown." Chester Himes, *Pinktoes* (1965).]

pin one's ears back, *idiom.* To punish someone verbally or physically.

pious, *adj.* Affecting morality hypercritically. ["He's a pious fraud—what Mencken called a Pithecantropus biblicus."]

pisher, *n.* An unimportant person or thing. [From the Yiddish word for a bed wetter.]

pipsqueak, *n.* A nobody. *Syn.*: nebbish, cipher, squirt.

pissabed, *n.* A lazy person. [From the allusion of one too lazy to go to the toilet.]

piss about or **piss around**, *idiom*. To goof off. ["Are you coming in? Or do we piss about all day?"—T. Lewis, *Jack's Return Home* (1970).]

piss artist, *n*. A glib person.

pissass, *n*. An unpopular wretch.

pissed, *adj*. Furious. *Syn*.: pissed at, pissed off at, hacked, hacked off.

piss-elegant or **pissy**, *adj*. A pretentious, self-obsessed gay man. ["... that pissy queen in Bloomindale's sampling fag water"—*Maledicta IX*.]

pisshead, *n*. A disgusting, stupid jerk.

pissing, *adj*. Worthless, very small. ["I'm only a pissing Sergeant." N. Freeling, *What Are Bugles Blowing For?* 1975.]

piss in it, *interj*. To hell with it!

piss-mean, *adj*. Cruel.

piss on, *idiom*. To denigrate someone or something.

piss-poor, *adj*. Extremely poor quality or performance.

pisspot, *n*. A real S.O.B.

piss someone off, *idiom*. To make someone very angry.

piss-ugly, *adj*. Repulsive. *Syn*.: ugly as cat shit.

piss-willie, *n*. A coward.

pits, the, *idiom*. The most loathsome place or situation imaginable; hence, a loathsome person. ["You're the pits" —John McEnroe to a tennis umpire, at Wimbledon.] *Syn*.: the armpit, the asshole, barf city.

pixy, *n*. A gay man.

pizzaface, *n*. A person with severe acne, redcaps, blackheads, or whiteheads *Syn*.: craterface, Swiss cheese, vomithead.

plagiarist, One who steals another's writings. ["When you take stuff from one writer, it's plagiarism; but when you take it from many writers, it's research"—Wilson Mizner.]

plastic, *adj*. Synthetic, false, phony, superficial.

plastic hippie, *n.* A hippie in appearance but not in substance. *Syn.:* pseudo hippie, hippie hypocrite.

player, *n.* A promiscuous person, or a pimp.

play with a full deck, not to, *idiom.* To be mentally unsound.

plebiocologist, *n.* One who flatters the common people.

ploot, *n.* A slut.

plunger, *n.* A Baptist.

po'buckra, *n.* A poor white. [Shortened form of "poor buckra."]

pocho, *n.* A Mexican-American. ["I am frequently labelled a *pocho,* a Mexican with gringo pretensions." *Saturday Review of Literature* (1975).]

Poindexter, *n.* A bookworm. ["Ohmigod, like Hillary's brother is like such a total Poindexter he's skipped two grades, I mean like he's in eleventh grade and he doesn't even have hair under his arms"—Corey and Westermark, *Fer Shurr! How to Be a Valley Girl—Totally* (1982).] *Syn.:* brainy geek, computer nerd, grind.

pointyhead, *n.* An intellectual seen as a grossly impractical person. ["Mr Wallace . . . dismissed it . . . as the most callous, asinine, stupid thing that ever was conceived by some pointy-head in Washington, D.C." *Times* (1972).] *Syn.:* egghead, double-dome.

poison, *adj.* An evil person or act.

poke, *n.* (1) A loose woman, a mistress, or a concubine. [From *poke* = copulate.] ["'Caroline,' said Derek . . . wouldn't make a good poke for a blind hunchback'"—C. Rae, *Few Small Bones* (1968).] (2) A lazy person. [Shortening of *slowpoke.*]

Polack or **Polock,** *n.* A person of Polish descent. ["You're some cheap Polack hooker that was tossed out of parochial school for diddling little boys." E. V. Cunningham, *Helen* (1966).]

polecat, *n.* A mean, treacherous man.

politically correct, *adj.* Authoritarian, against free speech (in the eyes of those called "politically incorrect").

politically incorrect, *adj.* Racist, sexist, homophobic, lookist, ageist, fatist, classist, ecologically wasteful (from the viewpoint of those who consider themselves "politically correct").

poltroon, *n.* A craven coward. ["Congress consists one-third, more or less, scoundrels; two-thirds, more or less, idiots; three-thirds, more or less, poltroons"—H. L. Mencken.]

pond scum, *n.* A really nasty person.

pong, *n.* A Chinese.

poodle-faker, *n.* A ladies' man. [From the image of a man who would behave like a poodle or other lapdog in order to seduce a woman.]

poontang or **poon,** *n.* A woman viewed as a sexual object ["... Why it's on patience and poontang that they built the West"—Norman Mailer, *Why Are We in Vietnam?* (1967).]

poop, *n.* A bore, an ineffectual person, a dumb person. [From *poop* = shit.] *Syn.*: poopbutt, poopchute, poophead.

poor-ass, *adj.* Mean, nasty, lousy.

poor-mouth or **bad-mouth,** *v.* To speak ill of others.

poor white trash, *idiom.* Particularly backward Southern rural whites.

poot around, *idiom.* To waste time in frivolous behavior.

pootbutt, *n.* An immature or inexperienced person. [From *poot* = a fart.] *Syn.*: junior flip, poot, rookie, rootiepoot, rumpskin, wethead.

popcorn, *n.* A mental lightweight or mediocre performer.

popcorn pimp, *n.* (1) A small-time pimp, or would-be pimp. (2) A fraud.

poper, *n.* A Roman Catholic. [From one who obeys the Pope.]

pop one's cork, *idiom.* To explode. *Syn.:* blow one's top.

pop-tart, *n.* A cheaply sexy, loose, pop music performer. ["Rock's richest pop-tart (Madonna) ... who made lingerie-and-crucifixes fashionable"—*Life* (1989).]

porker or **porky,** *n.* (1) A Jewish person. [A reverse spin on the fact that Jews are forbidden to eat pork.] (2) A fat person; more particularly, a fat and ugly woman.

pornocrat, *n.* A bureaucrat in a pornocracy. ["Pornocracy: governance by prostitutes or harlots, used contemptuously to indicate government corruption"—*A Feminist Dictionary* (1985).]

pornogenerian, *n.* A dirty old man.

Portugoose, *n.* A person of Portuguese nationality or descent.

poser, *n.* A fake or pretentious person, someone who tries to behave like people in a group but is rejected as a phony by that group. *Syn.:* poseur, wannabe.

poshlost, *n.* Shallow or hackneyed writing or opinion. [Vladimir Nabokov's term for a hack.]

posthole or **tollhole,** *n.* A hooker.

poski, *n.* A Pole or a person of Polish descent.

pothead, *n.* A heavy user of marijuana. *Syn.:* blower, blow top, bo-bo jockey, doper, freak, Fu Man Chu, gowster, grass-eater, grasshead, griefer, hay-burner, head, hophead, junkerman, lusher, oiler, pot lush, reeferhound, roach-bender, tea-blower, teahead, teo, T-man, toker, weed-eater.

pottymouth or **toiletmouth,** *n.* One who uses obscene language all the time.

pound salt up your ass, go, *idiom.* Go to hell! Stick it up your ass!

power tool, *n.* A student disliked because he studies too hard.

powder puff, *n.* An effeminate gay man.

pox box, *n.* A dirty woman, or one with a veneral disease. [From *pox* = syphilis and *box* = vagina.]

P.R., *n.* A Puerto Rican.

prat, *n.* A fool. [From *prat* = buttocks.]

prate, *v.* To harp on, or to talk nonsense. ["We may prate of democracy, but actually a poor child in England has little more hope than the son of an Athenian slave to be emancipated into that intellectual freedom of which great writings are born"—Quiller-Couch.]

press one's buttons, *idiom.* To anger someone.

prevert, *n.* A pervert. [From the movie *Dr. Strangelove* (1964).]

prick, *n.* An obnoxious man, or an idiot, a fool, an incompetent. ["...She said the difference between Mercedes owners and a cactus is that on a cactus the pricks are on the outside."]

prick-tease or **prick-teaser,** *n.* A woman who arouses a man but refuses to make love. ["He shouted after her; 'Prick-teasing bitch.'" J. Mann, *Mrs. Knox's Profession.*]

pricky or **prickish,** *adj.* Detestable.

prig, *n.* An overly fastidious and uptight person, hypercritical, supertraditional. ["Prig and philistine, Ph.D. and C.P.A., despot of English 218C and bigshot of the Kiwanis Club—how much at the bottom they both hate Art and how hard it is to know which of them hates it more" —Louis Kronenberger, *Company Manners* (1954).]

prima donna, *n.* A spoiled, temperamental person who must be the sole center of attention and who indulges in frequent temperamental displays. [Literally, "the first woman," used to describe lead female opera singers, who are noted for tempestuous outbursts.]

prissy, *adj.* Overly fastidious, finicky, fusspotty, fussy, persnickety, picky, prunish. ["...those do-gooding prissy women."]

profanity, *n.* Irreverent language. ["He had what one might call a preliminary recourse in his profanity, those 'scorching, singeing blasts' he was always directing at his companions"—Brooks.]

prole, *n.* A member of the working class. [Shortened from *proletariat.*]

prosty or **prostie,** *n.* A prostitute.

prude, *n.* A person who dislikes profane talk or sexy behavior. *Syn.:* bluenose, goody-goody, Mrs. Grundy, nice Nelly, prig, puritan.

prune, *n.* A disliked prude.

pseud or **pseudo,** *n.* Someone with intellectual pretensions, a fake. ["Get it together to put down pseuds, poseurs and general smart asses"—*Private Eye* (1977).]

psilology, *n.* Empty talk.

psilosophy, *n.* Superficial philosophy.

psittacism, *n.* Mindless, repetitive speech.

psycho, *n.* A psychopath, a truly crazy person, a strange or weird person. [" 'Keep that psycho away from me,' Wade yelled, showing fear for the first time"—Raymond Chandler, *The Long Goodbye* (1953).]

psychobabble, *n.* Nonsense language used by psychiatrists and psychologists.

P.T.A., *n.* A foul-smelling female. [From the acronym for "*p*ussy, *t*itties, and *a*rmpits."]

p.u. or **P.U.,** *interj.* An exclamation of revulsion over a fetid smell or something disgusting or botched. [Pronounced as separate letters.]

pucker-assed, *adj.* Timid, cowardly.

puckfist, *n.* A person given to boasting.

pudsy, *adj.* Plump, fat.

pug-ugly, *n.* An extremely ugly person.

pull a fast one, *idiom.* To take advantage of.

pull one's chain, *idiom.* To anger someone.

pull one's finger out, *idiom.* To get on with it, to stop stalling. ["Pull your finger out. I want that report on my desk now".]

pull the rug out from under, *idiom.* To undermine or disable an opponent, often quickly and by surprise.

pumpkin-roller, *n.* A rural dweller.

punch, *n.* Women deemed sexual objects.

punchboard, *n.* A very loose woman.

punch one's lights out, *idiom.* To trounce or hit someone severely.

punk, *n.* (1) A sexually loose woman. ["The play-house Punks, who in a loose undress/Each night receive some Cullie's soft address..."—John Dryden, "Poor Pensive Punck" (1691).] (2) An inexperienced person, or a nobody. (3) A petty hoodlum.

punk out, *v.* To chicken out, to act in a cowardly manner.

puppethead, *n.* A gullible conventional teenager who follows anything he hears in matters of current taste.

puppy, *n.* A wimp.

puppy's mamma, *n.* A bitch.

pusbag, *n.* A contemptible person, a scumbag.

pusgut or **pustlegut,** *n.* A fat-bellied person.

pushed out of shape, *idiom.* Angry. *Syn.:* bent, bent out of shape, out of shape.

pushover, *n.* (1) One who is easily defeated, imposed upon, persuaded. (2) A woman who is an easy lay.

pushy, *adj.* Overly assertive.

pusillanimous, *adj.* Cowardly.

puss gentleman or **gentleman puss,** *n.* A weak or effeminate man.

pussy, *n.* (1) A woman considered as a sexual object. (2) A harmless or passive person. ["He's a pussy, Frank./Yeah, but he's our pussy"—*Blue Velvet*, U.S. film, 1986.]

pussy-bumper, *n.* A lesbian. [An allusion to rubbing vulva against vulva.]

pussy-farter, *n.* A dirty, disgusting woman. [From one who emits vaginal farts.]

pussy-kisser, *n.* A weak man. ["You ain't seen the day when you was strong enough to unzip it out of your pants around me, pussy kisser"—Norman Mailer, *Why Are We in Vietnam?* (1967).]

pussy-Nellie, *n.* A male homosexual.

pussy-simple or **pussy-struck,** *adj.* A man obsessed with copulation.

put-down, *n.* An intentionally cruel insult. ["Evil-hearted you, you always try to put me down, with the things you do and the words you spread around"—Lyrics to "Evil-Hearted You," the Yardbirds, 1965.]

put it in your ear, *idiom.* The hell with you! *Syn.:* stick it up your ass, take it in the ear.

put it over on someone, *idiom.* To deceive.

put it where the monkeys shove their nuts, *idiom.* Shove it up your ass!

put-on, *n.* (1) An act or remark intended to fool someone. (2) A pretender. *Syn.:* put-on artist, phony.

put one's ass in a sling, *idiom.* To create big troubles for someone.

put one's foot in it, *idiom.* To blunder.

put one's foot in one's mouth, *idiom.* To embarrass oneself by saying something stupid.

put one's two cents in, *idiom.* To give unwanted advice, to kibitz. *Idiom:* add one's two cents.

put on the chill, *idiom.* To become distant and hostile. *Syn.:* put the chill on someone, give someone the cold shoulder.

put on the ritz, *idiom.* To make a vulgar display of wealth. *Syn.:* put on the dog.

put someone down, *idiom.* To criticize severely. *Syn.:* denigrate, dump on.

put someone's nose out of joint, *idiom.* To make someone jealous.

put someone on, *idiom.* To fool or tease.

put that shit down, *interj.* Stop acting that way!

put the clip on, *idiom.* To overcharge. *Syn.:* gouge, clip.

put the kibosh on someone, *idiom.* To stifle. *Syn.:* put the quietus to.

put the screws to someone, *idiom.* To be extremely coercive. *Syn.:* harass, put the heat on someone.

put the skids under someone, *idiom.* To arrange for someone to lose or fail.

put the slug on one, *idiom.* To criticize sharply, to knock.

put the wood to someone, *idiom.* To punish or coerce.

putz, *n.* An obnoxious or dumb man. [From the Yiddish *putz* = prick.] [" 'You,' she said, enunciating clearly, 'are a putz, a schmeckel, a schmuck, a schlong, and a shvantz. And a WASP putz at that.' " Judith Krantz *Scruples* (1978).]

putz around or **futz around,** *v.* To waste time, or to do something halfheartedly.

puzzlepate, *n.* One who is confused by very simple ideas.

pygian, *n.* A pain in the ass. [From the medical condition *pygia* a pain in the rectum.]

pygmy, *n.* An insignificant person.

quack, *n.* A fraudulent or incompetent doctor. ["Sigmund Freud was a half-baked Viennese quack. Our literature, culture and the films of Woody Allen would be better today if Freud had never written a word"—Ian Shoales.]

quail, *n.* (1) A woman viewed only sexually. (2) A prostitute. (3) A spinster.

quail-hunter, *n.* A woman-chaser.

quakebuttock, *n.* A craven coward.

quean, *n.* (1) A homosexual man. (2) A sexually loose woman.

queef, *n.* A fart.

queen, *n.* (1) An effeminate man. ["There once was a queen from Khartoum/Who invited a dyke to his room./They argued all night/As to who had the right/To do what, and with which, to whom"—Limerick adapted from Ed Cary, *The Erotic Muse* (1972).] (2) An effeminate male homosexual who prefers virile males and seeks a wide variety of sexual acts. *Syn.:* ace queen, African queen, alley queen, amyl queen, anus queen, ass queen, auntie queen, bean-juice queen, bean queen, benrus queen, big-dick queen, bitch queen, body queen, bondage queen, bone queen, boss queen, boy-scout queen, brownie queen, browning queen, budset queen, butch queen, butterfly queen, buy queen, car queen, catalog queen, chicken queen, clean queen, cleavage queen, closet queen, clothing queen, coffee queen, coffin queen, cold cream queen, come queen, crotch queen, crunch queen, cucumber queen, dairy queen, dalmation queen, dangle queen, dinge queen, dinge-rim queen, diplomat queen, dish queen, dishy queen, drag queen, drape queen, drip queen, dry queen, dyke queen, Easter queen, eclair queen, Egyptian queen, electric queen, encore queen, erector-set queen, express queen, eyeball queen, face queen, felch queen, fire queen, fish queen, fladge queen, flaming queen, flash queen, flip queen, foot queen, follow queen, frog queen, fruit bowl queen, fuchsia queen, golden queen, golden shower queen, goodrich queen, gray queen, green queen, hand queen, head queen, Hershey queen, jaw queen, jean queen, johnny queen, Jonathan queen, kaka queen, kitchen queen, KY queen, leather queen, Levi's queen, killer queen, link-sausage queen, love queen, lookout queen, macaroni queen, magnolia queen, main queen, marigold queen, midnight queen, mirror queen, mitten queen, morning dewdrop queen, movie queen, on-the-street queen, panty queen, park queen, payoff queen, penis-envy queen, pineapple queen, piss-elegant queen, posie queen, post queen, pot queen, poundcake queen, privy queen, queen bee, queen for a day, queenie, queen mother, queen of the gown, queen of clubs, railroad queen, raisin queen, ranch queen, rice queen, rim queen, road queen, rubber queen, rub queen, salt-and-pepper queen, screaming queen, shell queen, shrimp queen, shit queen, shower queen, sidesaddle queen, sissy queen, sixty-nine queen, size queen, skillet queen, skin queen, slap queen, war paint queen, Max Factor queen, snowball queen, snowflake queen, snow queen, social queen, spinach queen, spray queen, spud queen, spy queen, statue queen, steam queen, stomp-down queen, store queen, straight-arrow queen, street queen, string queen, stringbean queen, suck queen, Sunkist queen, taco queen, tattoo queen, tat queen, tearoom queen, throne queen, thumb queen, Tijuana queen, tired queen, tit queen, titty queen, toe jam queen, toe queen, toilet queen, triple-threat queen, tube queen, virgin queen, wall queen, watch queen, Xerox queen, zoo queen.

queer, *n.* A homosexual. ["All is not queer that titters" —Graffito.]

queer as a three-dollar bill, *idiom.* Obviously homosexual.

queer-beer, *n.* (1) A gay man. (2) Any strange person.

queer-basher or **queer-roller,** *n.* A member of a gang that beats up homosexuals.

queer fish, *n.* A strange person.

queer queen, *n.* A lesbian.

queervert, *n.* A homosexual. [A combination of *queer* + *pervert*.]

quibberdick, *n.* A person who quibbles.

quiff, *n.* A promiscuous young woman.

quince, *n.* An effeminate or gay man.

quisling, *n.* A traitor. [After Vidkun Quisling, who was Germany's cat's-paw in Norway during World War II.]

quockerwodger, *n.* A dupe. [From a marionette on strings.]

quoob, *n.* A misfit. [Rhymes with *tube*.]

 rabbi, *n.* A patron or influential political friend. [The religious persuasion is immaterial.] ["You're damn lucky to have come out of the thing pretty clean. You got a rabbi down at City Hall?"]

rabbit, *n.* (1) A timid, worthless person. (2) A white person.

racist, *n.* One who denigrates other peoples. *Syn.*: bigot, race-baiter.

radical, *n.* A person who believes in fundamental changes. ["The sterile radical is basically . . . conservative. He is afraid to let go of the ideas and beliefs he picked up in his youth lest his life be seen as empty and wasted"—Eric Hoffer.] *Syn.*: extremist, rad, revolutionary, ultraist.

radiclib or **rad-lib,** *n.* A political left-winger. ["I never dared to be radical when young for fear it would make me conservative when old"—Robert Frost.]

rag, *n.* (1) A weak or unpleasant person. [Shortening of *wet rag*.] (2) An unhappy or crabby woman.

rag doll, *n.* A slattern, a ragmop.

ragged-ass, *adj.* Nasty, disreputable.

raggedy, *adj.* (1) Unattractive or unkempt. (2) Out of control. (3) Out-of-date.

raggedy-ass, *adj.* Inferior. *Syn.:* half-assed, raggedy-pants.

raghead, *n.* (1) A black man who wears a scarf around his head to protect a fancy hairdo. (2) An Arab, a Hindu, or any Asian who wears a turban or other cloth headgear.

raisin, *n.* A wrinkled old person. ["He had more wrinkles than Auden, that other amazing raisin"—Paul Theroux, *Picture Palace* (1978).]

rakehell, *n.* A worthless, debauched person; generally male. *Syn.:* rake, rakehellion, rakel, rakeshame.

Ralph, *n.* A fool.

Rambo, *n.* A superhawk. ["Given the bomb-'em kill-'em suggestions pulsing from the typewriters of 100 literate Rambos, a boycott of the airport was the most reasonable act suggested"—*Washington Post* (1985).]

ram it, *interj.* Stick it! Shove it!

ramp, *n.* A wanton woman.

rampallian, *n.* A general term of abuse. ["Away, you scullion, you rampallian, you fustilarian"—William Shakespeare, *Henry IV.*]

randy, *adj.* Horny. ["Brandy makes you randy, but gin makes you sin."]

rare dish, *n.* An exceptionally attractive woman.

rascaglion, *n.* A eunuch.

raspy, *adj.* Unattractive.

rastus, *n.* A black man.

rasty, *adj.* Referring to a tough-looking young woman.

rat, *n.* (1) An extremely unpleasant person. (2) An informer. ["... dirty double-crossing rat"—Line spoken by James Cagney in the movie *Blonde Crazy* (1931).] *Syn.:* ratter, stool pigeon.

rat around, *v.* To loaf. *Syn.:* bat around, rat-fuck.

ratass, *n.* A curse, a term of abuse.

ratchetmouth, *n.* Someone who talks incessantly. [From a ratchet wrench, which can be operated continuously, making a rapid, rasping sound.] *Syn.:* ratchetjaw, motormouth.

rat fuck, *n.* A loathsome person. ["Stay away from that rat fuck. He'll act like your best friend and then stab you in the back."] *Syn.:* ratbag, ratface, rat fink, rat fucker, rat prick, rat's asshole, rat bastard.

rat fuck, *interj.* A curse of anger and exasperation.

rat on, *idiom.* To inform on someone, to squeal.

rat out, *idiom.* To desert. *Syn.:* fink out.

rats or **ratshit,** *interj.* An exclamation of disgust.

a rat's ass, *idiom.* Nothing, very little. [Used in the negative. "That thing's not worth a rat's ass."]

rattlebones, *n.* A very skinny person.

ratty, *adj.* Slovenly. *Syn.:* rat-ass, scruffy, tacky.

raunchy or **ronchie,** *adj.* (1) Racy, obscene, or off-color. (2) Disgusting or inferior. *Syn.:* cheap, crummy, grungy.

raven beauty, *n.* An attractive black woman. [From the blackness of a raven and a play on "raving beauty."] *Syn.:* banana, bit of ebony, black meat, black velvet, brown-skin baby, brown sugar, charcoal blossom, charcoal, lily, dange broad, dark meat, laundry queen, nigger-wench, redbone, sapphire, seal.

razzle-dazzle, *n.* Skillful deception. ["She was able to make her case without the usual razzle-dazzle."] *Syn.:* dipsy-do, dipsy-doodle, double shuffle, fancy footwork, fast shuffle, flamdoodle, hanky-panky, hokum, jive, quick shuffle, razzmatazz, ring-a-ding, smoke and mirrors.

reactionary, *n.* An enemy of revolution, progressivism, or liberalism. ["A reactionary is a somnambulist walking backwards"—Franklin D. Roosevelt.] *Syn.:* blimp, Bourbon, diehard, ultraconservative.

read the riot act, *idiom.* To rebuke or warn.

real bitch, *n.* A very annoying person.

real shit, a *n.* A despicable person

ream someone out, *idiom.* To scold someone harshly.

rebarbative, *adj.* Repulsive. ["As unappealing as a week's growth of beard."] from *Darba* = beard.

Rebecca, *n.* A Jewish woman or girl.

recreant, *n.* (1) An apostate, a renegade, a turncoat. (2) A coward.

rectalgiac, *n.* A pain in the ass. [From *rectalgia*.]

Red, *n.* A Communist or a presumed Communist.

red-assed, *adj.* Very angry. *Syn.*: pissed-off.

red-baiter, *n.* One who zealously seeks out or harasses alleged communists.

redbone, *n.* A light-skinned black or mulatto woman.

red-faced, *adj.* Embarrassed.

red-hot momma, *n.* An exciting and sexually attractive woman. ["Sophie Tucker was called the last of the Red-Hot Mommas."]

redneck, *n.* A poor, white, rural, racist Southerner. [Perhaps from the characteristic ruddy neck of an angry person, or the fact that pellegra, a deficiency disease associated with poor Southern whites, produces a dermatitis that turns the neck red.]

redskin, *n.* A Native American. *Syn.*: bow-and-arrow, breed, buck, Red Indian Injun, Uncle Tommyhawk, Vanishing American.

reject, *n.* A fool or useless person. [Implying that a person could not pass a physical or mental test.]

rent or **renter,** *n.* A gay man who charges for his services.

remo, *n.* A stupid person.

retard, *n.* (1) One who doesn't understand what's happening. *Syn.*: airhead, dork, jel, space cadet. (2) A stupid person.

retchsome, *adj.* Nauseating.

Reuben, *n.* An unsophisticated person. *Syn.*: hayseed, hick, rube.

R.F., *n.* A rat fink, a rat fuck, a royal fucking. [Pronounced as separate letters.]

rhetorical, *adj.* Pertaining to overblown speech or writing. *Syn.*: bombastic, florid, flowery, grandiloquent, highfalutin', high-flown, magniloquent, orotund, pompous, purple, sonorous, swollen.

rib, *n.* A woman. [From the biblical story of the creation of Eve from Adam's rib.]

ribald, *n.* A harlot or a whoremonger.

ribald, *adj.* Wanton. ["Their backs . . . shaking with the loose laughter which punctuates a ribald description" —Mary Austin.]

ribbon clerk, *n.* An amateur.

ricebelly, *n.* An Asian person. *Syn.*: rice man, riceburger, ricer, rice-grinder.

rich bitch, *n.* A rich woman.

ricky-tick, *adj.* (1) Old-fashioned, outworn, corny. (2) Cheap and flashy, ricky-ticky.

ridge-runner, *n.* A Southern Appalachian mountain resident.

riffraff, *n.* A very low person or group of people.

right-winger, *n.* A political conservative.

rig-mutton or **rig,** *n.* A wanton woman.

rigsby, *n.* A debauched young man or woman.

rimadonna, *n.* A gay man who prefers anilingus.

ringding or **ding-a-ling,** *n.* A stupid person.

ring-snatcher, *n.* A pederast.

ringtail, *n.* (1) An offensive person. (2) An Italian. (3) A Japanese. (4) A catamite.

rinky-dink, *adj.* Second-rate, crummy.

rip, *n.* (1) A libertine. (2) A hateful woman.

ripesuck, *n.* A bribable person.

rip-off artist, *n.* A thief.

roach, *n.* (1) A contemptible person. (2) A police officer. (3) An ugly girl or woman.

road whore, *n.* A slut.

robot, *n.* A mindless person. ["I thought it would be better having a fairly intelligent . . . girl instead of one of those little office robots." J. B. Priestley, *Daylight on Saturday* (1943).]

rockhead, *n.* A stubborn, mulish person, someone who seems to have rocks in his head.

romp, *n.* A wild female or a whore.

rook, *v.* To cheat, to swindle. ["With his angelic face, he could rook widows out of their life savings."]

room for rent, *idiom.* A very stupid person.

rooster, *n.* A lecher.

root-faced, *adj.* Solemn, sanctimonious. [From a face carved from the hard twists of a tree root.]

rooty-toot, *adj.* Corny, ricky-tick.

ropey, *adj.* Second-rate, inadequate, mediocre.

rotten apple, *n.* A single bad person, out of a group of supposedly good people. ["The rotten apple injures its companion"—American proverb.] *Syn.:* bad apple

rough around the edges, *idiom.* Crude.

rough-ass, *adj.* Harsh.

rough trade, *n.* A violent, sadistic sex partner to a homosexual man, often a man who is or who poses as a construction worker, serviceman, truck driver, or motorcyclist, with an appropriate costume, often of leather.

rounder, *n.* A lecher.

roundeye, *n.* (1) A white person. (2) A catamite.

roundhead, *n.* A Swede or a person of Swedish descent.

roundheel or **roundheels,** *n.* A promiscuous woman. ["Little Miss Roundheels ... specialized in gentlemen who were otherwise committed." G. Bagby, *Murder's Little Helper* (1963.)]

row with one oar in the water, *idiom.* To behave oddly or stupidly.

royal fucking, *idiom.* A complete defeat, bad treatment, or deceit at the hands of others. *Syn.:* raw deal, royal screwing.

rubber sock, *n.* A passive person.

rubbery, *adj.* Wishy-washy.

rube, *n.* An unsophisticated person. [... always a new crop of rubes waiting to be tricked out of their money.]

rude, *adj.* Insolent, lacking in social refinement. ["It seldom pays to be rude. It never pays to be only half-rude" —Norman Douglas.]

rug-muncher or **carpet-muncher,** *n.* A lesbian. [From *rug* = pubic hair.]

rugy, *adj.* Unattractive or unkempt.

rumdum, *n.* A chronic drunkard or a stupid person, especially when the condition results from habitual drunkenness; a rummy; a rumpot.

rump-ranger, *n.* A gay man.

rung-up, *adj.* Emotionally disturbed.

runnion, *n.* A wretch.

run off at the mouth, *idiom.* To talk too much, to shoot off one's mouth.

run something down, *idiom.* To denigrate, to bad-mouth.

runt, *n.* A contemptible person, or a short person.

rusty-dusty, sit around on one's, *idiom.* To waste time. ["Stop sitting on your rusty-dusty twiddling your thumbs."]

S

sack artist or **sack rat,** *n.* A person who loafs. [From *sack* = bed.]

sackmouth *n.* A blabbermouth.

sadie-maisie *n.* One whose bent is sadism and masochism.

sad sack, *n.* An ineffectual and unlucky person. ["... what a delight it was, what a crazy kind of privilege to call a fellow G.I. a goldbrick, a sad sack—really a sad sack of shit—a goof off, a fuck up." Leonard Silk in K. Odean's *High Steppers, Fallen Angels, and Lollipops* (1986).]

saltwater turkey, *n.* An Irish person who crossed the Atlantic to come to America.

Sambo or **Sam,** *n.* A conformist black person who meekly accepts his oppression. [From "Little Black Sambo," a story that perpetuates stereotypical subservient black behavior. "I wonder:—How many Little or Big Black Sambos totter-teeter-titter-tatter at the cake walk justice of their American dreams?"—Q. R. Hand, "I Wonder."]

sand-toter, *n.* An informer.

sanctimonious, *adj.* Simulating holiness. ["... if it only takes some of the sanctimonious conceit out of one of those pious scalawags"—Robert Frost.]

San Quentin quail, *n.* A girl below the legal age of consent for copulation, for which a person can go to jail. *Syn.*: jailbait, San Quentin jailbait.

sau, *n.* A repulsive person, a bastard. [Pronounced like *few*. From Vietnam War usage.]

Sapphire, *n.* An unattractive, unlikable black woman [From the character on the old popular "Amos 'n Andy" radio program. "It has been hard for black women to emerge from the myriad of distorted images that have portrayed us as grinning Beulahs, castrating Sapphires, and pancake-box Jamimahs"—Margaret Sloan, *Manifesto*, National Black Feminist Organization.]

sarcastic, *adj.* Sneering and ridiculing. ["Sarcasm I now see to be in general the language of the devil"—Thomas Carlyle, *Sartor Resartus*.] *Syn.:* acerbic, archilochian, bitter-tongued, caustic, corrosive, sarky.

satchelmouth, *n.* A person with a big mouth. [Louis Armstrong's nickname, Satchmo, came from this word.] *Syn.:* satch, satchel.

saucer-lip, *n.* Any black person.

sausage, *n.* A German.

scab, *n.* (1) A person who works while others are on strike, or who takes the job of a person on strike; a strikebreaker. (2) An exceptionally ugly woman.

scadger, *n.* A mean man.

scag or **skag,** *n.* An ugly woman.

scag hag, *n.* A heterosexual woman who hangs around gay men.

scalawag, *n.* A reprobate.

scam, *n.* A swindle, a confidence game, a fraud. ["They're know as 'scam' operators, promotors who set up ostensibly legitimate businesses, order a large amount of merchandise on credit, sell it fast . . . and then go bankrupt leaving their creditors unpaid." *Wall Street Journal* (1966).] *Syn.:* bill of goods, bite, bunco, bunco game, burn the C, clip game, the con, con game, dipsy-doodle, double shuffle, fast shuffle, flimflam, fucking, grift, gyp, hosing, hustle, hype, murphy, number, razzle-dazzle, rip-off, rooking, sell, shell game, skinning, slicker game, sting, sucker game, suckering, suck-in.

scamp, *n.* A troublemaker, a young schemer. *Syn.:* enfant terrible, rapscallion, rascal, ribald, rogue, scalawag, sly-boots, villain.

Scandihoovian, *n.* A Scandinavian.

scank, *n.* An unattractive female.

scapegoat, *n.* A person falsely blamed for someone else's error. *Syn.*: fall guy, goat, patsy, whipping boy.

scared shitless, *idiom.* Terrified, extremely worried. ["You're scared shitless this little affair will do you out of old Tanager's dough, aren't you?" Louis Auchincloss, *Rector of Justin* (1964).] *Idioms:* fudging one's undies, goose-bumpy, goose-fleshy, scared fartless, scared spitless, shitting one's drawers, scared witless.

scatterbrain, *n.* A forgetful, disorganized person. *Syn.*: birdbrain, featherbrain, harebrain, rattlebrain, rattlehead, shatterbrain.

scattergood, *n.* A person who squanders wealth. *Syn.*: high roller, profligate, spendthrift, waster, wastrel.

schizo or **schiz,** *n.* A person who is schizophrenic. ["If you talk to God you are praying, if God talks to you, you are a schizo"—adapted from Thomas Szasz.]

schlemazel, *n.* An awkward, bumbling loser.

schlemiel, *n.* A gullible, clumsy fool with consistently bad luck. ["Don't talk like a schlemiel, you schlemiel. Sounds like you're letting them push you around." Budd Schulberg, *What Makes Sammy Run?* (1941).]

schlep or **schlepper,** *n.* A stupid person, a bothersome person. ["I've got a message for all the Penelopes of this world. It is high time they said to their Ulysseses, 'Okay Schlepper, you've been around the world, your turn to keep the home fires burning. I'm splitting on my own trip for a while.'" *Rolling Stone* (1977).]

sclerat, *n.* A wretch.

schlimazl, *n.* An accent-prone, hard-luck, chronic loser. [From German *schlimm* = bad + Hebrew *mazl* = luck. "A schlimazl buys a shirt with two pair of pants and promptly burns a hole in the jacket"—Leo Rosten, *Treasury of Jewish Quotations.*]

schlockmeister, *n.* A person who sells inferior merchandise.

schlocky, *adj.* Shoddy or gaudy. *Syn.*: bargain-basement, cheap-shit, cheesy, crapoid, cruddy, crummy, mickey mouse, tacky, tatty, tinpot, trashy, two-bit.

schloomp, *n.* A lazy fool.

schlub or **zhlub,** *n.* A dull, unpolished person; often a moron.

schmaltzy, *adj.* Overly sweet, sentimental, corny. ["... a pianist whose schmaltz record of *Stardust* made him a Harlem juke box favorite." Leonard Feather, *Inside Be-bop* (1949)]

schmatte, *n.* A person who allows himself to be treated like a rag. [From the Yiddish word for a rag.]

schmearer, *n.* A person who gives a bribe. [Hence, "schmear-taker" means one who takes a bribe.]

schmeckel, *n.* A dope, a stupid person. [From the Yiddish word for a small penis.]

schmegeggy, *n.* A fool. ["And a liar like Nixon as President of the United States. Eisenhower's gift to America. That schmegeggy in his golf shoes—this is what he leaves for posterity"—Philip Roth, *Zuckerman Unbound* (1981).]

schmendrick, *n.* A stupid, inept, ineffectual nobody.

schmuck, *n.* A detestable, repellent, obnoxious person who is often stupid, a schmoo. [From the Yiddish word for penis.]

schnook, *n.* A timid dope or naive patsy who is often victimized. ["To be self-conscious about the possibility of error ... is to be a nerd, a schnook and a wimp." William Safire in *New York Times Magazine* (1980).]

schnorrer, *n.* A person who sponges off relatives and friends, a moocher, a sponger. ["The tale of the perfect schnorrer." Ezra Pound, *Eleven New Cantos* (1934).]

schnozzler, *n.* One who snorts cocaine. [From *schnozzle* = nose.]

schoolbook chump, *n.* A very studious person who is ridiculed.

schtoonk, *n.* A despicable person, a stinker.

schvartze, *n.* A black person. [From the Yiddish word for black.]

sciolist, *n.* A superficial or pretentious person who lays claim to great knowledge.

scorcher, *n.* A sexually aggressive female.

scortator, *n.* A womanizer.

scrag, *n.* An ugly woman.

scrape the bottom of the barrel, *idiom.* To be forced to use incompetent people as a last resort.

scrape-shoe, *n.* A sycophant, a brown-noser.

scrat, *n.* A hermaphrodite.

screaming fairy, *n.* A blatant homosexual.

the screaming meemies, *n.* A hysterical state of mind. *Syn.:* the heebie-jeebies, the meemies.

screaming queen, *n.* (1) A very obvious or blatant homosexual. (2) A lesbian.

screw, *n.* A person who is seen only as a sex object.

screwball, *n.* An eccentric person, a clown, an oddball.

screwed, blued, and tattooed, *idiom.* Completely victimized, cheated, or abused.

screwed up, *adj.* Confused, neurotic, or incompetent.

screw loose have a, *idiom.* Crazy or eccentric. ["Don't go near him, he has a screw loose."]

screw-off, *n.* A person who avoids work.

screw someone out of something, *idiom.* To cheat someone.

screw someone over, *idiom.* To cheat, exploit, or victimize someone.

screw someone up, *idiom.* To mess another person up.

screw up, *idiom.* To blunder, to fail to perform up to snuff, to spoil something, especially by bungling. *Idioms:* ass up, ball up, bitch up, flummox up, fuck up, goof up, gummix up, louse up, make hash of, mommix up, mung up.

screw you, *interj.* To hell with you! Fuck you!

scribblative, *adj.* Pertaining to hasty, verbose writing.

scrog, *v.* To cheat someone.

Scrooge, *n.* A a penny-pincher. [From the character in Charles Dickens's *A Christmas Carol.*]

scroungy or **scrungy,** *adj.* Crummy or grungy.

scrub, *n.* A slob.

scrubber, *n.* A promiscuous female.

scrubbers, *n.* A nasty person.

scrungy, *adj.* Filthy, disgusting.

scuffer, *n.* A prostitute.

scumbag, *n.* A vile, disgusting, worthless person. [From the slang word for a condom.] *Syn.:* scum, scumbucket, scumsucker.

scumbered, *adj.* Full of dog shit, full of baloney, full of crap.

scum-sucking, *adj.* Totally disgusting. [From the slang word for semen.]

scupper, *n.* A promiscuous woman.

scurve, *n.* A loathsome person.

scurvy, *adj.* Ugly, mean, unkempt. ["What difference betwixt this Rome and ours . . . between that scurvy dumbshow and this pageant sheen?"—Browning.]

scut, *n.* A mean, despicable person.

scuz, *n.* A truly disgusting person. ["Her cheating husband, Ernie, a crotch-grabber who brings new meaning to the word scuzzbucket."—*Newsday* (1989).] *Syn.:* scuzzbag, scuzzo, scuzzbucket.

scuzz someone out, *v.* To repel or nauseate someone.

seafood, *n.* A person regarded as a candidate for oral sex. ["Want some seafood, momma"—From the song "Hold Tight."]

seat cover, *n.* An attractive woman driver. [CB radio slang.]

second-fiddle, *n.* A subordinate or stooge, one who is not the best or most important.

section eight, *n.* An eccentric or crazy person. [From Section 8 of U.S. Army regulations relating to the discharge of such persons.]

seddity, *adj.* Pertaining to blacks attempting to imitate whites.

see no further than the end of one's nose, *idiom.* To be narrow-minded or to lack understanding.

seg, *n.* A shit-eating grin. ["Get that seg off your face, now!"]

seggy, *adj.* Altered, castrated.

sell a woof (or **wool**) **ticket,** *idiom.* To brag, bluff, or lie.

sellout, *n.* A person who abandons or betrays people or principles for money or advancement.

semiliterate, *adj.* Barely able to use language correctly.

semolia, *n.* A fool or idiot.

senile, *adj.* Showing the decay of old age. ["I'm in the prime of senility"—Joel Chandler Harris.]

sensual, *adj.* Lewd, voluptuous. ["A sloping meaty jaw, a large discolored bucktooth which showed unpleasantly in a mouth . . . always half open that gave his face its sensual, sly and ugly look"—Wolfe.]

septic, *n.* An American. [From *septic tank* = Yank. British rhyming slang.]

setup, *n.* One who is easily tricked.

sewermouth, *n.* A heavy user of obscenities.

sexist, *n.* One who is biased about, discriminates against, or stereotypes women. ["A sexist is one who proclaims or justifies or assumes the supremacy of one sex (guess which) over the other." S. Vanauken, *Freedom for Movement Girls* (1968).]

sex job, *n.* A provocative, promiscuous woman. *Syn.:* sex bunny, sex kitten, sexpot.

sexo or secho, *n.* A perverted man. [Australian usage.]

sexy, *adj.* Sexually appealing. *Syn.:* dang, foxy, ginchy, humpy, hunky, slutty, steamy, sultry, twisty, va-va-voom, voomy, zaftig

For words starting with *sh* see also *sch*.

shab, *n.* A nasty person.

shack job, *n.* An unmarried woman who lives with a married man.

shack man or **shack rat,** *n.* A man who lives with a woman who is not his wife.

shadmouth, *n.* A black person. [Slang for a person with prominent lips.]

shady lady, *n.* A sexually loose or dishonest woman.

shaft, *n.* A woman considered as a sexual object.

shaft, *v.* To cheat or abuse. ["She Got the Gold Mine, I Got the Shaft"—Jerry Reed song title.] *Idioms*: to give the shaft, to slip it to one where the rhinoceros got the javelin, to slip it to one where the monkey shoved his nuts.

shaft artist or **shaft man,** *n.* A cheat.

shagbag, *n.* A shabby, promiscuous woman. [From the slang word *shag* = copulate.]

shag-nasty, *n.* An evil or unpopular man.

shakebag, *n.* A detestable man.

shake down, *v.* To blackmail or extort.

sham, *n.* An Irish person. [Shortened from *shamrock*, a symbol for Ireland.]

shanty Irish, *idiom.* An Irish person. [From the term for the poorest Irish in America, as distinguished from the middle-class or lace-curtain Irish.]

shark, *n.* A particularly predatory and effective cheat or hustler. ["God save me from the sharks: the loan sharks, card sharks, land sharks, and pool sharks."] *Syn.*: sharp, sharpie, bloodsucker, leech, shakedown artist.

she-devil, *n.* An evil woman.

she-dog, *n.* A bitch.

sheepherder, *n.* A pederast. [From folklore that men who tend sheep use them sexually.]

she-he, *n.* An effeminate or gay man. *Syn.*: she-man, shim.

shellback, *n.* An ultraconservative, rather dumb person. [From the shell of a turtle, a rather slow, dumb creature.]

shemale, *n.* A hateful bitch.

shiksa, *n.* A non-Jewish woman. ["His mother, a lady of the old school, had repeatedly and solemnly warned him that there was a yellow haired, blue-eyed shiksa lying in wait for every good Jewish boy." Judith Krantz *Scruples* (1978).]

shine, *n.* A black person.

shit, *n.* (1) A wretched, despised, obnoxious, despicable person. ["She was a third-class harlot who made up for it by being a first-class shit." J.I.M. Stewart, *Young Patulo* (1976).] *Syn.*: shitass, shitbag, shitheel, shithook, shitepoke, shitface, shithead, shitpot, shitsack, shitsky, shitstick. (2) Boastful or idle talk. (3) Insulting or offensive treatment. ["I took a lot of shit from him before I decided to get a divorce."]

shit, *v.* To exaggerate or lie. ["Please, don't shit me!"]

shitass, *v.* To behave like a despicable or contemptible person, especially by betrayal of a duty or promise.

shit, bit of a, *idiom.* A disgusting person. ["There was a young fellow named Dave,/Who kept a dead whore in a cave/He said, 'I admit!/I'm a bit of a shit/But think of the money I save'"—*The Playboy Book of Limericks.*]

shit-eating grin, *idiom.* An annoying, gloating expression. ["Wipe that shit-eating grin off your face!"]

shitfire, *n.* A bully.

shit fit, *n.* A temper tantrum.

shit-for-brains, *n.* A truly stupid person.

shit for the birds, *idiom.* Nonsense, bullshit. ["That's pure shit for the birds."]

shit, give a, *idiom.* To care. ["I don't give a shit about Italian lira."—Richard M. Nixon, on being asked by H.R. Haldeman if he wanted to hear a report on the decline of the Italian lira.]

shitheaded, *adj.* Foolish and obnoxious.

shit-hunter, *n.* A pederast. *Syn.:* shit-packer, shit-stirrer, stirshit.

shit in your hat!, *idiom.* Go to hell! Go fuck yourself!

shit-kicker or **shit-stomper,** *n.* (1) A stupid person. (2) A rustic, a hick, a farmer. (3) A white person.

shit list or **crap list,** *n.* A list of people who are going to get it, but good. ["Watch your ass, man! You're on my shit list."]

shit one's pants or **shit one's drawers,** *idiom.* To become so terrified as to be unable to control one's sphincter.

shit on it, *interj.* Forget it!

shit on one, *v.* To treat someone very badly. ["Don't let them shit on you, open your mouth."]

shit on one, *interj.* An exclamation of rejection. ["shit on him!"]

shit out of luck, *idiom.* Ill-fated or ill-starred. ["You get nothing. You're shit out of luck."] *Syn.:* S.O.L. (pronounced as separate letters).

shit, piss, and corruption, *interj.* ["... is an early twentieth-century exclamation that with unhurried deliberation expresses a feeling of utter dismay. It keeps a close relation to its kindred 'Hell, fire, rape, and sodomy,' a nineteenth-century contribution"—Ashley Montagu, *The Anatomy of Swearing* (1967).]

shit-stirrer, *n.* A malicious busybody.

shits through his mouth, *idiom.* To bullshit. *Syn.*: he's doing a lot of shitting and his pants aren't even down.

shitter, *n.* A liar and a loudmouth.

shit-yellow, *adj.* Light-skinned. ["I killed you Malcolm/the first time I got locked/inside my shit-yellow complexion/ I laughed at all my black brothers"—Conyus, "Confessions to Malcolm."]

shitty, *adj.* Disgusting, rotten, malicious, nasty, lousy.

shonk or **shonky,** *n.* A peddler or a Jewish merchant.

shonnicker or **shon,** *n.* A Jewish man.

shoot oneself in the foot, *v.* To create one's own problems, to commit a major blunder. ["You just shot yourself in the foot. Now you're going to get it, but good!"]

shoot one down in flames, *v.* To defeat or badly hurt someone. ["I'm going to shoot you down in flames for dissing my woman."]

shoot out one's marbles, *idiom.* To go berserk.

shopaholic, *n.* A compulsive shopper. ["(The rumor) that Diana is a 'shopaholic' . . . was described as 'absolute rubbish' "—*Washington Post* (1984).]

shorteyes, *n.* A child-molester.

short-peckered, *adj.* Having a small penis. ["A skinny old maid named Dunn/Wed a short-peckered son-of-a gun./ She said, 'I don't care/If there is not much there./God knows it is better than none.' "—Limerick, *Immortalia* (1927).]

short-heeled wench, *n.* A promiscuous woman.

short-sheet, *v.* To play a dirty trick. [From the trick of doubling a bedsheet so that one can not fully get into the bed.]

shove it or **shove it up your ass,** *idiom.* A rude invitation intended as an insult. ["You can take your money and shove it!"] *Idiom:* stick it.

showcase nigger, *n.* A token black person conspicuously displayed in a white firm.

shower scum, *n.* A slimy, deceitful person. ["He is nothing but shower scum. He's running around with three women; each one thinks he is going to marry her."] *Syn.:* pond scum, bath scum.

shpos, *n.* An obnoxious hospital patient. [The acronym for "subhuman piece of shit," pronounced like "mahs."]

shrew, *n.* A nag, a cantankerous woman. ["Cursed be the man, the poorest wretch in life,/The crouching vassal to the tyrant wife,/Who has not sixpence but in her possession./Who must to her his dear friend's secret tell;/Who dreads a curtain lecture worse than hell./Were such a wife had fallen to my part,/I'd break her spirit or I'd break her heart"—Robert Burns, *The Henpecked Husband.*]

shtarka or **shtarker,** *n.* A thug, a hoodlum. ["Real shtarkas, dig, the kind that wear wool suits with no underwear" —Lenny Bruce.]

shtup, *n.* A sexually loose woman.

shuck and jive or **shuck,** *v.* To try to fool one with apparently sincere but dishonest talk. ["Yawhl jivin' . . . Yawhl Schuchin." Ed Bullins *Theme is Blackness* (1966).]

shuffler, *n.* A confidence man.

shut-eyes, *n.* A sexual pervert. [From the suggestion: "Just shut your eyes . . ."]

shuttlebutt, *n.* A woman with a fat behind.

shut your face, *imper.* A command to stop talking. *Idioms:* shut up, shut your bazoo, shut your shit, shut your yap, zip your lip, zip your mouth, button your lip, shut your ass.

shy-cock, *n.* A coward.

shylock, *n.* A usurer, a loan shark. [From the Shakespearean character in *A Merchant of Venice.*]

sickie or **sicko,** *n.* A mentally ill person, a psychopath.

sidewinder, *n.* A rotten, sneaky person.

siddity, *adj.* Arrogant.

signifier, *n.* A mischievous, gloating liar, a troublemaker. ["Deep down in the jungle where the tall grass grows/ Lived the signifyingest monkey that the world knows" —Wepman, Newman, and Binderman, *The Life* (1976).]

silk, *n.* A white woman.

silk and satin, *n.* A woman viewed as merely a sex object.

silk stocking, *n.* A wealthy person.

simp, *n.* Fool or imbecile. [Short for *simpleton.*]

simple Simon, *n.* A person who doesn't use drugs. [Considered a square by those who do.]

sink, *n.* A dirty place, either physically or socially. ["If you keep going to that sink, God only knows what you are going to catch."] *Syn.:* Augean stable, cesspit, cesspool, Sodom, sty.

sir echo, little, *n.* A yes-man.

sit down before you fall down, *interj.* Shut up and sit down.

sit on it and rotate, *interj.* General term of abuse. [From the TV series "Hill Street Blues."]

skank or **skang,** *n.* An ugly, smelly, sluttish woman. *Syn.:* skanky box.

skat, *n.* A heavy glob of shit. [Used at times as a more polite word for *turd,* as in "bear skat" or "dog skat."]

skeet, *n.* A despicable, disgusting person. [From a glob of nasal mucus.]

skeevy, *adj.* Sleazy and revolting.

skeezer, *n.* A slut, a ho.

skibby or **skippy**, *n.* An Asian, particularly a Japanese person. [From the word for an Asian mistress or prostitute.]

skillet, *n.* A black person.

Skimo, *n.* An Eskimo.

skin, *n.* An attractive woman viewed as a sex object.

skin dog, *n.* A womanizer.

skinhead, *n.* (1) A bald person or a person with a shaven head. (2) A neo-fascist.

skippy, *n.* A gay or effeminate man.

skirt, *n.* A woman considered as a sexual object; hence, "skirt-chaser" = womanizer. ["The two patriarchs never tired of chasing twenty-year old skirts in their old age." Kate Millett, *Flying* (1974).]

skrungy, *adj.* Disgusting.

skunk, *n.* A loathsome, hateful person.

sky pilot, *n.* A preacher or a missionary. *Syn.*: amen-snorter, bish, christer, cushion-thumper, devil-catcher, devil-chaser, devil-dodger, devil-driver, devil-pitcher, devil-scolder, devil-teaser, gluepot, god-botherer, gospel cove, gospel-grinder, gospel postilion, gospel-pusher, gospel shark, gospel sharp, gospel-shooter, gospel-whanger, haul-devil, jesus-screamer, jesus-shouter, parish bull, parish prig, pound-text, pulpit-cuffer, puzzle-text, sinhound, sky-rider, sky scout.

slack, *n.* (1) A unkempt man or woman. (2) A sexually promiscuous woman.

slant, *n.* An Asian. [From the epicanthic fold, which gives a slanty look to the eyes.] *Syn.*: slants, slant-eye(s), slit(s), slope, slopie, slopeeyes, squint-eye(s), tight, tight-eye(s).

slap-sauce, *n.* A parasite.

slattern, *n.* A sloppy, unkempt woman. *Syn.*: dowd, drab, draggletail, malkin, slamkin, slamtrash, slut, streel.

slave, *n.* A woman.

sleazebag, *n.* A disgusting, smelly person. ["We are not giving away any principles, because we do have a few on this side of the House, unlike the sleazebags over there" —*National Times* (1985).] *Syn.:* chili bowl, creep, crud, dirtbag, dirtball, douche bag, filthbag, fishball, geek, pusbag, scuzzbag, scuzzo, sleaze, sleez, sleezo, sleazoid, sleazeball.

sleeping Jesus, *n.* (1) A drug user who keeps nodding out. (2) A dull person.

sleepy-time girl, *n.* A promiscuous woman.

sleez or **sleaze,** *n.* A slut. ["Oh God, red nail polish—I look like a sleaze." *Time* (1977).]

slewfoot or **slobfoot,** *n.* A clumsy person.

slick, *n.* A tricky, crafty, unethical person. *Syn.:* slicker, slickster, smoothie, hustler.

slick, *adj.* Deceptive, glib, manipulative, cunning. ["A pair of slick operators had given the district a bad name by salting a barren claim"—Oscar Lewis.] *Syn.:* lubricious, sliddery, slippery, slippy, slithery.

slick chick, *n.* An attractive young woman.

slim, *n.* A police stool pigeon.

slimeball, *n.* A completely rotten, repugnant person. ["Like me and Kimberly go to this bitchen store on Ventura Boulevard, and like the slimeball owner is like totally spying on us in the dressing room"—Corey and Westermark, *Fer Shurr! How to Be a Valley Girl—Totally* (1982).] *Syn.:* slimebag, slime, slimebucket, muckbag, muckball, muckbucket.

sling it, *idiom.* To lie and exaggerate. *Syn.:* bullshit, shoot the bull, sling the bull.

sling mud, *idiom.* To malign someone.

slip one's trolley, *idiom.* To lose one's cool and act a little crazy.

slob, *n.* An unattractive, sloppy, mediocre person. ["Harding was not a bad man, he was just a slob"—Alice Roosevelt Longworth.]

sloomy, *adj.* Lacking energy or drive.

sloppy seconds, *n.* A woman who has just made love with one person and is ready to proceed with a second.

sloth, *n.* A lazy, worthless idler. ["... he would jog a slothful conscience and marshal its forces"—Vernon Parrington.] *Syn.*: slug, slugabed, slowpoke, a do-nothing.

slotted-job, *n.* A woman. [From reference to anatomy.]

sludge, *n.* Baloney. [From the feces in sewage.]

sludgeball, *n.* A repulsive and filthy person. *Syn.*: sludgebucket.

sluggard, *n.* A lazy, worthless person. ["Plough deep while sluggards sleep;/And you shall have corn to sell and to keep"—Benjamin Franklin, *Poor Richard's Almanack* (1756).] *Syn.*: bum, dolittle, lazybones, loafer, slouch.

slummy, *n.* A poorly dressed, unattractive woman.

slut, *n.* (1) A sexually loose woman or a prostitute. ["An apple, an egg, and a nut, you may eat after a slut"—John Ray, *English Proverbs* (1670).] (2) A promiscuous gay man. ["Of all the tame beasts, I hate sluts"—John Ray, *English Proverbs* (1670).]

slutch, *n.* A nasty, sluttish woman. [From a blend of *slut* + *bitch*.]

slyboots, *n.* A clever rascal who pretends to be dumb.

smack freak or **smackhead,** *n.* A heroin addict.

small change, *n.* An unimportant, no-account person. *Syn.*: small fry, small potatoes.

smarmy, *adj.* Unctuous, self-righteous, oily. ["He's a smarmy, ingratiating swine." S. Raven, *Close of Play* (1962).]

smartass, *n.* An impudent and arrogant person. ["You're too pretty to be such a smart ass. Just watch your step." P. Marks, *Collector's Choice* (1972).] *Syn.*: armchair general, bigmouth, hodad, know-it-all, smart aleck, smart guy, smartmouth, smarty, smartypants, wise apple, wiseacre, wiseass, wiseguy, wisehead, wisenheimer.

smellfest or **lickdish,** *n.* An uninvited guest at a meal.

smellfungus, *n.* A perennial complainer.

smellsmock, *n.* A lecherous man.

smoke, *n.* An American black person. *Syn.*: smoked Irishman, smoke stack, smoky, smudge, smear, smidget, smitbutt.

smoke and mirrors, *idiom.* Skillful lies or cover-ups.

smoker, *n.* One who smokes marijuana. *Syn.*: bushwhacker, grasshead, grasshopper, griefer, gashhead, hay-burner, hayhead, motter, mugglehead, pipe-hitter, pothead, reefer, reefing man, snake, tea-blower, teahead, teahound, tea man, viper, weedhead.

smurf, *n.* Someone who launders criminals' money.

smuthound, *n.* (1) One who sees obscenity everywhere; hence, a censor. [Coined by H. L. Mencken.] (2) A man who loves pornography.

smut peddler, *n.* A seller of pornography.

smut-slut, *n.* A sexually promiscuous woman.

snafu, *v.* To make a serious mistake, to foul up. [Acronym for "*s*ituation *n*ormal, *a*ll *f*ucked *u*p."] *Syn.*: commfu, fubar, fubb, fumtu, gfu, imfu, jaafu, jacfu, janfu, mfu, nabu, sabu, samfu, sdapfu, snefu, snarasfu, susfu, tabu, tafubar, tarfu, tasfuira, tccfu.

snag, *n.* An ugly woman.

snake, *n.* (1) A deceitful, treacherous person; a snake in the grass. ["All modern men are descended from a worm-like creature, but it shows more on some people"—Will Cuppy.] (2) A promiscuous or ugly young woman. (3) A white person.

snap it up, *imper.* Hurry up!

snarge, *n.* An unlikeable person.

snarky, *adj.* Irritable.

snatch, *n.* A woman considered sexually.

sniffer, *n.* A cocaine user.

sniffy, *adj.* Haughty and hypercritical. [From smelling something nasty.] *Syn.*: disdainful, snifty, fault-finding.

snippy, *adj.* Griping hypercritically or cutting people down.

snit, *n.* A fit of agitation or anger.

snitch, *n.* An informer, a stool pigeon. ["Lopez was an informant . . . a paragon among snitches." S. Rifkin, *Mc-Quaid in August* (1979).] *Syn.*: bat carrier, beefer, bleeter, bogus, buzzman, canary, cheese-eater, dime-dropper, dimer, finger, geepo, nark, nightingale, nose, pigeon, rat, singer, snitcher, squawk, squealer, stool, stoolie, weasel.

snitzy, *adj.* Ritzy.

snobbish, *adj.* Acting like a snob. *Syn.*: dicty, high-hat, potty, snobby, snooty.

snollygoster, *n.* A clever, but dishonest person.

snookered, *adj.* Deceived.

snool, *n.* A cringing person.

snooser, *n.* A Scandinavian.

snot or **snotty,** *n.* A rotten, contemptible, often contemptuous person. [From the word for nasal mucus. "A British Naval Party under the command of a snappily saluting little snotty." P. Dickenson, *Poison Oracle* (1974).] *Syn.*: bugger, cur, puke, skunk, snake, snotnose, snottynose, stinkard, stinkaroo, stinker, toad, wretch.

snotnose or **snotnosed kid,** *n.* A young, inept, inexperienced person. [From one who can't wipe his own nose.]

a snowball's chance in hell, *idiom.* No possibility whatever of something happening or succeeding. ["You have about as much as a snowball's chance in hell of my going out with you."]

snow, *v.* Cheat, do out of.

snow job, *n.* A flattering and false story intending to deceive. ["That was some snow job you gave her to get her to go away with you."]

snudge, *n.* A tightwad.

snurge, *v.* To shirk work by disappearing or sneaking off.

soap-crawler, *n.* A toady.

soch or **sosh,** *n.* A social climber, a parvenu. [Pronounced like "posh."]

sock it to someone, *idiom.* To criticize vigorously. ["I'm going to sock it to him at the meeting. I'm really going to let him have it!"]

soft and nasty, *adj.* Pertaining to an unpleasant or difficult situation. ["This job is getting soft and nasty like cat shit."]

soft-jaw, *n.* A promiscuous woman. [From a woman whose mouth cannot form the word *no.*]

soft-roll, *n.* A woman who is easily available for sex.

soft soap, *idiom.* Flattery, sweet talk. *Syn.:* applesauce, banana oil, butter, eyewash, grease, oil, salve.

soft stuff, *n.* Nonsense. [From *soft stuff* = feces.]

so mad one can spit nails, *idiom.* Extremely furious.

someone blew out his/her pilot light, *idiom.* Being confused, high on drugs, or vague.

son of a bitch, *n.* A despicable, disgusting, mean-hearted, troublesome person. *Syn.:* S.O.B. (pronounced as separate letters), son of a whore, son of a bitch of a bastard, sombitch, sonovabitch, son of a b, son of a female canine, son of a sow, son of a whore, whoreson.

sorry-ass(ed), *adj*. Inferior, incompetent, half-assed.

sow, *n*. A fat woman.

space cadet or space case, *n*. (1) An eccentric who is removed from the real world, one who lives far out in outer space. (2) A heavy drug user.

spaced-out, *adj*. Giddy.

spade, *n*. A black person. ["... one quiet church went to extra ordinary lengths to rid itself of the 'dicty spade' who wore his learning on his sleeve." Darryl Pinckney, *High Cotton* (1992).]

spado, *n*. A man who has been castrated.

spaghetti, *n*. A person of Italian descent. *Syn.*: spaghetti-bender, macaroni.

spaghetti-bender, *n*. An Italian. *Syn.*: dago, dingbat, ding, eytie, eyto, ghin, gingo, ginney, ginzo, greaser, guin, guinea, guinie, guinnee, hikes, itie, macaroni, organ-grinder, ringtail, spic, walliyo, wop, zool.

spaginzy, *n*. A black person. ["... predicted I would come to no good among the ... cows, monkeys, jungle bunnies, jigabors spaginzy-spagades, mole skins ..."—Darryl Pinckney, *High Cotton* (1992).

spaniel, *n*. A toady.

spare, *n*. A female who engages in extramarital sex.

spare prick, *n*. A totally useless person. ["He's as much use as a spare prick at a lesbian wedding."]

spare rib, *n*. A married man's mistress. *Syn.*: belly-lass, belly-piece, jug, kept woman, lady-bird, leveret, lie, piece of stray, poke, side dish, smig.

spare tire, *n*. A worthless, unhelpful person.

sparrow fart, *n*. A pipsqueak.

spastic, *n*. An incompetent, a social reject. *Syn.*: spas, spaz.

spaz around, *v*. To fool around.

spazzy, *adj*. Weird.

spear-chucker, *n.* An American black.

specious, *adj.* False, deceptive.

spic or **spick,** *n.* A Spanish-American or any person of Hispanic extraction. *Syn:* Spig, spiggoty.

spider, *n.* An evil, cleverly scheming person.

spigot-sucker, *n.* One who practices fellatio.

spill, *n.* A black person, a Puerto Rican, or a black Hispanic.

spindleshanks, *n.* A tall, skinny man.

spin one's wheels, *idiom.* To waste time, to be stuck in a rut.

spinster, *n.* An older, unmarried woman. ["Merely a bit of spinster-baiting." Louis MacNeice, *Modern Poetry* (1938).] *Syn.:* maiden lady, old maid, spinstress, tabby.

spitfire, *n.* A hot-tempered woman.

spiv, *n.* A small-time, flashily dressed hustler. ["Mad Kidd was an ex-plumber made good; a total spiv down to the last camel hair in his coat"—Kate Saunders, *Evening Standard* (1989), British usage.]

splib, *n.* An American black.

splinter your toupee, *idiom.* To go crazy.

split stuff or **split tail,** *n.* A woman seen only as a sexual object.

sponge, *n.* A parasite.

spook, *n.* A black person.

spookerican, *n.* A person of mixed black and Puerto Rican descent.

spread it on thick, *idiom.* To embellish, to exaggerate. [From *it* = shit.] *Syn.:* spread the bull.

spurge, *n.* A wimpy or effeminate man.

spud, *n.* A jerk.

squab, *n.* A chick, a young woman.

squabash, *v.* To crush with scathing criticism.

square, *n.* An old-fashioned, conservative, unsophisticated person. ["So I didn't expect it to be that good, not from the square dude you are." Bernard Malamud, *Tenants* (1971).] *Syn.*: citizen, clone, clyde, cornball, cube, drip, drizzle, drizzlepuss, droid, Elk, flat hoop, flat tire, foursquare, fuddy-dud, fuddy-duddy, Jeff, Ken, shim, square john, square apple, straight, straight-arrow, Zelda, zoid.

square, *adj.* Conventional in attitudes and behavior. ["Canada is so square even the female impersonators are women"—*Outrageous,* film (1983).] *Syn.*: bogus, burbed-out, buttondown, clonish, gray-flannel, icky, lame, plastic, squeaky-clean, uncool, unhep, unhipped, white-bread, Wonder bread.

squarebrain, *n.* A conservative fool.

squarehead, *n.* A Scandinavian or a German.

square peg (in a round hole), *idiom.* A misfit. ["I'm sorry to say that I'm going to have to let you go. You're a square peg. You don't fit into our program."]

square to the wood, *n.* Very immature.

squash that, *interj.* Forget it! *Syn.*: squash that melon.

squaw, *n.* One's wife or girlfriend.

squid, *n.* A student who studies all the time.

squirrel, *n.* (1) A strange or eccentric person. (2) A young woman. [From *squirrel* = vulva.]

squirt, *n.* A short, insignificant, or unpleasant person.

squishy or **squooshy,** *adj.* Overly sentimental, schmaltzy, soppy.

squit, *n.* Silly talk.

stacked like a brick shithouse, *idiom.* Having a sexually attractive body. [From the fact that a homemade brick privy is generally poorly built and curvy, not straight.] *Syn.*: built like a brick shithouse.

stallion, *n.* A tall, attractive, sexy female.

stand around with one's finger up one's ass or **in one's ear,** *idiom.* To do nothing while others are busy or need help.

stank, *adj.* Ugly.

stanky, *adj.* Smelly.

star, *n.* An especially attractive female.

star-fucker, *n.* One who offers sex to rock performers, a groupie.

startenated fool, *n.* Someone as stupid now as when dropped from the womb.

steal a rotten doughnut out of a bucket of snot, *idiom.* To be dishonest.

steamy, *adj.* Very sexy.

steatopygian, *n.* One having a big fat ass.

stepinfetchit, *n.* An Uncle Tom. [From a black actor of the 1930s and 1940s, whose stereotype included bulging eyes, smiling, shuffling, and saying "Yassuh, boss, I'se coming."]

stick, *n.* A stiff, overly formal person; a stick-in-the-mud.

stick it, *imper.* Take it and shove it! *Idioms*: cram it, put it in your ear, ram it, stow it, stick it where the sun doesn't shine, stick it up your jumper.

stick it to one, *idiom.* To attack someone violently, verbally or physically.

sticky-fingered, *adj.* Thieving.

stiff, *v.* To fail to pay a bill or tip.

stiff-assed, *adj.* Haughty, nitpicking.

stiff prick, *n.* A strict boss.

sting, *v.* To swindle.

stinker, *n.* A rotten person, or a promiscuous woman.

stinking rich, *idiom.* Very rich. *Syn.*: stinky-pie rich.

stinko, *adj.* Malodorous. ["Your stinko breath is like wolf pussy."]

stink on ice, *idiom.* To be terrible, foul.

stinkpot, *n.* A smelly object, condition, or person. ["Go away you stinkpot." James Joyce, *Portrait of an Artist as a young Man* (1916).]

stink to high heaven, *idiom.* To be particularly rotten.

stitch someone up, *idiom.* To deceive. ["Leched over by managers, stitched up by agents, girls in the music biz have traditionally paid a high price for succumbing to the lure of lurex"—*Ms.* London magazine (1959).]

stomp-ass, *adj.* Nastily violent.

stone fox, *n.* A sexy woman.

stooge, *n.* A completely acquiescent underling, a Charlie McCarthy, a dummy, a yes-man. ["(they) branded the moderate African leaders as 'Swary Stooges' of Premier Smith (of Rhodesia)." *Detroit Free Press* (1978).]

stool on someone, *v.* To inform or rat.

stow it, *imper.* Stop it, stick it.

strabismic, *adj.* Cross-eyed.

straight, *n.* A heterosexual person or one who does not use drugs. *Syn.:* apple, brown shoes, do-righter, John, lame duck, square, square apple, breeder, citizen, vanilla.

strawberry, *n.* A slut who engages in sex for drugs. ["All the vice girl victims (of a Los Angeles serial killer) were known as strawberries—American slang for hookers who trade sex for drugs"—*Sunday Mirror* (1989).]

strictly from hunger, *idiom.* Very poor quality, mediocre product or performance.

stroker, *n.* A sycophant.

strommocks, *n.* A big, mannish woman.

struggle and strife, *n.* A wife.

strung out, *adj.* Heavily addicted to drugs.

strunz, *n.* Nonsense, bullshit. [From the Italian.]

strut fart, *n.* An arrogant, conceited man.

stub, *n.* A fool.

stubble-jumper, *n.* An Okie. [Canadian usage.]

stud, *n.* A promiscuous and sexually prodigious man. ["A notorious seducer; a ladies'-man; a cuckolder of the rich; in short a stud." Salman Rushdie, *Midnight's Children* (1981).] *Syn.*: Casanova, chaser, cocksman, Don Juan, gashhound, heavycake, horndog, hot nuts, hound dog, jelly roll, meathound, pistol Pete, rooster, stallion, stud hammer, wolf.

stud-muffin, *n.* A vain, good-looking guy.

stuff, *n.* A woman defined by her sexual potential.

stuff a sock in it, *idiom.* Shut up!

stuffed shirt, *n.* A conservative, dull man. *Syn.*: blimp, Colonel Blimp, fuddy-duddy.

stultiloquence, *n.* Empty talk.

stump-jumper, *n.* A farmer, a shit-kicker.

stump water, your head is full of, *idiom.* Not overly bright. *Idioms:* an idea would bust your head wide open, you have about as much sense as you could slap in a gnat's ass with a butter paddle.

stunted, *adj.* Underdeveloped, mentally slow.

stupe or **stoop,** *n.* An idiot.

stupid, *adj.* Dumb. ["Ordinarily he was insane, but he had lucid moments when he was merely stupid"—Heinrich Heine.] *Syn.*: beefheaded, beef-witted, beetleheaded, blockish, chuckleheaded, doltish, fatheaded, hammerheaded, numskulled, thick-witted, air-brained, ass-brained, barmy-brained, bird-brained, blubber-brained, buffle-brained, clay-brained, cock-brained, culverheaded, emptyskulled, feather-brained, fuck-brained, harebrained, leather-brained, maggot-brained, scramble-brained, shit-brained, squiffy.

sub, *n.* (1) A slow-witted person. (2) A promiscuous person.

subhuman, *n.* A stupid, gross person; a social reject.

suck, *v.* To be revolting. ["This job sucks."] *Syn:* sucks rope.

suck ass, *idiom.* To curry favor via flattery.

suck-ass, *adj.* Totally bad.

suck eggs, *idiom.* (1) To be mean and irritable. (2) To be totally rotten. (3) To be told off nastily. ["Tell your husband to go suck huge eggs"—*Village Voice.*]

sucker, *n.* (1) A victim of fraud, a dupe, a mark, a patsy. ["There's a sucker born every minute"—P. T. Barnum.] (2) One who curries favor. (3) A woman who performs oral sex.

suck hind tit, *idiom.* To be in a losing position, to get the last and least attractive items or treatment.

suck it and see!, *imper.* Don't ask such stupid questions.

suck-off, *n.* An obsequious person, a brown-nose.

suck one in, *idiom.* To deceive by promising things you won't deliver.

suck up to one, *idiom.* To use flattery in order to gain influence. [" 'sucking up to the stars' " is a way of doing business in Hollywood.]

sucky, *adj.* Awful. ["This food is sucky. It really sucks."]

sugar daddy, *n.* (1) A man who keeps a mistress or girlfriend. *Syn.*: daddy, John, old man, poppa, Santa Claus, sugar papa. (2) An elderly gay man who keeps a younger man.

sugar pants, *n.* A gentle person, a pussycat.

suggin, *adj.* Having inherited deficiencies. ["They's a family over Whistleberry that's all suggins. They've married each other so much they all got six toes an' six fingers."]

superpatriot, *n.* A strong nationalist; a severe critic of those who question his country's policies, particularly abroad; a hard hat. ["The 100% American is 99% an idiot" —George Bernard Shaw.]

superspade, *n.* A very race-conscious black.

superstrap, *n.* An overly serious student.

surd, *n.* A dumb and insensitive person.

swashbucket, *n.* A slattern.

swatchel, *n.* A fat slattern.

sweat hog, *n.* A fat, unattractive, or promiscuous woman.

Swede or **big dumb Swede,** *n.* An awkward fool.

sweet or **a sweetie,** *n.* A gay man.

sweet chocolate, *n.* A sexy, appealing black woman.

sweetie, *n.* A gay man.

sweet mama, *n.* A girlfriend.

sweet man, *n.* A lover of a married woman. ["A woman down in Georgia/Got her two sweet-men confused./One knocked on the front do'/One knocked on de back" —Blues Song, Langston Hughes.]

sweet meat, *n.* A female.

swellhead, *n.* A vain person.

swensker, *n.* A Swede.

swillbelly, *n.* One who eats like a pig.

swine-eater, *n.* A white person.

swing the lead, *idiom.* To shirk one's duties.

swish, *n.* An effeminate or gay man, especially a homosexual.

swivel-neck, *n.* A nerd.

swivet, *n.* An angry fit, a snit.

Sylvester, *n.* A white man.

tabby cat, *n.* A shrew.

table-grade, *n.* A sexy female who looks good enough to eat. ["Where I come from we call that kind of stuff 'table pussy' "—William Saroyan, "Jim Dandy" (1947).]

tacky, *adj.* Lacking good taste. *Syn.:* inferior, shabby, vulgar, icky, ratty.

taco or **tacohead,** *n.* A Mexican or Mexican-American. *Syn.:* taco-bender, tacohead.

tad, *n.* An Irish Catholic.

taffeta phrases, *idiom.* Flowery speech or writing.

taig, *n.* A Roman Catholic. [Used by Protestants in Northern Ireland.] ["This week a new slogan appeared . . . (in) Protestant West Belfast. It read: 'All Taigs are targets.' "—*Observer* (1982).]

tail, *n.* A woman viewed strictly as a sexual object. *Syn.:* article, bit of goods, bit of rough, brush, bush, calico, cooler, coot, crumpet, goose, gusset, hair, hat, hole, jazz, kippy-dope, meat, muff, nooky, piece of Eve's flesh, piece of mutton, piece of tail, pork, punch, pussy, rabbit pie, saddle, screw, shaft, skirt, split stuff, tit, trim, whisker.

tailgunner, *n.* A male homosexual.

take a flying fuck, *imper.* Go to hell! *Idioms:* take a flying frig, take a flying fuck at a rubber duck, take a flying fuck at a rolling doughnut.

take it, *imper.* A demand for fellatio.

takeoff artist, *n.* A drug addict who robs other addicts and pushers.

take shit, *idiom.* To permit humiliation, bullying. *Syn.:* eat shit, eat dirt.

take someone down a peg, *idiom.* To deflate a vain or pompous ass. *Idioms:* cut off at the knees, cut off one's water, prick one's balloon, put a tuck in one's tail, settle one's hash, take someone down a notch, take the shine out of, take the wind out of one's sails, turn off one's water.

take the piss out of someone, *idiom.* To stop someone's cocksure behavior, sometimes violently.

taliped, *n.* Awkward. [From the word meaning "clubfooted."]

talk one ragged, *idiom.* To bore someone to death. *Syn.:* talk one's ear off, talk one's head off.

talk out of the side of your mouth, *idiom.* To exaggerate.

talking shit, *idiom.* Talking foolishness. *Idioms:* talking trash, talk through one's ass, talk through the back of one's neck, talk through one's hat.

talk to hear one's own voice, *idiom.* To talk excessively and egotistically.

tapinosis, *n.* Particularly nasty name-calling.

tar brush, touch of the, *idiom.* A person having, or believed to have, some black ancestry. ["And did you know that I have a tinge of the tar brush"—Paul Robeson.]

tard, *n.* A mentally deficient person. [Short for *retard.*]

tattoo, *n.* A boob. ["... you feel like a faggot window dresser schlepping the naked mannequin in and out while the dumb tattoo gape at you from the street"—Lenny Bruce.]

tchotchke, *n.* A woman seen as a toy or plaything.

tease, *n.* A woman who seems to want sexual activity but stops short of intercourse.

tear one a new asshole, *idiom.* To engage in a vicious verbal or physical attack.

teddy bear, *n.* A short sexy woman.

teenybopper, *n.* An adolescent or preteenager. *Syn.*: bubble-gummer, grommet, the teen tribe, teeny-rocker, tweenager.

tell it to the marines, *idiom.* I don't believe you. *Syn.*: tell it to Sweeney.

tell owlshit from putty without a map, can't, *idiom.* Very stupid. *Idioms*: doesn't know how to scratch his ass, doesn't know frogshit from pea soup, doesn't know sheepshit from cherry seeds.

termagant, *n.* A loud vixen, a ball-breaker.

terrier, *n.* An Irish person.

the hell you say, *idiom.* I don't believe you!

theroid, *adj.* Savage.

thersitical, *adj.* Speaking loudly and insultingly.

thick-lips, *n.* A black person.

thicko, *n.* A dumbbell, dimwit. ["The midwife laid her hand on his/Thick Skull,/With this Prophetick blessing/Be Thou Dull"—John Dryden.]

thing, *n.* A gay or effeminate man.

think one's shit doesn't stink, *idiom.* To be extremely egotistical.

third-sexer, *n.* A homosexual.

thithy, *n.* A effeminate male.

thoroughbred, *n.* A stylish hooker.

three-balls, *n.* A Jewish person. [From the three brass balls that hang outside a pawnshop.]

three bricks shy of a load, *idiom.* Very dumb.

three-letter man, *n.* A gay man.

throttlebottom, *n.* An unfit politician.

throw attitude, *idiom.* To act rude or angry. *Syn.*: give attitude, throw tude, give tude.

thrumster, *n.* A lecherous male.

thumbsucker, *n.* An inept person. ["I ain't followin' a bunch of thumbsuckers—you want to run a national firm, friend, you put your arse in gear behind us"—"The Firm," British TV play (1989).]

tib, *n.* A whore.

ticky-tacky, *adj.* Poorly made or done.

tiger, *n.* A cruel person.

tight, *adj.* Greedy, stingy. ["He was tight, and, as was characteristic of him, he soon dropped any professional discretion that he might have been supposed to exercise" —Edmund Wilson.] *Idioms:* so tight when he grins his pecker skins back, so tight she makes pancakes so thin they've got just one side, so tight that when you blink your toes curl.

tight as a tick, *idiom.* Frugal.

tight as Kelsey's balls, *idiom.* Parsimonious, stingy. *Syn.:* tight as Reilly's balls.

tightass, *n.* A tense, rigid person; a prude.

tinhorn, *n.* A flashy and despicable person, especially a politician.

tio taco, *n.* A Chicano Uncle Tom.

tired-ass, *adj.* Overused, clichéd. ["... thinking in tired-ass racial clichés."]

tired woman, *n.* A naive female.

tit-kisser, *n.* A seducer.

titless wonder, *n.* A woman with small breasts.

titotular bosh, *n.* Rubbish.

tits on a bull or **tits on a boar,** *idiom.* Something that is of no value or use.

titty, *n.* A woman.

T.L., *n.* A toady, a sycophant, an ass-kisser. [Pronounced as separate letters. From the Yiddish phrase *tochus-licker,* meaning ass-licker.]

toad, *n.* A nasty person or a parent of a teenager.

toffee, *n.* Flattery.

toilet talk, *n.* Obscene talk.

Tom, *n.* A black person who has sold out to whites. ["By installing 'American Nigger Toms' as the Third World Elite, the U.S. has controlled the angry hunger of the poor populace." *Publishers Weekly* (1975).] *Syn.:* Tom-a Lee, Uncle Tom.

tomcat, *n.* A womanizer.

tomfool, *n.* A fool.

Tom slick, *n.* A black who informs on other blacks.

Tom tart, *n.* A loose woman.

tomtit, *n.* Shit. [British rhyming slang.] ["You can cut the Tom Tit, Sergeant." J. Gardner, *Madrigal* (1967.)]

tongue, *n.* An attorney, a mouthpiece.

tonto, *n.* A black man who fails to support the causes of his people. [From the TV character Tonto, Indian sidekick to the Lone Ranger.]

tony, *adj.* Very stylish and snooty.

tool, *n.* (1) A hardworking student, a grind. (2) A dupe.

toolhead, *n.* A fool. [From *tool* = penis.]

toot, *n.* A dope.

tooti-frutti, *n.* An ineffectual man.

tootle, *n.* Feeble, overblown talk or writing.

tootsie, *n.* A lesbian.

top sergeant, *n.* A mannish lesbian.

torqued, *adj.* Pissed off, angry.

tosser, *n.* A dummy. [From the folklore of one who sustains brain damage from excessive masturbation.]

toss-prick, *n.* A useless man.

a total loss, *n.* A useless person.

totally clueless, *idiom.* Ignorant.

tottie or **totty,** *n.* A sexually available girl.

tough cat, *n.* A successful womanizer.

tough shit, *interj.* So what! See if I care! My heart bleeds for you! *Syn.*: T.S., tough nibs, tough noogies, tough rock, tough tiddy, tough titty, tough titties.

touron, *n.* A troublesome tourist. [From a blend of *tourist* + *moron.*]

tout, *n.* An informer. [Irish Republican Army usage.]

town bicycle, *n.* A very promiscuous female. *Syn.*: town pump, town punch.

toy boy, *n.* An attractive male sex tool of an older, rich women. ["At 48 she is like a teenage girl again—raving it up with four different lovers including a toyboy of 27!"—*News of the World* (1987).]

trade, *n.* A muscular man attractive to homosexuals.

tramp, *n.* A loose woman. ["Girls who put out are tramps. Girls who don't are ladies. This is however, a rather archaic use of the word. Should one of you boys happen upon a girl who doesn't put out, do not jump to the conclusion that you have found a lady. What you've probably found is a lesbian"—Fran Lebowitz, *Metropolitan Life.*]

transy, *n.* A transvestite.

trapes, *n.* A slattern.

trash, *n.* (1) Low-level, scruffy people, such as Southern poor whites; white trash. (2) A slut. (3) A promiscuous gay man.

trashmouth, *n.* A heavy user of profanity or obscenity.

trash-toter, *n.* A gossip.

trat, *n.* (1) An old lady. (2) A tart. [Back slang.]

treddle, *n.* A promiscuous woman. [From a word for rabbit shit.]

tree-hugger, *n.* A lobbyist for environmental causes.

trendoid or **trendy,** *n.* A devotee of current fashions.

trick, *n.* (1) A prostitute's client. [From tricking or conning a client into parting with money.] (2) Any casual gay sex partner. (3) An unpopular person. (4) A sexy female. ["She's a cute trick."]

trifflin', *v.* Low-life, acting as a leech.

trifflin' trash, *n.* Common as dishwater, sorry as owl bait.

trim, *n.* A woman viewed as a sexual object.

tripe, *n.* Worthless expression.

tripple clutcher, *n.* A motherfucker.

trippy, *adj.* Bizarre. [From LSD trips.]

troglodyte, *n.* A staunch conservative; a right-winger; or a boorish, backward person.

troll, *n.* (1) An ugly girl. (2) A dirty old man.

trollybags, *n.* A sleazy person.

troppo, *adj.* Insane. [Australian usage from the effect of tropical heat.]

trot or **trat,** *n.* An old whore.

Trot, *n.* An extreme hard-core leftist. [From *Trotskyist,* meaning a follower of Leon Trotsky.]

troublemirth, *n.* A spoilsport.

trout, *n.* A woman. [From *trout* = vagina.]

truck driver, *n.* A straight or very masculine homosexual. [From being dressed as or looking like a truck driver or similar macho male.]

truckler, *n.* A toady.

trumpery, *n.* Worthless or trifling statements or objects.

trust him any further than I can see up an alligator's ass at midnight, can't, *idiom.* He's completely untrustworthy. *Syn.:* can't trust him any further than I can throw a bull by his prick.

tub of lard, *n.* An obscenely fat person. ["She used to call you buttercup?/What's so funny about that, Norton?/You were a little cup of butter, now you're a whole tub of lard"—"The Honeymooners," U.S. TV comedy series, 1950.] *Syn.:* tub of guts, tubby.

tub-thumper, *n.* A passionate advocate or religious preacher.

tude, *n.* Negative attitude or one who exhibits such an attitude. ["My English teacher is like this total tude, the airhead, he goes like 'Tiffany, I think you talk funny.' I'm shurr, I'm shurr!"—Corey and Westermark, *Fer Shurr! How to Be a Valley Girl—Totally* (1982).]

tuft-hunter, *n.* A womanizer.

tuna or **tuna fish,** *n.* A woman.

turbobitch, *n.* A bitchy female. *Syn.:* turboslut.

turd, *n.* A rotten person. ["Somebody . . . called him a great turd." D. Welch, *In Youth Is Pleasure* (1944). From the word for a piece of excrement.]

turd-packer, *n.* A homosexual.

turf-cutter, *n.* An Irishman.

turgid, *adj.* Unnecessarily ornate, complicated. ["The turgid intricacies the modern foundation gets itself into in its efforts to spend millions"—Dwight MacDonald.]

turk, *n.* (1) A gay who enjoys anal intercourse. (2) A cruel man. (3) An Irishman.

turkey, *n.* An incompetent or dull person, a lemon, a loser. ["I decided I had enough of that turkey." *Tampa Tribune* (1984).]

turkey on a string, *n.* A person who is so infatuated that he or she can be led around and used easily.

turncoat, *n.* A renegade from a cause or party.

turnoff, *n.* Something that repels someone, a sexual or emotional depressant.

turpid, *adj.* Vile.

turpiloquence, *n.* Obscene speech.

turquoise, *n.* An easy sexual conquest.

turtle, *n.* Women defined as sexual objects.

tush, *n.* A light-skinned upper-class black.

tush hog, *n.* A hoodlum who collects protection money.

twaddle, *n.* Meaningless speech or writing, twaddling.

twank, *n.* (1) An older man whose sexual gratification comes from watching whores at work but who has no personal interest in sex. (2) An effeminate or gay man.

twat, *n.* (1) A woman regarded only as a sexual object. [From *twat* = vagina.] ["Divorce me and you'll have a slot for this new twat, what's her name"—John Updike, *Coup* (1979).] (2) A despicable person. [" 'We hate tense people,' says guitarist John Squire. 'The tense people are the twats who are only interested in making money and who ruin things for everybody else' "—The Stone Roses, *The Observer* (1989).]

twat-faker, *n.* A lecher or pimp. [*Fake* is probably from a gypsy word meaning "to mend."]

tweaker, *n.* One who uses crack. ["Then there are wounds inflicted with knives, baseball bats and other weapons when drug users are 'tweaking,' the street jargon for the volatile behavior that accompanies crack"—*New York Times* (1989).]

twerp or **twirp,** *n.* A minor and unpleasant person. *Syn.*: idiot, jerk, nerd, pup, puppy, sprat, squirt.

twiddle-poop, *n.* An effeminate man.

twink or **twinkie,** *n.* (1) An attractive but rather dumb person, a chicklet. (2) A homosexual.

twirl, *n.* A woman, a girl. [From *twist* + *twirl.*]

twist, *n.* An attractive young woman.

twit, *n.* A very stupid and unimportant person, a spectacular fool. ["There is no need to get so worked up about it, you twit." C. McCullough, *Thorn Birds* (1977.) British usage.]

twixter, *n.* An effeminate man, or a mannish woman.

two-bagger or **double-bagger,** *n.* An extremely ugly person. [From the notion that someone can be so ugly that you have to put one bag over his head and one over yours just in case his breaks.]

two-bit, *adj.* Cheap, vulgar.

U

ucker-say, *n.* A victim. [Pig Latin for *sucker.*]

ugh *interj.* How horrible! How disgusting!

ugly as sin *adj.* Very ugly. ["Beauty is only skin deep; ugly goes right down to the bone" —American proverb.]

ug-may, *n.* A sucker. [Pig Latin for *mug.*]

um-bay, *n.* A bum. [Pig latin for *bum.*]

ultra-, *prefix.* Extreme, beyond normal limits (e.g., ultraleft, ultraliberal, ultranationalistic, ultrapatriot, ultraright).

un-American, *adj.* Acting against the dominant values of the United States. ["They'll (the Un-American Activities Committee) nail anyone who ever scratched his ass during the national anthem"—Humphrey Bogart.]

unbleached American, *n.* An Native American or black person.

Uncle Tom, *n.* A servile black or one who accepts so-called white values and life-styles. [From a character in the novel *Uncle Tom's Cabin* by Harriet Beecher Stowe.]

Uncle Tommyhawk, *n.* The Native American equivalent of an Uncle Tom.

undercover man, *n.* A male homosexual.

underwit, *n.* A halfwit.

unhep or **unhip,** *adj.* Conventional, unimaginative, naive.

unk-pay, *n.* A dupe. [Pig Latin for *punk*.]

untogether, *adj.* Mixed-up, ineffectual, screwed up.

up against the wall, *idiom.* Ready to be excoriated or physically attacked.

uppity, *adj.* (1) Pertaining to blacks who fought discrimination. (2) Obnoxious, stuck-up. [From a bumper sticker: "Uppity Women Unite."]

up shit creek without a paddle, *idiom.* In deep trouble, in hot water, faced with a situation of grave difficulty. ["After he blew the whistle on the graft, he was up shit creek without a paddle."] *Idioms:* between a rock and a hard place, between the devil and the deep blue sea, in the soup, on the hot seat, painted into a corner, sucking canal water, up to one's ass in alligators, up to one's ass in rattlesnakes.

upstart, *n.* Relating to a new member of society, not acceptable to old society. *Syn.:* arriviste, nouveau riche, parvenu, roturier.

upta or **upter,** *adj.* Useless. [From "up to shit." Australian usage.]

up the kazoo, *idiom.* To an overwhelming degree. ["I've had it with you up to the kazoo."] *Syn.:* up the gazoo.

up thine with turpentine, *idiom.* Fuck you! Stick it!

uptight or **tight-assed,** *adj.* Very tense or scared. ["By starving emotions we become humorless, rigid, and uptight; by repressing them we become literal, reformatory, and holier-than-thou; encouraged, they perfume life; discouraged, they poison it"—adapted from Joseph Collins.]

up to here, I've had it, *idiom*. I'm disgusted with your behavior.

up your gigi, *idiom*. Go to hell! *Idioms*: shove it, up your fur-lined shit chute, up yours and give it a left turn, up your bunny with an open umbrella, up your brown with a Roto-Rooter—and spin it, stick it up your ass and holler fire!

up yours, *interj*. Go to the devil, don't bother me. *Idioms*: up you, up your ass, up your butt.

urning, *n*. A gay man.

uzzard, *n*. A third-generation bastard. [From Ivor Brown.]

vacuous, *adj*. Emptyheaded, not thoughtful.

vampire *n*. A woman who seduces and ruins men. ["Made whores facinating vampires instead of poor, stupid, diseased slobs they really are." Eugene O'Neill, *Long Day's Journey Into Night* (1953).]

vanilla, *adj*. Plain.

vanilla, *n*. (1) A white woman. (2) A sexually straight person.

vegetable, *n*. A person who acts as if brain-damaged. ["That ditz acted like a vegetable, and couldn't complete a sentence."] *Syn*.: veggie, veg.

velcrohead, *n*. A black person. [From the plastic adhesive strips now used for clothing, shoes, luggage, etc.]

ventripotent, *adj*. Big-bellied.

viper, *n*. (1) A treacherous person, a villain. (2) A prolonged marijuana user.

virago, *n*. (1) A scold. ["Mild-mannered men often are attracted to viragos."] (2) A mannish woman. *Syn*.: amazon, fishwife, harpy, shrew, vixen, Xanthippe.

vixen, *n*. A shrew.

vomity or **vomitrocious,** *adj*. Extremely unpleasant.

voracious, *adj.* Extremely greedy, hard to satisfy. ["The nineties finally caught up with the voracious bankers and real estate operators."] *Syn.*: gluttonous, rapacious, ravenous.

voyager, *n.* An LSD user. [From LSD use as taking a trip.]

voyeur, *n.* One whose sexual kicks come from watching others perform. ["I was brought up to be a spectator . . . I was raised to be a voyeur." John Irving, *World According to Garp* (1978).] *Syn.*: picker, peeping Tom.

vulgarian, *n.* A Bulgarian.

vulture, *n.* A person who victimizes other people. ["Only a few S & L vultures were penalized; many, including the politician's son, were just slapped on the wrist."]

vup, *n.* A very unimportant person. *Syn.*: pup (pretty unimportant person).

wacky, *adj.* Crazy, silly, offbeat. *Syn.*: whacky, wacked-out, wacko.

wad *n.* An unpopular person.

waffle *n.* A homosexual.

waffle *v.* To double-talk, to hedge. ["Congressmen first have to learn how to waffle without seeming to."]

wagtail, *n.* A hooker.

wagwit, *n.* A joker.

walk heavy, *v.* To carry oneself proudly or vainly.

walk-up fuck, *n.* An easy woman.

wall-eyed, *a.* Shortsighted.

wallflower, *adj.* A woman who attracts no attention at a dance, party, etc.

wally, *n.* A drab, unsophisticated suburbanite.

Walter Mitty, *n.* An ordinary person who always daydreams about becoming famous or having great adventures. [Based on the movie *The Secret Life of Walter Mitty.*]

walyo, *n.* A person of Italian descent. *Syn.:* goombah.

wand-waver, *n.* A sexual exhibitionist. *Syn.:* flasher.

wanker, *n.* A lazy, poor performer. [From *wanker* = masturbator.] ["They're such a bunch of wankers . . . you can't trust them to do anything right." P. Niesewand, *word of gentleman* (1981).]

wannabe, *n.* A person who aspires to a higher or different life-style. ["The film (*School Daze*) is set in the Deep South divided into the politically active 'Jigaboos' who want the college to divest itself of South African holdings and the lighter-skinned 'Wannabes' (as in 'Wanna be white') who are all for partying, parading, pledging to fraternities and raising hell generally"—*Evening Standard* (1989).]

wanton, *n.* A promiscuous woman. [". . . wanton little creatures without character or depth of feeling"—Nordhoff and Hall.] *Syn.:* baggage, bimbo, hussy, jade, jezebel, pig, slattern, slut, strumpet, tramp, trollop, trull, wench, doxy, harlot, prostitute.

wantwit, *n.* A fool.

war-horse, *n.* A strong aggressive woman.

warm bit, *n.* A sexy woman. *Syn.:* warm baby.

warm body, *n.* A completely unimpressive, unnoticeable person who simply takes up space, a chair-warmer. ["The governor's girlfriend was hired as a warm body."]

warm member, *n.* (1) A prostitute. (2) A womanizer.

warped, *adj.* Distorted, confused. ["Their lives and minds have been warped, twisted, and soured"—Lardner.] *Syn.:* mentally twisted, perverted.

wart, *n.* A pest. ["I'm going to hire a hit man and have the little wart rubbed out"—Cynthia Heimel, "L.A. Blues."]

washout, *n.* A fiasco. *Syn.:* flop.

WASP, *n.* A White Anglo-Saxon Protestant, usually middle-class or upper-class, traditional in politics and social values. ["That's the thing you gotta understand about WASPS—they love animals. They can't stand people" —*Wall Street*, U.S. film (1987).]

waspish, *adj.* (1) Characteristic of wasps. ["... well, they say people in the corporate life shoot their urine straighter than an '03 Springfield. We ain't wasp-like for nothing, Y'hear Rangoon?"—Norman Mailer, *Why Are We in Vietnam?* (1967).] (2) Irritable, sassy, malicious. ["A little waspish woman who ... snapped out at a man who seemed to be with her"—C. S. Lewis.]

wastoid, *n.* A person who wastes his or her life and money on drugs and alcohol.

watermelonhead, *n.* An unsophisticated rural dweller.

weak in the head, *idiom.* Slow, dull.

weaker sex or **weaker vessel,** *n.* Women.

weak sister, *n.* A weak, timid man.

weasel, *n.* A sneak who reneges on his obligations, an informer or rat.

webfoot, *n.* A person devoted to the protection of the environment.

wedded wench, *n.* A wife.

weedy, *adj.* Spineless.

weekend warrior, *n.* A part-time prostitute. *Syn.*: weekend ho.

weenie, *n.* A stupid, despised, incompetent person. *Syn.*: jerk, weeny, weiner.

weird, *adj.* Frighteningly peculiar. *Syn.*: creepy, double-gaited, far out, fruity, kinky, off the wall, psycho, queer, sick, spazzy, strangioso, way out, wigged out.

weird or **weirdie,** *n.* A peculiar or unpleasant person with odd tastes. ["When the going gets weird—the weird get going"—Hunter S. Thompson.]

weisenheimer or **wiseacre,** *n.* A smart aleck.

welcher or **welsher,** *n.* One who refuses to pay debts or meet one's obligations.

welfare mother, *idiom.* Any poorly dressed woman.

wench, *n.* (1) A woman. (2) A slut.

wencher, *n.* A man who likes prostitutes.

wenchy, *adj.* Bitchy.

wetback, *n.* (1) A person of Mexican nationality or descent. (2) An illegal Mexican immigrant to the United States. [From Mexicans getting wet backs from swimming the Rio Grande River to sneak into the United States.]

wet blanket, *n.* A person who spoils others' fun.

wetfoot, *n.* A naive person.

wethead, *n.* A novice.

wet noodle, *n.* A wimp or an effeminate man.

wetnose, *n.* A snotnose.

wet one's pants, *idiom.* To panic, to be very frightened. [From involuntary urination, which can accompany fright.] *Syn.:* to piss one's pants.

wet sock, *n.* A wimp. *Syn.:* wet rag.

whacked out, *adj.* Crazy. *Syn.:* whacky, wacko, whack-a-do.

whacker, *n.* A male masturbator.

whale, *n.* A fat person.

whale the piss out of, *idiom.* To beat severely. *Idioms:* whale the shit out of; whale the bejesus out of; I'd slap you, but shit splatters.

the whammy, *n.* The evil eye, a crippling curse. ["He said he'd put the whammy on me if I didn't pay up soon."] *Syn.:* hex, the Indian sign.

what or **(something) the cat dragged in,** *idiom.* A disagreeable person or object.

wheeler-dealer, *n.* A person who is engaged in many deals at the same time, or pretends to be doing so most ostentatiously. *Syn.*: big macher, big shot, big-time operator, ganze macher, operator, wire-puller.

whelp, *n.* A brash youth.

whiffet, *n.* A nobody. [Someone who is as light as a breath or whiff of air.]

whip one's ass, *idiom.* To rout, either in competition or in physical conflict.

whippersnapper, *n.* A young person who defies elders.

whip the dog, *idiom.* Fuck the dog.

whisker-splitter, *n.* A whoremonger.

whiskey dick, *n.* A man who can't get an erection due to liquor.

whistle-blower, *n.* A person who exposes illegal acts, particularly in government.

white bread, *adj.* Dull. [Refers to Wasp styles, presumably very straight or bland.]

white knuckler, *n.* A tense and frightened person. [From knuckles becoming white when one clenches one's fist in fear.]

white liver, *n.* A gay man without any interest in women.

white meat, *n.* A white woman viewed as a sexual object by blacks.

white Negro, *n.* A black or white who adopts the life-style of the other race.

white nigger, *n.* (1) A French-Canadian. [Their own term to describe their earlier inferior position relative to "English" Canada.] (2) Whites who work for civil rights. (3) Any menial white.

white Paddy, *n.* A white person.

white spot, *n.* A white person who spends great amounts of time with blacks.

white trash, *n.* Poor Southern whites. *Syn.*: peckerwood, redneck.

whitey, *n.* A white person. ["The white race is the cancer of human history. It is the white race, and it alone, its ideologies and inventions, which eradicate autonomous civilizations wherever it spreads. It has upset the ecological balance of the planet which now threatens the very existence of life itself"—Susan Sontag, *Partisan Review.*] *Syn.*: Anglo, blue-eyed devil, bright-skin, buckra, chalk, Charlie, Chuck, devil, face, fay, ghost, gray, hack, hay-eater, honky, Jeff, the man, marshmallow, milk, Mr. Charley, Mr. Eddie, ofay, Paddy, paleface, peck, peckerwood, pink, silk, vanilla, white meat, wood, yacoo.

wholemeal, *n.* A heterosexual woman.

whole wheat bread, *idiom.* A light-skinned black person.

whoops boy, *n.* An effeminate man. ["Whoops" is allegedly used often by homosexuals.]

whopstraw, *n.* A boor.

whore, *n.* (1) A woman who charges for sex, or any promiscuous gay man or woman. ["Aren't women prudes if they don't, and prostitutes if they do?"—Kate Millett, Speech given to the Women's Writer's Conference, Los Angeles (1975).] (2) Anyone who sells out for money or other gain.

whore bitch, *n.* A prostitute.

whore-hopper, *n.* A frequent patron of prostitutes or a womanizer.

whorehound, *n.* A whoremaster.

whoreson, *n.* A contemptible man. [The bastard son of a whore. "The seed of a whore/Thou whoreson seed" —William Shakespeare, *King Lear.*]

wienie-wagger, *n.* A man who exposes himself, an exhibitionist. [From *wienie* = penis. "He's just a wienie-wagger . . . that's what the cops call them"—*Lady Beware*, U.S. film (1987).]

wife, *n.* A passive gay partner, a catamite.

wigged out, *adj.* Out of one's mind, crazy. *Syn.:* flipped out.

wiggy, *adj.* Bizarre, disturbing.

wild-ass, *adj.* Unbalanced.

wildcat, *n.* An ill-tempered woman. ["The old Jean (Harlow) would have turned on him spiting and screeching like a wildcat . . ."—Eve Goldin, *Platinum Blonde* (1991).] *Syn.:* spitfire, catamount.

willie, *n.* A catamite or any gay man. *Syn.:* painted willie, winking willie, willie boy.

willing-tit, *n.* A sexually available female.

wimp, *n.* A jerk, a coward, or a repulsive person, usually a man. ["It's official, George Bush is a wimp. He admitted it himself last week—to David Frost, of all people—'We Bushes cry easily,' he told the veteran broadcaster"—*Sunday Times* (1989).] *Syn.:* baby, big baby, bimbo, candyass, Caspar Milquetoast, chicken, chickenheart, cream puff, cry baby, daisy, doormat, drip, drone, drool, dweeb, Ethel, featherweight, flower, goody-goody, gutless wonder, jellyfish, jerk, limp-dick, limp dishrag, loser, mama's boy, milktoast, Milquetoast, nebbish, nervous Nellie, nobody, nothing, ook, paperass, Percy, puppy, pushover, pussycat, putz, rabbit, sad sack, schlemiel, schmendrick, schmo, softass, tootie-fruttie, turkey, weak sister, whimp, wuss.

windbag, *n.* An extremely boastful and talkative person. ["Mr. Kinnock appears to be sinking under a barrage of criticism to the effect that he is an ill-educated Welsh windbag carried high by chippy class hatred"—*Evening Standard.*]

windfoggery, *n.* Bombastic expression. [Coined by Theodore Bernstein.]

windy, *adj.* Relating to flatulence.

wingy, *n.* A cripple, particularly a one-armed person.

winner, *n.* Loser or stupid. ["You're a real winner, Joe. We file for Chapter 11 tomorrow morning."]

win the porcelain hairnet, to, *idiom.* To accomplish something minor that merits a trivial and useless award. ["For that brilliant idea you win the porcelain hairnet."] *Syn.:* win the barbwire garter, win the cast-iron overcoat, win the furlined bathtub, win the hand-painted doormat, win the solid gold chamberpot.

winger, *n.* A political extremist.

wipe up the floor with someone, *idiom.* To beat an opponent badly. *Syn.:* mop up the floor with someone, clobber.

wired, *adj.* High on drugs, or very tense.

wiseacre, *n.* A know-it-all.

wiseguy, *n.* (1) A person who is smug about his cleverness. (2) A "made" member of the Mafia.

witch, *n.* A woman who claims magical influence; or a nasty, sordid woman. *Syn.:* bruja, enchantress, hag, hex, lamia, sorceress.

wittol, *n.* A man who accepts his wife's infidelity.

wog, *n.* Someone from the Near East or Far East. [Presumably from "*w*onderful *O*riental *g*entleman" or "*w*ily Oriental *g*entleman," or the acronym printed on work uniforms, which stands for "*w*orking *o*n *g*overnment *s*ervices."]

wolf, *n.* A sexually aggressive gay or heterosexual man or a lesbian. ["A gentleman is a patient wolf"—Henrietta Tiarks.] *Syn.:* cocksman, Casanova, chaser, Don Juan, lady-killer, masher, philanderer, womanizer.

wolfess, *n.* A flirtatious woman.

wolverine, *n.* A female who likes to flirt.

woman, *n.* An effeminate man.

woman-chaser, *n.* A lecher, one who seeks out women for sex. ["Fat generally tends to make a man a better husband. His wife is happy in the knowledge she is not married to a woman-chaser. Few fat men chase girls, because they get winded too easily"—Hal Boyle.]

woman-flesh, *n.* A woman deemed sexually available.

womanizer, *n.* A promiscuous man. ["Hogamous, Higamous, men are polygamous,/Higamous, Hogamous, women monogamous"—Lois Gould, *Such Good Friends.*] *Syn.*: Casanova, chaser, Don Juan, lady-killer, masher, philanderer, wolf.

woman jessy, *n.* A coward.

wombat, *n.* An odd person. *Syn.*: geek, freak.

wompster, *n.* An enthusiastic preacher, a bible pounder.

wong, *n.* An Asian. ["Two wongs don't make a white" —Arthur Calwell, expounding on his antiimmigrant stand. Australian usage.]

wonk, *n.* An intense, serious student. *Syn.*: greasy grind.

wonky, *adj.* Anxious about one's academic performance.

wood, *n.* A white person or a redneck.

woodchuck, *n.* A Northern farmer, a Northern redneck.

woodman, *n.* A lecher. [From the slang word *wood* = erection.]

woodpecker, *n.* A poor Southern white. [A reversal of *peckerwood.*]

woof, *v.* To brag or talk nonsense. *Syn.*: bat one's gums.

woofie, *n.* A wimp.

wool, *n.* A female viewed as a sexual target. [From *wool* = pubic hair.]

wooly bear or **wooly-wooly,** *n.* A woman.

woolyhead, *n.* A black person.

wooly-headed, *adj.* Excessively idealistic or impractical.

wop, *n.* A person of Italian descent. *Syn.*: dago, dino, eytie, ginzo, greaser, guinea, spaghetti.

working girl, *n.* A prostitute. ["They call themselves 'working girls.' ... By the prostitute's code, prostitution is moral." *New York Times* (1971).]

work one over, *idiom.* To threaten or beat up someone.

worm out, *idiom.* To sneakily avoid a difficult situation or problem.

worry and strife, *n.* A wife.

worrywart, *idiom.* A perennial worrier.

worth a damn, not, *idiom.* Worth little or nothing, incompetent, of poor quality. ["Your promises aren't worth a damn."]

worthless, *adj.* Contemptible, mediocre, without character. *Idioms:* not fit to carry guts to a bear, ain't worth a milk bucket under a bull, ain't worth shuck, not worth dried spit, not worth a shit, not worth a bucket of warm spit.

worth wiping your ass on, ain't, *idiom.* Useless, incompetent. *Idiom:* you ain't worth trading for a shit-ass pup, you don't amount to a fart in a whirlwind.

wowser, *n.* A puritan, a prude.

wrap, *n.* A girlfriend.

wrapped around the axle, *idiom.* Hung up on trivial issues or arguments.

wrapped tight, not, *idiom.* Crazy or dumb.

wren, *n.* A prostitute.

wretch, *n.* A nasty person. *Syn.:* blighter, low-life, mucker, no-good, worm.

wrinkle, *n.* A woman.

wrong, *adj.* Bad, evil, immoral, iniquitous, reprobate, sinful, vicious, wicked.

wrong gee, *n.* A devious, dishonest man.

wrong guy, *n.* A bumbler or deceitful person, an informer. *Syn.:* wrong 'un.

wrongo, *n.* A crook.

wump, *n.* White, urban, middle-class Protestant.

wuss or **wussy,** *adj.* Weak, indecisive.

XYZ

Xanthippe, *n.* A scold or a shrew. [After Socrates' venomous wife.]

yack *n.* A silly person or silly talk. *Syn.:* yock, yuck, yuk.

yacoo, *n.* A racist or white person.

yahoo, *n.* An ignorant lout. [From Jonathan Swift, *Gulliver's Travels.*]

yak, *n.* A Pole or a person of Polish descent.

yancy, *adj.* Nervous. *Syn.:* antsy.

yang-yang, *n.* Foolishness.

yank someone around, *idiom.* To give someone a hard time. *Syn.:* yank someone's chain.

yank someone's crank, *idiom.* To engage in sexual teasing.

yard dog, *n.* An uncouth person.

yawn, *n.* A boring person. ["Dan Quayle's brain is gone, Debbie Gibson gives good yawn"—Julie Brown, *The Village Voice* (1991).]

yazzihamper, *n.* A fool or despicable person.

yeah-man, *n.* A bore.

yech or **yecch,** *interj.* Horrible!

yeller-feller, *n.* A light-skinned or racially mixed aborigine.

yellow bastard, *n.* A Japanese person. ["In the Pacific theater . . . the sobriquets applied to the Japanese were particularly hateful, as ringtails, yellow bastards and a host of unprintables." *American Speech* (1947).]

yellowbelly, *n.* (1) A craven person. ["I'm a cowardly yellow belly." John Steinbeck, *East of Eden* (1952).] (2) An Asian. or a Eurasian. ["They're Eurasians—sons of white fathers and native mothers. Yellow-bellies is our friendly nickname for them"—George Orwell, *Burmese Days* (1934).]

yellow-black, *n.* An American black with yellowish skin.

yellow boy, *n.* A Chinese.

yellow dog, *n.* A very cowardly person. *Syn.*: Candyass chicken, chickenheart, craven dastard, jellybelly, lilyliver, Milquetoast, pansy, pantywaist, piker, pussycat, rabbit, ringtail, shy-cock, sissy, sop, weak sister, wheyface, yellow heel, yellow liver.

yellow girl, *n.* A light-skinned black woman.

yellow nigger, *n.* An East or Southeast Asian.

yellow streak down one's back, a, *idiom.* Cowardice.

yenta, *n.* A nagging, gossipy woman.

yentzer, *n.* A heavily sexed man or woman.

yes-girl, *n.* A sexually acquiescent female.

Yid or **yiddle,** *n.* A Jewish person.

Yid-kid, *n.* A Jewish boy.

ying-yang, *n.* A fool.

yodeling in a canyon, *idiom.* (1) Meaningless talk. (2) Performing oral sex on a woman.

yokel, *n.* A stupid country resident.

yola, *n.* A light-skinned black girl.

yold or **yuld,** *n.* A sucker.

yo' mama, *interj.* So you say! Say what! Listen up! Same to you!

yoo-hoo boy, *n.* An effeminate homosexual.

you and who else, *Idiom.* What makes you think you can lick me? *Syn.*: you and what army.

you asked for it, *interj.* I'm going to whack you for what you did.

youngblood or **blood,** *n.* A young black man.

young in the head, *idiom.* Childish.

young squirt, *idiom.* An ignorant, sassy, adolescent man. *Syn.*: pootbutt, punk, punk-kid, pup, snotnose, squirt, young punk.

your mother, *interj.* Whatever you say applies double to your mother. *Syn.*: yo' mama.

your mother wears army boots, *idiom.* Dismissive retort in answer to an insult, slur, or put-down.

yo-yo, *n.* A fool, or a vacillator. [From the toy on a string that rises and falls.]

yuck or **yeck,** *interj.* Disgusting! Revolting! Ugh!

yucky, *adj.* Disgustingly sticky or smelly.

yug, *n.* A Yugoslav.

yummy, *n.* A pretty teenage girl, "good enough to eat."

yutz, *n.* A fool, a failure.

zany, *n.* Someone who makes a fool of himself.

zarf, *n.* A repulsive man.

zebra, *n.* A radically mixed (black and white) individual or couple.

Zelda, *n.* A boring woman.

zerk, *n.* A jerk.

zerking, *adj.* Strange.

zero, *n.* A nothing.

zhlub, *n.* A jerk, a slob.

zigaboo, *n.* A black.

zilch, *n.* Little or nothing. *Syn.*: bubkes, chopped liver, diddly-damn, diddly-shit, diddly-squat, doodle-shit, a goose egg, nada, nix, one red cent, one thin dime, a plugged nickel, poop, a rat's ass, a row of pins, a shit, two hoots in hell, a whoop, zippo, zotz.

zip, *n.* A fool [Acronym for "*z*ero *i*ntelligence *p*otential."]

zipperhead, *n.* A person who will not entertain a new idea.

zipper morals, *idiom.* Loose morally.

zip up your lip, *imper.* Shut up! *Syn.:* zip it up, zip up your mouth.

zob, *n.* A nonentity.

zod, *n.* An extremely disgusting person. ["Like I just got my hair streaked, OK, and like Brian throws me in the pool, and like the chlorine turns my hair like totally green, I mean I look like such a zod!"—Corey and Westermark, *Fer Shurr! How to Be a Valley Girl—Totally* (1982).] *Syn.:* creep, nerd.

zoid, *n.* A misfit.

zone, *n.* A nodding, stupified person. [Probably from excessive use of narcotics.] *Syn.:* space cadet, zoner.

zooie, *n.* Noisy, chaotic. *Syn.:* zooey.

zook, *n.* A worn-out hooker.

zool, *n.* An Italian, especially someone from the old country.

zoophiliac, *n.* An animal lover or someone who copulates with animals.

zot, *n.* Zero, zotz, zilch, zip.

zuch, *n.* A stool pigeon. [Pronounced like "mooch".]

BIBLIOGRAPHY

Abrahams, Roger D. *Deep Down in the Jungle: Negro Narrative Folklore from the Streets of Philadelphia.* Chicago: Aldine Publishing Company, 1970.

Adams, Ramon F. *Western Words*, 2nd. rev. ed. Norman, Okla.: University of Oklahoma Press, 1968.

American Speech, University, Ala.: University of Alabama Press, 1925.

Andrews, Malachi and Paul T. Owens. *Black Language*, 3rd edition. West Los Angeles, Calif.: Seymour-Smith, Publisher, 1979.

Barltrop, Robert and Jim Wolveridge. *The Muvver Tongue.* London: The Journeyman Press, 1980.

Behan, Brendan. *Borstal Boy.* New York: Alfred A. Knopf, 1959.

Bernbach, Lisa. *The Official Preppy Handbook.* New York: Workman Publishing, 1980.

Berrey, Lester V. and Melvin Van Den Bark. *The American Thesaurus of Slang: A Complete Reference Book of Colloquial Speech*, 2nd edition. New York: Thomas Y. Crowell, 1960.

Bierce, Ambrose. *The Devil's Dictionary.* New York: Dover Publications, 1958.

Bruce, Lenny. *How to Talk Dirty and Influence People.* Chicago: Playboy Press, 1965.

Burchfield, R.W., editor. *A Supplement to the Oxford English Dictionary*, 4 vols. Oxford, Clarendon Press, 1972–1986.

Cassidy, Frederic G. *Dictionary of American Regional English.* Cambridge, Mass.: The Belknap Press of Harvard University Press, 1985.

Cassidy, Frederic G. and R. B. Le Page. *Dictionary of Jamaican English.* London: Cambridge University Press, 1967.

Chambers English Dictionary. Cambridge, Eng.: Chambers, 1988.

Chambers Thesaurus; A Comprehensive Word-finding Dictionary. Cambridge, England: W.R. Chambers and Cambridge University Press, 1988.

Chapman, Robert L., editor. *New Dictionary of American Slang.* New York: Harper & Row, 1986.

Chapman, Robert L., editor. *Thesaurus of American Slang.* New York: Harper & row, 1989.

Ciardi, John. *A Browser's Dictionary and Native's Guide to the Unknown American Language.* New York: Harper & Row, 1980.

Claerbaut, David. *Black Jargon in White America.* Grand Rapids, Mich.: William B. Eerdmans, Pub. Co., 1972.

Claire, Elizabeth. *An Indispensible Guide to Dangerous English! for Language Learners and Others.* Dundee, Ill.: Delta Systems Co., 1990.

Cohen, John, compiler and editor. *The Essential Lenny Bruce.* New York: Douglas Books, 1970.

Corey, Mary and Victoria Westermark. *Fer Shurr! How to be a Valley Girl—Totally!* New York: Bantam Books, 1982.

Daly, Mary and Jane Caputi. *Webster's First New Intergalactic Wickedary of the English Language.* London: The Women's Press, 1988.

Dickson, Paul. *Slang!: The Topic-by-Topic Dictionary of Contemporary Lingoes.* New York: Pocket Books, 1990.

Dickson, Paul. *Words.* London: Arrow Books, 1983.

Dillard, J.L. *Lexicon of Black English.* New York: The Seabury Press, 1977.

Dundes, Alan, editor. *Mother Wit From the Laughing Barrel: Readings in the Interpretation of Afro-American Folklore.* Englewood Clifs, N.J.: Prentice-Hall, 1973.

Elting, John R., Dan Cragg, and Earnest L. Deal. *A Dictionary of Soldier Talk.* New York: Charles Scribner's and Sons, 1984.

Farmer, J.S. and W. E. Henley. *Slang and its Analogues.* 7 vols. New York: Arno Press, 1970.

Flexner, Stuart Berg. *I Hear America Talking: An Illustrated Treasury of American Words and Phrases.* New York: Van Nostrand Reinhold Co., 1976.

Flexner, Stuart Berg. *Listening to America: An Illustrated History of Words and Phrases from Our Long and Splendid Past.* New York: Simon and Schuster, 1982.

Folb, Edith A. *Runnin' Down Some Lines: The Language and Culture of Black Teenagers.* Cambridge, Mass.: Harvard University Press, 1980.

Gold, Robert S. *Jazz Talk.* Indianapolis, Ind.: The Bobbs-Merrill Company, 1975.

Goldin, Hyman E., Frank O'Leary, and Morris Lipsius. *Dictionary of American Underground Lingo.* New York: The Citadel Press, 1962.

Goodwin, Joseph P. *More Man Than You'll Ever Be: Gay Folklore and Acculturation in Middle America.* Bloomington, Ind.: Indiana University Press, 1989.

Grahn, Judy. *Another Mother Tongue: Gay Words, Gay Worlds.* Boston: Beacon Press, 1984.

Grambs, David. *The Random House Dictionary for Writers and Readers.* New York: Random House, 1990.

Green, Jonathon. *The Dictionary of Contemporary Slang.* London: Pan Books, 1984.

Green, Jonathan. *The Slang Thesaurus.* London: Penguin Books, 1986.

Green, Jonathan. *Newspeak: a Dictionary of Jargon.* London: Routledge & Kegan Paul, 1984.

Gwaltney, John Langston. *Drylongso: A Self-Portrait.* New York: Vintage Books, 1980.

Holder, R.W. *The Faber Dictionary of Euphemisms.* London: Faber & Faber, 1989.

Homer, Joel. *Jargon: How to Talk to Anyone About Anything.* New York: Times Books, 1979.

Hudson, Bob. *The First Australian Dictionary of Vulgarisms and Obscenities.* London: David and Charles, 1987.

Hughes, Geoffrey. *Swearing: A Social History of Foul Language, Oaths and Profanity in English.* Oxford, England: Basil Blackwell, 1991.

Jackson, Bruce. *"Get Your Ass in the Water and Swim Like Me": Narrative Poetry from the Black Oral Tradition.* Cambridge, Mass.: Harvard University Press, 1974.

Johansen, Lenie (Midge). *The Dinkum Dictionary: A Ripper Guide to Aussie English.* Ringwood, Victoria, Australia: Viking O'Neil, 1991.

Jonson, Helen. *Kangaroo's Comments and Wallaby's Words: The Aussie Word Book.* New York: Hippocrene Books, 1988.

Kramarae, Chris and Paula Treichler. *A Feminist Dictionary*. London: Pandora Press, 1985.

Kochman, Thomas, ed. *Rappin' and Stylin' Out: Communication in Urban Black America*. Urbana, Ill.: Univ. Of Illinois Press, 1972.

Laird, Charlton. *Webster's New World Thesaurus*. New York: New American Library, 1975.

Landy, Eugene E. *The Underground Dictionary*. New York: Simon and Schuster, 1971.

Lewin, Esther and Albert E. Lewin. *The Random House Thesaurus of Slang*. New York: Random House, 1988.

Maggio, Rosalie. *The Non-Sexist Word Finder: A Dictionary of Gender-Free Usage*. Boston: Beacon Press, 1989.

Major, Clarence. *Black Slang, A Dictionary of Afro-American Talk*. London: Routledge and Kegan Paul, 1971.

Maledicta: The International Journal of Verbal Aggression. Waukesha, Wisc.: 1977.

Maurer, David W. *Language of the Underworld*. Lexington, Ky.: University of Kentucky Press, 1981.

McConville, Brigid and John Shearlaw. *The Slanguage of Sex*. London: Macdonald and Company, 1985.

Mencken, H. L. *The American Language: An Inquiry into the Development of English in the United States*, 4th edition. New York: Alfred A Knopf, 1937.

———Supplement I, 1966.

———Supplement II, 1967.

———Abridged edition by Raven J. McDavid, 1982.

Mezzerow, Milton "Mezz" and Bernard Wolfe. *Really the Blues*. New York: New American Library, 1946.

Mills, Jane. *Womanwords: A Vocabulary of Culture and Patriarchial Society*. London: Virago Press, 1991.

Montagu, Ashley. *The Anatomy of Swearing*. New York: The Macmillan Co., 1967.

Morton, James. *Lowspeak: A Dictionary of Criminal and Sexual Slang*. London: Angus and Robertson, 1989.

Moss, Norman. *British/American Language Dictionary*. Lincolnwood, Ill.: Passport Books, 1984.

Munro, Pamela. *Slang U*. New York: Harmony Books, 1989.

Murray, J.A.H., H. Bradley, W.A. Craigie, and C.T. Onions. *The Oxford English Dictionary*, 13 vols. Oxford England: Oxford University Press, 1933.

Neaman, Judith and Carole S. Silver. *A Dictionary of Euphemisms.* London: Unwin Paperbacks, 1984.

Partridge, Eric. *A Dictionary of Catchphrases: British and American from the Sixteenth Century to the Present.* New York: Stein and Day, 1977.

Partridge, Eric. *A Dictionary of Slang and Unconventional English: Colloquialisms and Catch-phrases, Solicisms and Catachreses, Nicknames and Vulgarisms.* {Edited by Paul Beale} 8th edition. New York: Macmillan Publishing Company, 1984.

Partridge, Eric. *A Dictionary of the Underworld: British & American, Being the Vocabularies of Crooks, Criminals, Racketeers, Beggars and Tramps, Convicts, the Commercial Underworld, the Drug Traffic, the White Slave Traffic, Spivs.* New York: Bonanza Books, 1961.

Partridge, Eric. *Slang Today and Yesterday: with a Short Historical Sketch; and Vocabularies of English, American and Australian Slang.* 3rd edition. New York: Bonanza Books, [n.d.]

Randolph, Vance and George P. Wilson. *Down in the Holler: A Gallery of Ozark Folk Speech.* Norman, Okla.: University of Oklahoma Press, 1953.

The Random House Thesaurus, College Edition. Edited by Jess Stein and Stuart Berg Flexner. New York: Random House, 1984.

Random House Webster's College Dictionary. New York: Random House, 1991.

Rawson, Hugh. *A Dictionary of Euphemisms and Other Doubletalk.* New York: Crown Publishers, 1981.

Rawson, Hugh. *Wicked Words, A Treasury of Curses, Insults, Put-Downs and Other Formerly Unprintable Terms from Anglo-Saxon Times to the Present.* New York: Crown Publishers, 1989.

Rodgers, Bruce. *The Queen's Vernacular; A Gay Lexicon.* San Francisco: Straight Arrow Books, 1972.

Roget's International Thesaurus, 4th edition, revised by Robert L. Chapman. New York: Thomas Y. Crowell, 1977.

Rosten, Leo. *Hooray for Yiddish: A Book About English.* New York: Simon & Schuster, 1982.

Rosten, Leo. *The Joys of Yiddish.* New York: McGraw-Hill, 1968.

Saussy, George Stone. *The Oxter English Dictionary: Uncommin*

Words Used by Uncommonly Good Writers. New York: Facts on File, 1984.

Scott, George Ryley, editor. *Swan's Anglo-American Dictionary.* London: Gerald G. Swan, Ltd., 1950.

Smitherman, Geneva. *Talkin and Testifyin: The Language of Black America.* Boston: Houghton Mifflin Company, 1977.

Spears, Richard A. *Forbidden American English.* Lincolnwood, Ill.: Passport Books, 1990.

Spears, Richard A. *NTC'S Dictionary of American Slang and Colloquial Expressions.* Lincolnwood, Ill: National Textbook Company, 1989.

Spears, Richard A. *Slang and Euphemism.* Middle Village, N.Y.: Jonathan David Publishers, 1981.

Syatt, Dick. *Like We Say Back Home.* Secaucus, N.J.: The Citadel Press, 1987.

Tulloch, Sara *The Oxford Dictionary of New Words: A Popular Guide to Words in the News.* New York: Oxford University Press, 1991.

Webster's Collegiate Thesaurus. Springfield, Mass.: G & C Meryiam Co., 1976.

Webster's New Collegiate Dictionary, 9th edition. Springfield, Mass.: G & C. Merriam Co., 1984.

Webster's II New Riverside University Dictionary. Boston: Houghton Mifflin Co., 1988.

Wentworth, Harold and Stuart Berg Flexner. *Dictionary of American Slang: Second Supplemental Edition.* New York: Thomas Y. Crowell, 1975.

Wessen, Maurice. *A Dictionary of American Slang.* New York, Thomas Y. Crowell Company, 1934.

Wilder, Roy, Jr. *You All Spoken Here.* New York: Viking Penguin, 1984.

Wilkes, G. A. *A Dictionary of Australian Colloquiallisms.* Sydney, Aus.: Sydney University Press, 1985.

Wilson, Robert A. *Playboy's Book of Forbidden Words.* Chicago: Playboy Press, 1973.